Welcome to

Our future!

"What a fresh and forward-looking read. Jeanne C. Meister and Karie Willyerd have tackled recruitment, motivation, learning, and leadership in the new and evolving 'connected world,' and they have offered best practices and their own thoughtful approaches for companies and leaders to consider."

—John W. Gill, vice president, human resources,
Rolls-Royce Energy Systems

"Meister and Willyerd have blazed a trail with *The 2020 Workplace*. Using real data and valuable business examples to bolster their case, they provide the brand-new vocabulary and game plan your company needs to get started. With key insights on how to manage tomorrow's workforce—one that is beginning to show up to work today—this book is a must-read for all in our profession!"

—Matthew Peters, chief learning officer,
Defense Intelligence Agency

"The workplace is evolving faster than ever before, reinventing everything from how employees connect with an organization to how they learn, leverage information, and lead. Managers, don't miss this opportunity to get a jump start on the 2020 workforce before it's too late. "

—Lynne C. Lancaster, coauthor of
*The M-Factor: How the Millennial Generation Is
Rocking the Workplace*

"*The 2020 Workplace* is a thought-provoking guide to the emerging workplace trends and how they will shape business in the future."

—Peter Cappelli, George W. Taylor Professor of
Management and professor of education,
Wharton School of the University of Pennsylvania

"*The 2020 Workplace* provides tremendous insights, not only into the emerging workforce, but also into the changes that enterprises will have to make to effectively recruit, develop, and retain what will become increasingly scarce human resources. Here is a look into the future that today's leaders can use to map what is certainly going to be a journey down a different road."

—Stanton D. Sloane, president and
chief executive officer, SRA International

THE 2020 WORKPLACE

THE 2020 WORKPLACE

HOW INNOVATIVE COMPANIES ATTRACT, DEVELOP, AND KEEP TOMORROW'S EMPLOYEES TODAY

JEANNE C. MEISTER AND KARIE WILLYERD

HARPER
BUSINESS

An Imprint of HarperCollins*Publishers*
www.harpercollins.com

Designed by Renato Stanisic

Library of Congress Cataloging-in-Publication Data.
Meister, Jeanne C.
    The 2020 workplace : how innovative companies attract, develop, and keep tomorrow's employees today / Jeanne C. Meister, Karie Willyerd.
        p. cm.
    Includes bibliographical references and index.
    ISBN 978-0-06-176327-4
    1. Employees—Recruiting. 2. Employee retention. 3. Manpower planning. 4. Personnel management. I. Willyerd, Karie. II. Title.
    HF5549.5.R44M45 2010
    658.3'01—dc22

                                                        2009045458

    12 13 14   ov/rrd   20 19 18 17 16 15

For Bob, Danielle, and my parents: everything is possible with you by my side.

Jeanne Meister
New York, 2010

To my tribe: the friends, family, and neighbors who provided emotional support but sacrificed playtime with me for the last two years and occasionally insisted on restorative time at a beach house, a fly-fishing expedition, a boat ride around the lagoon, playing with grandchildren, or a trip to wine country. You make life so much more interesting.

Karie Willyerd
Redwood City, 2010

CONTENTS

Introduction: The 2020 Workplace

Who could have guessed that one of the big differences between life now and ten years ago would be our growing dependence on a mathematician who died nearly 250 years ago? If you've ever used Google, then you have relied on the work of Thomas Bayes, whose theorem is the basis of everything from running Google's search engine to predicting which door to choose on *Let's Make a Deal*. Although the complex theorem largely belongs in the provenance of mathematicians, engineers, and scientists, for the rest of us, it can be simply stated: the likelihood that something will happen can be plausibly estimated by how often it occurred in the past.[1] From this simple premise comes the revolution we have all experienced in the last ten years.

Think back to ten years ago: in the year 2000, a presidential election was determined by malfunctioning paper voting cards; millions if not billions of dollars had just been invested in averting the software code ambiguity threat known as Y2K; joint ventures with China were just getting started for most global companies; and the dot-com boom was on its way to becoming the dot-com bust. Google had just moved out of its garage office in Menlo Park, California; Apple was considered to be on the skids; YouTube was still five years away from being invented; and Facebook's creator was still in high school. What a difference a decade makes, not only in the tools we use to remain productive but in how we live our day-to-day lives. Who could have imagined the profound changes of the last ten years? Is there any reason to believe the changes during the next ten years will not be just as profound?

Ludwig Mies van der Rohe, a leader of modern architecture, once said, "Architecture is the will of an epoch translated into space." One of his crowning achievements was the Toronto Dominion Tower, where the executive floor and boardroom remain gloriously pristine and painstakingly maintained to his original, *Austin Powers*–like vision of the late 1960s. The boardroom table seats eighty-eight people. Made from one solid piece of wood, it is so large it had to be lifted in while the skyscraper was under construction, and it has never been moved since. When needed, replacement carpet is loomed on the same mills, according to the original specifications. Yet even an absolute commitment to historical authenticity faces the need for progress. In 1967, no one envisioned the need for people to sit around a table to collaborate together on the executive floor. After all, the hierarchy was clearly defined as the chairman, the board of directors, and the CEO; there was no need for collaborative space. Times have changed, though, and one of the few concessions to the original architectural vision for the floor has been to bring a round table into the former chairman's office, to allow dining and collaboration in a more egalitarian environment.

Likewise, organizations translate the will of the epoch not only into the physical spaces they create but also into the decisions about the talent they select and the structure they create within the firm. These decisions are crucial because although employees no longer stay at one company for life, the decisions that are made about who is hired, developed, and promoted endure for years. As such, we argue that a forward-thinking mind-set is a mandate for business executives, and too little is done to ground the discussion of the future in the needs and requirements of today. Our goal with this book is to stimulate that conversation.

WHY YOU NEED THIS BOOK NOW

For years, the much-feared and overly publicized war for talent has been predicated on the assumption that the Baby Boomers (those people born between 1946 and 1964) would follow the same retirement schedule as the prior generation, the Traditionalists (those born prior to 1946), and begin retiring in large numbers in 2007.[2] However, with a decade's worth of wealth obliterated in the financial crisis of 2008–2009, that assumption is no longer valid. Men and women who are healthy at 60, according to the World Health Organization, will on average be physically capable of working until they are 74 and 77, respectively.[3] If Baby Boomers now work as long as possible, that means that the leading edge of the Boomers may not begin retiring until 2020, when the quest for top talent will assuredly be in full swing.

All the major factors that will define this 2020 workplace are already in play. The future new employees, whom we call Generation 2020, are now in their middle school years. The technologies that will define the 2020 workplace are in design stages today. Emerging large-scale economies are rapidly entering as major forces. The workplace of tomorrow is being shaped today, driven primarily by globalization, the introduction of new ways of working, the usage of emerging technologies, and the shifting demographics of the workforce.

> **The 2020 workplace**: An organizational environment that provides an intensely personalized, social experience to attract, develop, and engage employees across all generations and geographies.

The best companies are already preparing their strategies to win the quest for top talent. The 2020 workplace will be defined by this acute vision—20/20 vision—with regard to recruiting strategies, customizable employee development and benefits, agile leadership, and the power of social networks.

In this book, "the 2020 workplace" means one that provides an intensely personalized, social experience to attract, develop, and engage employees across all generations and geographies. The organizations that create a competitive advantage in the 2020 workplace will do so by instituting innovative human resource practices—by first defining an authentic core set of organizational values and then augmenting these by leveraging the latest tools of the social Web to reimagine learning and development, talent management, and leadership practices.

This book pays special attention to the use of social media to attract, motivate, connect with, engage, develop, retain, and listen to employees. The marketing profession has realized the potential of social media to connect with prospective and current customers, as popularized in books such as *Groundswell*.[4] We believe that as more and more of the workforce is made up of "digital natives," the need for business executives to speak the language of their employees in the form of social media will become a requirement.[5] Yet at its core, the social media revolution is not about technology—it's a social movement that is all about creating a community. This makes it even more imperative for business executives to be in the game.

The landscape is exciting and dynamic, and it promises to redefine much of the conventional wisdom about work, organizational success, personal accomplishment, and so much more. As we scan the workplace of the future, we see that everything we know about work—where we work, how we work, what skills we need to stay employable, what technologies we use to connect with colleagues—is changing. And these changes will only continue to accelerate as we move toward 2020 because the Millennial Generation, which refers to the 88 million people born between the years 1977 to 1997, will make up nearly half of the workforce by 2014. Employers must prepare *now* for this multigenerational workforce, and if organizations are to be ready, it will take the foresight and actions of those who are most responsible for preparing the leadership and employee implications of the organizational strategy.

WHY WE WROTE THIS BOOK

The 2020 Workplace revolves around the premise that the increased focus on talent is making the human resources function within organizations more integral to an organization's success. Do the top leaders of an organization realize this? Are human resources and learning professionals ready to deliver? Are you ready to embrace this future and create a workplace that the employees of the future will choose?

Possibly. Yet many organizations continue to view the future as a linear progression from the past years. The business literature covering strategies for people, culture, and talent is filled with the same stories of a few companies that seem to be featured again and again, from decade to decade, indicating little change. We beg to differ for many reasons:

- Never in the history of the modern world have there been four generations—much less five—in the workplace that bring such vastly different sets of values, beliefs, and expectations.
- Never has a generation entered the workplace using technologies so far ahead of those adopted by its employer.
- Never has it been possible to acquire, use, and seamlessly integrate talent from around the world.
- Never has technology made it so possible to connect anyone anywhere asynchronously as a collaborator.
- Never before has society put as much pressure on organizations to be socially responsible.

The list goes on, but we hope you can see that the world of work is changing faster than ever.

Still, we needed validation of these beliefs, and we got it from the companies and working professionals from several generations we surveyed. Forward-thinking organizations are using innovative practices to address the changing marketplace, and we provide examples, such as Millennials coaching executives at Burson-Marsteller, corporate social networks at Cerner, new ways to engage employees of all ages in the Deloitte Film Festival, performance support on demand at IBM, power shifts from the top of the hierarchy to networked, connected decision makers at Cisco, and dozens of other case studies to demonstrate that the principles of *The 2020 Workplace* are in action now.

The 2020 Workplace takes a bold step into the future and serves as a practical guide for companies of all sizes to transform their workplace so they can compete more effectively in a global marketplace—one defined by an economic climate in flux and by powerful demographic, technological, and generational forces. Even though we feature companies of all types as examples throughout the book, by the nature of their business, technology and professional services firms provide many of the examples we use since they are at the leading edge of what will come next. Technology firms tend to "eat their own dog food," meaning they experiment with the newest technologies inside their own companies. Professional services firms rely heavily on fresh college graduates and thus have had to adapt to the needs of the Millennial Generation before those organizations that have a more age-diverse employee base. However, even though these changes are originating in technology and professional firms, their experiences are relevant to businesses of all shapes and sizes.

We believe that in the rapidly changing world of business, a best practice may be short-lived. The practice reflects an activity that delivers results in the context of the market conditions of the time. Our strategy in this book has been to focus on the next practice, not on sweeping generalizations of the company, while also researching the sustainability of the company's culture and values. We hope the companies featured in this book provide some helpful insights in preparing for the future workplace.

WHO WE ARE

As coauthors, we each bring a set of unique experiences that shape our view of the future and what is needed now to prepare for it. Jeanne has consulted with organizations on how to build effective learning organizations for more than twenty years, both through her own consulting firm as well as with Accenture. As the author of two books on the design and management of corporate universities and a widely read blog, she has consulted with hundreds of organizations on how they reinvent their learning functions and reimagine their talent management capabilities. Karie has been both a chief learning officer and a chief talent officer for global Fortune 200 organizations in Silicon Valley, as well as head of executive development and organization development in the defense and food industries. She has developed and implemented practical approaches to building talent around the globe for the future and has led her organizations in winning more than thirty awards for functional excellence. Finally and most important, as mothers of both Millennial and Generation X daughters, we have experienced firsthand the shift needed to communicate effectively across the generations.

Our combined experience has left us with the belief that it is time to make a transformational leap in organizational practices if we are to be relevant to a world that is changing so rapidly around us. The glimpses we have into the expectations of the next generations of workers and some of the practices of leading-edge companies motivated us to open the dialogue for the 2020 workplace. We purposefully use the word "dialogue," because when this book is released, there will already be new developments in technology, changes in companies, and emerging new best practices. We invite you to join that continued dialogue to ensure that what might be static instead becomes dynamic as we collaborate together to prepare for the future.

WHAT YOU WILL FIND IN THIS BOOK

The 2020 Workplace combines exclusive research with practical tools and resources. Some of the features include:

- Key findings from two global surveys. The first surveyed 2,200 working professionals from around the world on what they seek from employers, both now and in their anticipated future. The second survey queried 300 employers from around the world on the practices they have in play now and those they expect to use in the future. We look at where there is alignment, as well as gaps, in expectations. These findings will help organizations make strategic choices about where to invest their resources now to best prepare for the future of the workplace. The results of these surveys guided our search for relevant, leading-edge case studies.
- More than 50 case studies developed through more than 100

personal interviews with companies that are leading the way in the use of innovative practices for attracting, developing, and retaining talent for the future, including Deloitte, IBM, Cisco, Bell Canada, JetBlue, Nokia, and NASA.

- Real examples of how companies are using social media today to recruit, engage, develop, and connect employees.
- Practical tips and advice on how to prepare for 2020 both organizationally and personally.
- Twenty predictions for the 2020 workplace.
- The 2020 glossary, making it easy to read through the book with a ready reference at hand, for those who have never texted or posted a message on a Facebook wall, or don't know the difference between sending a tweet on Twitter and using Delicious to store and share bookmarks.
- A summary at the end of each chapter to help those of you who are inundated, as we are, with books and magazines stacked up at your bedside or on your Kindle.

Entire books could have been written about topics we cover in a single chapter, so we realize that we can only begin to touch the practices that people have spent their entire lives putting into place. Our intent is to weave a story of how the world is changing as we all interact with coworkers, friends, and family in new ways. In our notes, we have recommended other sources for more in-depth understanding of each area.

Part I, "The Changing Workplace," describes what is happening now and how organizations are responding to the changing workplace, starting with chapter 1, "Ten Forces Shaping the Future Workplace Now." In chapter 2, "Multiple Generations @ Work," we discuss our research findings around the several generations in the workplace, including some counterintuitive findings about what each generation prefers.

In part II, "Practices in Action Today," we bring to life real-world examples of what companies are doing now to incorporate social media across a range of practices that directly affect employees, and we offer a set of unifying principles for the 2020 workplace. Chapter 3,

"Principles of 2020 Engagement," covers the core fundamentals of how an organization can make the move to the workplace of the future. We introduce a model called Workplace Engagement 2020 that provides a guide for how to adopt workplace practices and processes to attract and retain top talent. In chapter 4, "Social Recruiting Emerges," we address innovative practices in reaching, recruiting, and nurturing the best talent in the global marketplace and offer examples of these practices in action. Chapter 5, "Über-connect Your Organization," examines how progressive organizations are using various types of social media and virtual collaboration, effectively creating an individualized yet social employee experience. In chapter 6, "The Social Learning Ecosystem," we start with the observation that although classrooms will be around for a long time, they are already becoming too expensive for all but the most strategic of training needs. We then explore ways organizations can move beyond classrooms and build learning within the context of any job, rather than as a separate and formal process. In chapter 7, "Accelerated Leadership," we focus on the qualities needed to build an agile leadership pipeline and argue that both management and leadership will need to fundamentally change to address the needs of the future organization.

Finally, part III, "Envisioning the 2020 Workplace," looks to the future and how to prepare for it now. Chapter 8 profiles our "Twenty Predictions for the 2020 Workplace." We proceed here warily and with full awareness of the difficulties inherent in any attempts at forecasting the future. To prepare, we relied on dozens of interviews with experts, queried thousands of working professionals in a diverse mix of organizations for their thoughts, established a Web 2.0 collaboration space to open a dialogue, leveraged our memberships in futurist societies, and became some of the online book retailers' favorite customers as we ordered books from far-reaching fields to understand what others are saying about the future. Our predictions are based on glimpses into a future we can already see in play at some of the most leading-edge companies. We hope they provide an imagination-expanding view of what life will be like in organizations in 2020.

Organizations at their simplest are societies, made up of individuals with a common set of goals. In our final chapter, "Get Ready for the Future Workplace," we help unify individuals in an organization through providing guidance on how to do just that. We offer advice to individuals on how to develop the necessary skills, as well as thoughts on how to prepare organizations to face the future. Throughout the book we include practices ranging from creating a strong employer brand to launching a corporate social network, all geared to attracting, developing, and engaging the best talent possible for the future.

Since many of the terms we use throughout the book may be new for some readers, we have provided a glossary of social media terms, along with a timeline and a list of key Web sites and online tools.

WHO SHOULD READ THIS BOOK

In the end, our essential goal is this: to get you and your workplace ready for 2020. You will benefit most from this book if you are in a position to influence the design of the workplace. Leaders at the tops of organizations will want to read the best practices revealed here and plot a strategy for preparing for the 2020 workplace. In addition, every business leader who manages a team will want to read this book to understand how to best attract, develop, and retain talent, as will practitioners in the field of organization and talent development who lead from within.

ALIENUS NON DIUTIUS

Alone no longer. The crest of Pixar University bears this Latin motto.[6] The research and best-practice examples that make up the core of this book are here for you to translate into appropriate actions for your organization—whether your business is a Fortune 500 multinational or an Inc. 500 firm. Thanks to the power of social media, we can all help one another as we transform for the future.

We welcome your thoughts and stories, and we invite you to join us in an adventure to create the future. Share with us at www .the2020workplace.com.

PART I

The Changing Workplace

CHAPTER ONE

Ten Forces Shaping the Future Workplace Now

Imagine the life of a new employee at a Fortune Global 1000 firm in the year 2020.

The alarm in her apartment starts out quietly, easing Katya into the morning with the latest release from her favorite musician. After sixty seconds, the alarm asks Katya if she is awake. "Barely," Katya mumbles in response.

"Okay," her alarm answers. "I'll let you rest another two minutes before checking in again."

"Make it five," Katya replies.

"I shouldn't have stayed up so late last night," she thinks, "not on the night before my first day of work." Who would have guessed that José, her best friend from childhood, was going to be in town? If her phone hadn't alerted her that José's phone was within ten miles, she would never have known. Serendipity, a program that matched her social networking profiles with those of others with similar interests, also alerted her that a close match had just moved into the same apartment building. After she and José checked out Elisa's profile, the three of them headed out to play the latest version of Celebrity City. Wearing their Cisco virtual-world contacts, they had tracked down five virtual celebrities. Her last one, John Lennon, had been worth 1,000 points and put her on the leaderboard. And that reminded her: she needed to bring along her virtual-world contacts for her new-hire orientation that morning.

"Well," the apartment alarm observed, "I see you are out of bed. Shall I turn on the morning news and start the espresso machine?"

"Sure," Katya replied, contacts in hand as she headed off to the bathroom to get ready.

Today, finally, was her first day of work at D&Y, one of the Big Two auditors. In her eighth year of schooling, D&Y had visited her middle school and talked to her about what was involved in pursuing a career in auditing. She'd had an education consultant from D&Y assigned to her well before she attended university, and they'd had a monthly video chat on Facebook to discuss her progress and whether D&Y still fit into her plans. Katya was also interested in nanobiotechnology, but in the end she'd decided a career in auditing at D&Y was a better fit.

In her freshman year at university, Katya shadowed a manager at D&Y. Then, after her third year, Katya spent the summer at the firm's office in Romania before accepting a full-time position at the end of the summer. Because Katya had a high grade point average at university, she was eligible to perform community service, spending three months in Tanzania before starting work at D&Y.

Glancing up at the instant messaging section on the monitor on the wall, she noticed that a few of her new coworkers were IM'ing as they also got ready. Sophie, already one of her best friends, was looking forward to meeting up later in the day.

"Breakfast is ready!" her apartment monitor cheerfully announced, so she headed toward the kitchen to grab a fresh egg sandwich and her coffee to have on the way to work.

The human resources meeting was blissfully short. She ran

her thumbprint and mobile phone under a scanner, which confirmed her citizenship and uploaded all her data to her custom benefits plan. For the next few hours, a series of managers presented the projects and jobs she could consider for her first assignment. Potential managers described their working styles, their commitment to the careers of new recruits, and the exciting work they had to offer. Katya especially liked the presentation by Bhaskar in Hyderabad and pulled out her smart phone so she could search the internal company social network to see how other new employees had rated Bhaskar and what they had to say, along with his 360-degree manager review.

"Not bad," she thought as she looked over a presentation he had done for a client in the nanobiotechnology field. That would allow her to merge both her interests, and besides, if it didn't work out, D&Y's promise was that she could select her first three jobs, so she would be able to explore a few fields before settling in a bit. "WDYT," she IM'd Sophie, wondering what her new friend thought of the idea. Sophie, sitting next to her, quickly IM'd back "G4I" to show her support.*

Three learning programs, each two minutes long, popped up on her smart phone while she listened to the next potential manager. She responded while she updated her employee record, verifying completion of the learning programs. After the managers completed their presentations, she put on her headphones and virtual-world contacts to watch a job preview by each manager. By lunchtime, she had selected and won Bhaskar as her new manager.[1]

Welcome to the 2020 workplace! If you think this scenario is farfetched, think again.

In the year 2020, our office will be everywhere; our team members will live halfway around the world. How, where, when, and for whom we work will be up to us—as long as we produce results.

---

* WDYT, "What do you think?" G4I, "Go for it."

By the year 2020, the rules of the employee-employer contract will have to be rewritten by the best employers if they are to compete for top talent.

After interviewing, researching, and speaking with people at scores of companies, as well as with members of the four generations currently in the workplace, we have identified ten forces that will define the new world of work in 2020. These forces will impact the lives of all those who work, whether they work in large companies, midsize not-for-profit firms, or public organizations.

Companies will experience the most daunting challenges as they compete for the best talent in 2020 in order to maximize their organizations' success. Senior executives, keenly aware that the world around them is changing and already recruiting a new breed of employee, must adapt their workplace policies to appeal to all generations. By looking at the road maps of birthrates, technological changes, social behaviors, and the evolution of the knowledge economy, we observe ten global forces at work in the workplace to come in 2020.

1. SHIFTING WORKFORCE DEMOGRAPHICS
Shifting U.S. Demographics

As we examine the shifting demographics of the U.S. workforce, we see the following:

- The number of U.S. workers over the age of 40 has increased significantly: 51 percent of the U.S. workforce in 2010 is expected to be 40 years of age or older, a 33 percent increase since 1980.[2]
- The number of workers aged 55 years and older will grow from 13 percent of the labor force in 2000 to 20 percent in 2020.[3]
- At the same time, Millennials (individuals born between 1977 and 1997) will be entering the workforce in record numbers. While they currently represent 22 percent of all workers, by 2014 they will make up almost 47 percent of the workforce.[4]
- The gender composition will also change, as more women are entering the workforce and staying in it.[5]

• Finally, Latinos, who currently make up 15 percent of the U.S. population, will account for up to 30 percent of the U.S. population by 2050.[6]

Taken together, these shifts will present significant challenges and opportunities. How companies prepare for these changes will be crucial to attracting, developing, and keeping top talent.

A Worldwide Shift in Demographics

The United States is not the only country facing a major shift in demographics, as the birth of Baby Boomers, those born between the years 1946 and 1964, was a global phenomenon following World War II. In Europe, the current aging of the population, combined with a significant falloff in fertility rates, has translated into a 1 percent decline in the overall population during the 2000–2010 decade. After 2010, the trend is projected to accelerate over the next forty years, with Germany, Italy, and Spain all expected to experience population declines ranging from 14 to 25 percent, according to the United Nations Population Division.[7]

These demographic trends are producing a workforce that is both aging and shrinking. It is estimated that in 2020 Germany will have a workforce that is 20 percent smaller than it was in 2000 and a retired population that is 50 percent larger.[8]

In many Asian countries the demographic situation is similar to or more pronounced than that seen in Europe. Fertility rates in Japan, Taiwan, Korea, Hong Kong, and China are all well below the replacement level. Consequently, estimates indicate that major East Asian countries will also face a sizable reduction in their working population over the next half century. For example, in Japan the working-age population has already peaked, with 3 million fewer workers in 2010 than in 2005. And in China, which has four times the population of the United States, the situation is much the same. By 2030, China will have nearly as many senior citizens aged 65 or older as children aged 15 and younger.[9] In the global economy, shifts happening globally will impact how and where companies in all countries source new talent.

What Will the Workforce Look Like in 2020?

In the United States, recent data show that older workers are staying in their jobs longer or returning after retiring. As a result, the Bureau of Labor Statistics estimates that 56 percent of those 65 and older now work full-time, as compared to 44 percent thirteen years ago. In addition, the Pew Research Center's Social & Demographic Trends project reports that half of all working adults in the United States between the ages of 50 and 64 say they will delay retirement, and another 16 percent report that they never expect to stop working.[10]

Dubbed by the Pew Research Center "the Threshold Generation," this generation is on the threshold of retirement, but they either want or need to continue working. According to a *Wall Street Journal* article, "While it is difficult to quantify just how many Americans are retiring earlier now amid weak job prospects, recent work from two Wellesley College economists, Courtney Coile and Phillip B. Levine, suggests the effect is large. In a new working paper, they estimate 378,000 workers will be pushed into retirement as a result of the weak labor market—almost 50% more than will end up working longer because of stock-market losses."[11] As Kris Moser, a 62-year-old member of the Threshold Generation and a producer of computer games who was recently laid off from her position, says, "While the fastest-growing area in gaming is social gaming and the fastest-growing demographic on Facebook is over fifty, it's ironic that those of us over fifty who want to continue working in the gaming industry are having a difficult, if not impossible, time finding work."

What does this mean? Although some older workers will find themselves pushed out of the job market, those who retain jobs may stay in them longer. As we move into the future, most workplaces will have five generations working side by side—Traditionalists, born before 1946; Baby Boomers, born between 1946 and 1964; Generation X, born between 1965 and 1976; Millennials, born between 1977 and 1997; and Generation 2020, born after 1997 (see figure 1-1). While human resource executives are trained to address many forms of diversity, they must now be prepared to manage extreme age diversity as well.

Gender

With the recession that began in 2008, one of the longest in the post–World War II era, there is a new milestone emerging. Though women still face other issues when it comes to equal employment, women are now about to surpass men on the nation's payrolls for the first time in history. This has arisen from a pattern in which the bulk of the layoffs experienced in the recession that began in 2008 fell on men, who accounted for 82 percent of the job losses.[12] One of the reasons for this is that predominantly male industries, such as construction and manufacturing, faced layoffs in higher numbers than did other industries. Heather Boushey and Ann O'Leary of the Center for American Progress estimate that women are now half of all U.S. workers, and mothers are the primary breadwinners or co-breadwinners in nearly two-thirds of American families. Compare this to 1967, when women made up only one-third of all workers.[13]

Ethnicity

The U.S. workforce is in the midst of a transformation. From 1980 to 2020, Caucasian workers in the United States will decline from 82

Figure 1-1: Generations as Percentage of U.S. Population

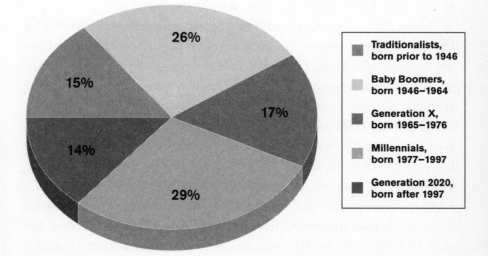

26%

15%

17%

14%

29%

Traditionalists,
born prior to 1946

Baby Boomers,
born 1946–1964

Generation X,
born 1965–1976

Millennials,
born 1977–1997

Generation 2020,
born after 1997

Source: U.S. Census Bureau, 2007 American Community Survey.

percent to 63 percent. During the same period, the non-Caucasian portion of the workforce is projected to double from 18 percent to 37 percent, with the Latino portion almost tripling from 6 percent to 17 percent.[14] Thus minority workers, who will largely be Generation Xers and Millennials, will account for most of the net growth in the workforce.

The workforce of 2020 will place new demands on employers as they manage a workforce with greater diversity in age, gender, and ethnicity.

2. THE KNOWLEDGE ECONOMY

The shift in the demographics is related to a larger issue: the changing skill and knowledge levels needed to get and keep a job in the global economy. In the next five to ten years, a growing number of jobs will require a significantly more complex set of interdisciplinary skills. The Employment Policy Foundation estimates that 80 percent of the impending labor shortage will involve a skills shortage. McKinsey Research calls this the "rise of the tacit workforce," referring to employees in jobs that require a complex set of skills such as problem solving, judgment, listening, data analysis, relationship building, and collaborating and communicating with coworkers.

These tacit jobs are opposed to transactional ones, which involve fewer conceptual duties. The tacit segment of the workforce is growing two and half times faster than the transactional segment. Today, 48 million of the more than 137 million U.S. workers are knowledge workers, making knowledge workers the fastest-growing talent pool in most organizations.[15] Put another way, 70 percent of all U.S. jobs created since 1998—4.5 million jobs, or roughly the combined workforce of the fifty-six largest public companies by market capitalization—require a set of conceptual tacit skills.

Part of the reason for the realignment of the workforce toward tacit jobs is that companies have been revising how they manage the least complex jobs, by streamlining processes, automating job tasks, and outsourcing some work. According to Forrester Research, at least

3.3 million white-collar jobs and $136 billion in wages will shift from the U.S. to lower-cost countries such as India and Russia by 2015.[16]

The types of transactional jobs that have been outsourced range from Nortel's software development centers to Boeing's aerospace engineers and Thomson Reuters' editorial assistants. As Thomas Friedman noted in *The World Is Flat*, Thomson Reuters outsources a number of journalist functions to India because it is a job that can be done anywhere in the new "flat world." Tom Glocer, the CEO of Thomson Reuters, points out that the value-added work of a journalist involves "someone in the market with contacts, who knows who the best industry analysts are and has taken the right people to lunch."[17] By outsourcing other functions of the job, Thomson Reuters is able to preserve as many high value-added journalist jobs as possible.

How, where, and when work is done is changing dramatically as more companies shift the composition of their workforces to lower-cost countries while creating a greater percentage of tacit jobs in the United States.

3. GLOBALIZATION

Globalization. The world is flat. Outsourcing. Today they're givens, but this was not always the case. Changes in the world in which we live and work in are happening at a rate that does not afford organizations the luxury of managing one major change at a time. The evidence is all around us, but a telling example can be found in the companies making up the annual Fortune 500 list. If a company was on the list in 1980, there was a 56 percent chance that it was still listed in 1994. But for a company listed in 1994, there was only a 30 percent chance of its still being on the list in 2007. And look how rapidly new innovations are reaching a penetration of 50 million households: it took radio thirty-eight years, television thirteen years, the Internet four years, iPods three years, and Facebook only two years to reach a penetration of 50 million households.[18]

More dramatically, a look at the headquarters locations of the *Financial Times* Global 500 rankings shows us just how globalized we are becoming in today's "flat world." Consider the shifts that have taken place in the top fifteen countries on the Global 500 rankings over the past five years. Over the period 2005 to 2009, the number of Global 500 companies headquartered in Brazil, Russia, India, and China (collectively known as BRIC) has significantly increased. As shown in table 1-1, the total number of companies represented by the top fifteen countries remains fairly constant. The United States shows a sharp decline with a net loss of thirty-eight companies, while countries filling the gap include China, with a net gain of thirty-five companies; Russia, with a net gain of two companies; India, with a net gain of five companies; and Brazil, with a net gain of four companies in the top 500.[19]

TABLE 1-1: TOP FIFTEEN COUNTRY HEADQUARTERS LOCATIONS

Country	2005	2006	2007	2008	2009	Percentage Change, 2005–2009
United States	219	197	184	169	181	−17
Japan	43	60	49	39	49	14
United Kingdom	33	36	41	35	32	−3
China	8	11	16	35	43	438
Canada	22	22	23	24	27	23
France	28	30	32	31	23	−18
Germany	19	19	20	22	20	5
Australia	8	8	11	11	14	75
Spain	9	8	12	14	13	44
India	5	4	8	13	10	100
Switzerland	12	11	12	12	10	−17
Brazil	5	8	7	11	9	80
Netherlands	9	8	10	8	8	−11
Italy	12	11	8	7	7	−42
Russia	4	8	8	13	6	50

Source: *Financial Times* Global 500—Top Fifteen Countries.[20]

By 2020, the BRIC countries will be the dominant centers of economic influence. What will this mean for how work is being sourced? Just ask Manish Modi, the president of the Business Resource Group of Pidilite Industries, who says, "Any job that is English-based can be done in India—you are only limited by your creativity and imagination." The list of professions that are being outsourced even includes lawyers. Forrester Research of Cambridge, Massachusetts, estimates that the number of U.S. legal jobs moved offshore will increase from 35,000 in 2010 to 79,000 by 2015.[21]

More striking, though, is how the nature of work is changing in a global marketplace. Regardless of whether your firm is an established multinational or a high-tech start-up, you are likely tapping into a global talent pool and—at least to some extent—managing a virtual workforce. Virtual workplaces such as these have fewer on-site employees and leaner headquarters facilities. Instead, they have workers organized in global teams who do not report to offices, do not keep set hours, and are compensated more in cash than in benefits. We call these individuals transient white-collar workers because they are working when, where, and how they want. According to an IBM spokesman, Clint Roswell, roughly 40 percent of IBM's staff is mobile, meaning they have no office and telecommute from home or a client location.[22] So how do they do their work? By collaborating electronically, in global conference calls with participants from three or four continents, through instant messaging, or by using password-protected document-sharing sites.

This global workplace increasingly places a premium on speed to market, local decision making, collaboration, and open-source innovation. For example, A. G. Lafley, the chairman of Procter & Gamble (P&G), says his company's goal is to get half of new product innovations from worldwide entrepreneurs, outside traditional P&G labs.[23] P&G has taken a visionary stance on product innovation and development. Lafley says, "We want P&G to be known as the company that collaborates—inside and out—better than any other company in the world."[24] Companies like P&G are becoming more agile, and leaders such as Lafley are requiring collaboration, agility, and open innovation as the levers for future growth.

Organizations that accomplish these goals will undoubtedly do so by leveraging an array of tools and technologies allowing employees the ability to share knowledge instantly and work in virtual teams.

4. THE DIGITAL WORKPLACE

Have you ever wondered how much digital content is passing through companies on any given day? Surprisingly, the answer may lie with a little-known nineteenth-century Italian scientist named Amedeo Avogadro, who defined the number of carbon atoms in twelve grams as $602,200,000,000,000,000,000,000$, or 6.022×10^{23}, known as Avogadro's number. The digital universe is not that big yet, but it's getting there.

According to a research study, "The Diverse and Exploding Digital Universe," the number of "atoms" in the digital universe—meaning the amount of digital content in bytes captured, created, and replicated during the year—was less than a hundredth of Avogadro's number.[25] However, "the number of digital 'atoms' in the digital universe is already bigger than the number of stars in the universe. And, because the digital universe is expanding by a factor of 10 every five years, in 15 years it will surpass Avogadro's number."[26]

Social Web: The cluster of Web 2.0 tools, such as blogs, wikis, and social networks, that drive community building and collaboration.

Blog: An individual or group online Web log maintained with regular entries on the subject of the contributors' choosing.

Wiki: A page or collection of pages designed to allow anyone with access to contribute or modify content.

The rapid expansion of the digital universe—defined as information that is created, captured, or replicated in digital form—will lead to tremendous challenges in the workplace for both individual employees and their employers. This digital information includes using the social Web and a host of social media tools, such as blogs, wikis, and video-sharing sites—in other words, all the tools you and I take for granted in how we communicate in our work and personal lives.

Currently hundreds of millions of people actively construct, maintain, and communicate their identities using Facebook and a host of other networks such as MySpace, Twitter, Friendster, Orkut, LinkedIn, and Bebo.[27] Though this number is substantial, what is even more impressive is how fast it is growing. An estimated 250,000 new users each day are creating online profiles and maintaining them on a social network. In addition to this, last year more than 125 million Americans watched more than 7 billion online video streams per month on sites such as YouTube, Metacafe, Vimeo, and Daily Motion. This audience represented almost a twofold increase from the previous year. YouTube itself is considered to be the largest online video library in the world and in 2007 was estimated to hold more than 70 terabytes, or 70,000 gigabytes, of data. Given that in 1993 the sum of all Internet traffic for the year combined amounted to approximately 100 terabytes, or 100,000 gigabytes, this is a fairly impressive accomplishment.[28] Some suspect that this number has grown at a rate of 18 terabytes a month. If so, YouTube is now more than four times the size of the Library of Congress, the largest physical library in the world.[29]

How Will the Digital Workplace Affect Us in the Twenty-first Century?

While individuals generate nearly 70 percent of digital content, it is their employers who have the responsibility for managing the security and privacy of this content with regard to the workplace.[30] Organizations must grapple with a host of issues on how to manage all this digital content in the workplace, especially when the software, platforms, and infrastructure are operated by others—often called cloud computing. This growth in digital content will affect every part of corporate life, from how employees contribute new knowledge and how they communicate with one another on the job and at home to the type of policies, standards, and guidelines created by organizations to manage this explosion of digital content. Increasingly, employees are carrying their own connection platforms with them in devices such as laptops, iPods, mobile phones, and flash drives, each one suited to a different aspect of their busy lives. The challenge for employers will be to walk a fine line between making it easy for employees to create and access content while securing the accuracy and appropriateness of this content in the mobile world in which we live.

5. THE UBIQUITY OF MOBILE TECHNOLOGY

Workers are demanding a new deal from their employers. Employees want a choice in how and where they work. On September 7, 1987, fifteen phone companies signed an agreement to build mobile networks based on the Global System for Mobile Communications, or GSM. This date was the birth of the global mobile phone industry.

Once feasible only for the affluent, mobile phones are now everyday communications tools essential to our modern lives. In a number of countries around the world there are now more mobile phones than people. For example, as of 2009, for every 100 individuals in the United Kingdom there were 123.64 mobile phone subscriptions.[31] It took twelve years for the first billion mobile connections to be made, but only thirty months later there were more than 3.5 billion subscriptions globally. GSM projects that by 2012, there will be 4.5 billion mobile subscriptions out of a global population of 7 billion, and by 2020 mobile devices will be the primary way people access the Internet.

As explained by Dr. Mike Short, a vice president of Telefónica Europe and former chairman of GSM, "We measure subscriptions because there is a growing trend for consumers to have more than one mobile phone—one mobile for personal use and one for professional business. So we see a trend of more mobile phones than people in the world." Among other things, Short sees the potential for mobile technology to one day revolutionize health care. For example, in London today, a hemophilia patient can text his or her status to a hospital via a mobile phone. More pervasive uses of mobile technology can have significant impact on the quality of health care delivery. The ubiquity of mobile phones is shown in the following list.

THE UBIQUITY OF MOBILE COMMUNICATIONS

- Globally, more than 2.5 trillion text messages were sent in 2008.[32]
- New users of mobile technology are signing up at the rate of 1,000 per minute for mobile services that support music, TV, video, and learning.
- Mobile technology has more users in the developing world than in the developed world, with 64 percent of mobile users living in emerging markets.
- China is the country with the most mobile users totally—445 million.
- There are now more mobile phones in the world than computers and TVs combined.[33]

Source: GSM Association, 2008; *New York Times*, 2008; and the *Guardian*, 2009.

All this growth in mobile phones has brought with it a surge of innovative uses for mobile devices in learning, starting in primary school. For example, the Kauffman Foundation, an organization that exists at the intersection of education and entrepreneurship, funded a program called Sports Bytes, where mobile phones delivered math and science quizzes to students attending sporting events in stadiums across the United States. According to Julia Holland, education manager of the Kauffman Foundation, "more than 100,000 people participated in Sports Bytes with the goal of inspiring a new generation to use their mobile phones as a learning device."

One can envision how mobile phones could become the most important wearable learning platform in our lifetime. All you have to do is view the long list of iPhone applications to see more than 7,200 applications in the education section alone, in areas such as learning a new language or brushing up on math skills. The most popular educational application is a free Spanish tutorial program offered by the 24/7 Tutor series. This program teaches a set of the most common and useful words and phrases, with audio recordings by native speakers and a learning system that allows you to quiz yourself as you progress.[34]

Finally, mobile devices are becoming an important tool for corporate learning as well. Companies such as Bank of America, Invitrogen, and Wachovia have pilots under way to deliver corporate training on mobile smart phones. In a survey of 125 heads of human resources conducted by Human Capital Institute, nearly 70 percent of respondents reported that they were working on mobile learning pilots to be launched in 2011. Among the areas of corporate training ripe for delivery on mobile devices are sales training, compliance training, product knowledge, and online performance support.

6. A CULTURE OF CONNECTIVITY

If you have a teenager in your household, you will most likely recognize the following scenario: on a typical weekday evening, your teenager is doing homework while also texting a friend from class, sending a message on Facebook to let everyone know about a party that evening, listening to music on an iPod, and engaging with at least ten instant messages. Welcome to the connected world we live in.

In a white paper by IDC, those who participate in this culture are called the hyperconnected. The hyperconnected are defined as those who are always connected regardless of where they physically happen to be—at work, home, on vacation, in a restaurant, in bed, or even in a house of worship. Increasingly, their personal and business lives are blurring into a single extended conversation. The more devices they carry in their arsenal, the better. According to IDC, these hyperconnected professionals currently make up 16 percent of the workforce and will increase to 40 percent of the workforce in next few years.

A new phrase has been coined to refer to how the hyperconnected spend their time: It is "weisure time," the next step in the evolving work-life culture. Weisure refers to the blurred line between work and fun. Family, friends, and coworkers are all constantly in touch, using an arsenal of the latest technologies from mobile phones to laptops. As we become increasingly connected, our lives become less rigidly divided.[35]

At Zappos, an online shoe retailer known for customer service, managers dedicate 20 percent of their time to after-hours, nonwork activities with their team, according to Aaron Magness, the head of business development and brand marketing. "You're building trust by spending time outside the office with your team," says Magness, "and trust leads to faster decisions. The line is blurring between work and free time at our company."

WHO ARE THE HYPERCONNECTED?

- They are found in all countries but more in Latin America and the Asia Pacific region.
- They are found in all industries, with higher concentrations in banking and high technology.
- They are found in all jobs but predominantly in IT and research and development.
- They come from all levels of the corporation but most likely are in management.
- They can be any age—what matters is attitude, not age—but 60 percent are under 35.
- They include both men and women, but 60 percent of them are male.
- They have wired homes; 63 percent have Wi-Fi at home.
- They tend to live in urban areas.
- If they have to leave the house on short notice, they will take their laptop before they reach for their wallet.
- They tend to work for companies that are early adopters of new technologies.

Source: IDC, "The Hyperconnected: Here They Come!," www.nortel.com/promotions/idc_paper/index.html.

But does all this hyperconnectivity have a dark side? Two recent federal lawsuits in the United States raise questions as to how hyperconnectivity impacts hourly employees when they are asked to use company smart phones to respond to e-mails and voice mails after hours and without pay. When the federal Fair Labor Standards Act was passed in 1938, "work" was easy to define for hourly employees, but as new technologies have blurred the line between work and

Corporate social network: A Web site behind a company's firewall that allows users to construct a profile they use to interact with others using social media tools such as messaging, journaling, photo sharing, tagging, and searching.

RSS feed: A Web publisher feature that allows readers to subscribe to view posts from a frequently updated Web site without visiting the site itself. RSS stands for "really simple syndication." RSS feeds collect the posts and push them to the reader through an e-mail update, or an RSS reader, or to a custom portal.

Mash-up: A Web application combining data or tools from more than one source into a single interface.

free time, the workplace has become a 24/7 environment.[36] Human resource officers need to understand these issues and their impact on various segments of the workforce in order to map out a strategy for how to manage hyperconnectivity in the workplace.

Hyperconnectivity is becoming a business issue. The McKinsey global survey of 1,700 executives from around the world reports significant value realized from social media deployments. Of the 1,700 executives surveyed, 69 percent gained measurable business benefits from usage of social media, including the implementation of more innovative products and services, more effective marketing, better access to knowledge, lower cost of doing business, and higher revenues.[37]

The McKinsey study found that companies are using social media to address a variety of stakeholders:

- 41 percent of companies use social media for internal purposes.
- 34 percent of companies connect with customers through social media.
- 25 percent of companies work with external partners and suppliers using social media.

Companies that successfully adopt social media understand that employees are looking for ways to work smarter; if social media tools can help them accomplish this, employees will adopt them as part of their natural workflow. Since we are in the early stages of the hyper-connected world, challenges remain: there are multiple systems, multiple passwords, and information stored in places that are not always connected. Some companies, such as Nortel, are addressing the need for businesses to unify their communication systems to leverage the potential that hyperconnectivity can yield to the bottom line.[38]

Companies are forming cross-functional teams to examine how and why to support the hyperconnected workforce. One of the compelling business drivers is the amount of time that knowledge workers spend looking for answers to their questions. According to a recent white paper by Socialtext, a social networking software provider:

- Knowledge workers spend up to one day a week looking for information, and half the time they may not find what they need. The costs associated with lost productivity are enormous.
- Knowledge workers want help finding the information they need to do their jobs. The days of hoarding knowledge are over.
- Knowledge workers recognize that just asking around may not yield the necessary results.[39]

When you consider that people need to be able to find and use knowledge to stay competent on the job, it's no surprise that they are using the same tools they use as consumers and then bringing their digital expectations into the workplace. The McKinsey study found that the tools leveraged most widely inside organizations are blogs, social networking, wikis, and video sharing—the same technologies consumers use in their personal lives. When used inside an organization, these social media tools foster collaboration, help identify and recruit talent, and enable rapid dissemination of learning, among a host of other uses. While organizations must develop a strategy for integrating these tools into their workflow, the rewards are significant and have the potential to drive improved business results.

In the 2020 workplace, work is becoming a place to collaborate, exchange ideas, and communicate with colleagues and customers. Your value as an employee will be determined not only by how well you perform your job but also by how much you contribute your knowledge and ideas back to the organization. The ways in which companies develop this culture of collaboration will become a significant competitive factor in attracting and engaging top talent in the twenty-first century.

7. THE PARTICIPATION SOCIETY

How can companies improve collaboration and knowledge sharing to achieve improved business results? Increasingly they are creating groundswells, a social trend whereby people use technologies to get the things they need from one another, rather than from traditional institutions.[40]

Scott Cook, the founder of Intuit and a former Bain & Company consultant, calls this the "contribution revolution," in which companies tap the creativity of their consumers and turn the knowledge gained into new products, new services, and improved business results. This concept of user contributions is not a new one. In 1979, Tim and Nina Zagat founded the Zagat Survey, which compiles consumer ratings of restaurants, airlines, hotels, zoos, shopping centers, and movies. Their success in New York City led them to expand to scores of cities though the world.[41]

There are numerous examples of how this contribution revolution is redefining businesses. Procter & Gamble leverages user contributions in an online forum called BeingGirl, which is geared toward preteen girls looking to learn from and share their experiences with feminine hygiene products. This has become four times as effective as television ads for building market share for products such as the Always and Tampax brands. Similarly, Sprint, in partnership with the Suave line of personal care products, created the Web site Motherhood, where users share stories and tips about being a mom. To date, more than three thousand stories have been created, and they serve as possible plotlines for an online comedy series. Unilever research found that the Web site increases users' intent to purchase a Suave product while positioning the brand as one that is in touch with the lives of consumers.[42]

These contribution systems are also used inside the company. Best Buy, the U.S. retailer, is doing this in an employee contribution system called Blue Shirt Nation. Launched in June 2006 by the marketing managers Steve Bendt and Gary Koelling, Blue Shirt Nation was originally created as a way to gather insight on what type of advertising was working in the store. Blue Shirt Nation has now become an online corporate social network for retail associates to help one another solve store operational issues, discuss best practices on what works and what doesn't on the sales floor, and even share jokes. Today Blue Shirt Nation, with more than 24,000 registered employee users, is moderated by the Blue Shirts themselves.

What Bendt and Koelling did not anticipate when they created Blue Shirt Nation was how the Web site could be used in human resources in addition to marketing. For example, Blue Shirt Nation ran an employee contest in which employees submitted videos to spur employee participation in 401(k) plans. The result was a 30 percent increase in plan enrollment, improved awareness of company human resources programs, and increased employee engagement. Blue Shirt Nation has also played a factor in reducing employee turnover. Whereas company turnover rates for retail associates were previously approximately 60 percent, the self-selected members of Blue Shirt Nation have a turnover rate below 10 percent. Perhaps as retail associates become engaged in Blue Shirt Nation, they become more satisfied with their jobs.[43]

8. SOCIAL LEARNING

If we think of the 1990s as the "e" decade, as in e-learning, e-books and e-libraries, we can envision 2010 to 2020 as the "s" decade, as in social networking, social media, and social learning. We are seeing that corporate learning does not have to be designed and delivered in a top-down fashion. Instead, learning is becoming participatory, social, fun, engaging, and, most important, integrated with work. Whereas Learning 1.0 relied heavily on classroom learning, Learning 2.0 added computer based e-learning, and now Learning 3.0, or social learning, incorporates social media, gaming, real-time feedback, and simulations. Social learning yields new knowledge from a social interaction: a text message, a post on a Facebook wall, a comment on a blog post, an entry on a wiki, a lecture accessed on a mobile phone, or an insight gained from viewing and commenting on a YouTube video.

Social learning: Learning that is collaborative, immediate, relevant, and presented in the context of an individual's unique work environment.

John Seely Brown, a consultant and author, tells this story: John King, the associate provost for academic information technology of the University of Michigan, asked Brown a seemingly straightforward question about how many students Brown thought the University of Michigan taught each year. In response, Brown says, "I knew that the university had approximately 40,000 students, give or take a few thousand, so that was my answer." Though King agreed that Brown had gotten the university enrollment correct, he explained that the number of students touched was much closer to 250,000. Here's his rationale: "Each year the incoming students bring their social networks with them. These networks reach back into UM students' communities and schools. Using the social software and social network tools of SMS, IM, Facebook, MySpace, they extend the discussions, debates, bull sessions and study groups that naturally arise on campus to encompass this broader constituency, thus amplifying the effect the university is having across the state."[44]

These networks are being used to brainstorm ideas, propose questions, conduct research, and extend the debate in the classroom. Today, you have to consider the larger social environment each student belongs to when assessing how and where learning occurs.[45]

If learning at the university level is becoming more of a social experience, what about corporate learning? There are a growing number of companies profiled in chapters 5 and 6 that are reinventing and reimagining learning to make it more personal and social, to increase its availability via various formats, and to blend it into work. Companies that are following this model are developing more engaging and collaborative learning experiences, which have greater appeal across generations and are creating a competitive advantage in sourcing and retaining top talent.

9. CORPORATE SOCIAL RESPONSIBILITY

If learning is becoming social, so is corporate philanthropy, which is now business-driven and integrated into the social, ethical, and environmental agendas of a growing number of companies. This is known as corporate social responsibility (CSR). Some companies are taking CSR one step further by embedding leadership development opportunities into a number of these programs. Companies such as IBM, Pfizer, and Ernst & Young are creating CSR programs that work in the following way: they select a small number of high-potential managers and send them to work in a local business for one month in a region of the world where the company anticipates future growth. Though these programs are rooted in philanthropy, they give the sponsoring organizations an opportunity to build future global leaders with work experience in a country targeted for growth.

While the programs are branded by each organization under various names, such as IBM's Corporate Service Corps, Ernst & Young's Corporate Responsibility Fellows, and Pfizer's Global Health Fellows, the goal is the same: corporate citizenship as a vehicle to further strategic business goals while building a new pool of global leaders.

The most extensive of these programs is IBM's Corporate Service Corps (CSC). Under this program, founded in July 2008, IBM sends roughly 100 employees each year from thirty-one countries to Romania, Turkey, Vietnam, Ghana, and Tanzania to work in teams of eight to ten on such projects as helping entrepreneurs access microloans, designing learning labs, and training teachers in the most effective uses of information and communication technologies.[46]

To date, IBM is committing $6 million over the next three years, with the goal of having six hundred IBMers participate in the Corporate Service Corps. According to Kevin Thompson, senior program manager for the IBM Corporate Service Corps, "The idea behind the Corporate Service Corps grew out of IBM's desire to have more employees develop a global perspective in the countries where IBM sees long-term growth opportunities for the next decade. At IBM we refer to this as building global citizenship." Corporate Service Corps is part of the new IBM global citizenship arena, responsible for building global citizenship skills among young leaders.

Global citizenship: Involves understanding how to conduct business in a foreign country, developing an increased cultural intelligence and a deeper appreciation of the relationship between business and society, and being able to understand complex policy environments and how to work in virtual teams with people from all over the world.

Though CSC is described as philanthropic, employees selected for the six-month-long programs are not volunteers. They draw their regular salaries, and they are reimbursed for travel and expenses during their time overseas. Thompson shares the broader vision of the CSC: "to build global citizenship skills among our high-potential leaders." Thompson continues, "It's no longer enough to have our employees read about how to conduct business in an emerging market. We believe they must have hands-on experience in how to live, work, and communicate in an emerging country."

One of those accepted to IBM's CSC program was Dr. Stefan Radtke, a systems architect for thirteen years at IBM. Radtke, based in Germany, was selected to join a five-person CSC team in Ghana to work for Yeboah Afihene Industries Limited, a family-run business that manufactures spring mattresses, steel beds, steel chairs, and other furniture. The company is currently involved in a project to manufacture more environmentally friendly products. Radtke prepared for his international assignment by participating on an IBM password-protected social networking site where the other members of his team got to know one another by posting photos, sharing expectations of participating in the CSC, becoming familiar with the local customs and the local economy, and completing a series of online courses relevant to the objectives of the assignment in Ghana.

After Radtke returned from Ghana, he concluded that "the biggest lesson for me in working in Ghana was not the technical aspect of the job or helping the company with its strategic plan, but it was the cultural aspect, meaning being aware of the cultural differences in Ghana and how to refrain from attempting to convince my team members that IBM's way was the only *right* way to work. Rather we learned how to all work together to find the *best* way to get things done."

Now IBM is using its corporate social investment program as a recruiting tool for the company. This makes good sense because 94 percent of new college hires expect to work across geographic borders, and 88 percent will seek out employers with social responsibility values that reflect their own, as revealed in a PricewaterhouseCoopers (PwC) survey of 4,271 new college hires entitled "Managing Tomorrow's People: Millennials at Work." This survey also reports that another 86 percent of new college hires will consider leaving an employer whose social responsibility values no longer reflect their own.[47]

Given this level of commitment to corporate social responsibility among new college hires, it is not surprising that companies such as IBM, Pfizer, and Ernst & Young are ensuring that their corporate social responsibility programs have greater impact. They are embedding opportunities for their employees to enhance their global leadership skills while working in emerging countries and then using these programs as a way to attract, develop, and engage high potential talent.

10. MILLENNIALS IN THE WORKPLACE

Millennials, those born between 1977 and 1997, are called by many names: the Net Generation, Gen Y, Digital Natives, even the Google Generation, to name a few. But regardless of the term used, these individuals share a common trait: they have grown up using technology as part of their everyday lives, and they will expect employers to provide them with the same tools to collaborate, brainstorm, and network on the job that they use in their personal lives.

As Don Tapscott tells us in his book *Grown Up Digital: How the Net Generation Is Changing Your World*, "If you understand the Net Generation, you will understand the future. You will also understand how our institutions and society need to change today."[48] As the first generation to be wired from birth, he says, "Net Geners are smarter, quicker, and more tolerant of diversity than their predecessors. They care strongly about justice and the problems faced by their society."[49] These young people are transforming every institution of modern life. They are requesting opportunities for personalized learning through mentors, and inquiring about opportunities to have virtual coaches or e-coaches in their pursuit of developing a career.

If companies want to attract and engage the best Millennial talent, they need to place more emphasis on providing these young working professionals what they value most, argues Tapscott. Eight norms or defining characteristics of Net Geners are critical to understanding the needs and expectations of this generation. According to Tapscott, Net Geners:

- Want freedom in everything they do: from freedom of choice to freedom of expression.
- Love to customize and personalize their experiences.
- Are the "new" scrutinizers.
- Look for corporate integrity and openness when deciding what to buy and where to work.
- Want to find entertainment in their work, educational, and social lives.
- Are focused on collaboration and relationship building.
- Have a need for speed—and not just in video games.
- Are innovators and are constantly looking for innovative ways to collaborate, entertain themselves, learn, and work.[50]

Organizations that understand what is important to Millennials in the workplace will have a competitive advantage in attracting and engaging them. Consider the experience of NASA's Johnson Space Center (JSC). One of its goals in 2007 was to design a new communications strategy explaining the Constellation Program, a $124 billion space exploration project to return humans to the surface of the moon. Rather than develop a one-way corporate marketing message and then push it out, NASA created a small group of Millennials in a multi-generational task force to develop new strategies to connect an age-diverse employee population with NASA's mission. Garret Fitzpatrick, a 26-year-old shuttle crew escape engineer at JSC who joined this effort, says this about his experience: "I felt honored to be part of this team charged with recommending a new way of communicating at NASA. I got to know other Millennials at NASA while being part of a major initiative and interacting with senior management."

One of the suggestions from the small group was "to open up avenues to allow NASA employees to share their amazing stories and perspectives on their jobs and the future of the space program," says Fitzpatrick. Open NASA (www.opennasa.com) is a collaborative group blog where NASA employees share insights about what is and could be happening inside the U.S. space program. Fitzpatrick continues, "The blog posts range in topics from how NASA is using social media to ways NASA is recruiting new hires and news about the next Space Shuttle launch. This is one of the reasons I joined NASA, to be on the cutting edge of making a lasting difference and to inspire people to be part of the adventure." For NASA, involving Millennials to create a more open, collaborative, and innovative workplace is starting to pay off: NASA was ranked number sixteen on the 2008 *BusinessWeek* Best Places to Launch a Career.

For each of the five generations in the workplace, these ten forces, which span shifting demographics, globalization, and the increasing usage of technology via the social Web, require a diverse set of solutions to attract, develop, and engage employees. Just as Katya in the opening of this chapter relied on a myriad of new ways to contribute to and collaborate in the workplace, so will every employee. The companies that are proactive in understanding the forces at play here will have an advantage in attracting the talent they need to be successful in the new world of work.

SUMMARY

- **Shifting workforce demographics.** Changes in the composition of the workforce based on shifts in gender, ethnicity, and generational breakdown will require employers to learn to manage an increasingly diverse workforce.

- **Rising knowledge economy.** As more and more companies attempt to cut costs by streamlining and outsourcing where possible, knowledge-intensive work will require an increasingly complex set of skills.

- **Globalization.** Corporations will rely on the global marketplace to fuel growth. More and more of the top global companies will be based in emerging-economy countries, fueling global competition for talent.

- **Soaring hyperconnectivity.** In our increasingly connected world, the lines between work and free time are blurring. While employers harness the tools of the social Web, some employees may find it difficult to achieve work/life balance.

- **Expanded corporate social responsibility.** In today's market, companies are including leadership development activities that incorporate a CSR opportunity. Employers that do this are building global leaders in emerging markets where they are experiencing growth.

CHAPTER TWO

Multiple Generations @ Work

InVentiv Health Inc. has a global workforce of 7,000 ranging in age from 18 to 78. And it is not just the older ones who are managing projects. Take Sandra Russo. She is 28 years old and a member of three different employee teams where the ages span from 31 years to 65 years old. With a multi-generational workforce, inVentiv Health is very aware of age diversity in the workplace and consequently offers learning and communications in various modes of delivery from classroom and online, to podcasts and webinars. More important, we never assume the older generation is not as tech savvy as the younger workers. It is very easy to bucket individuals just based on their age, but we prefer to allow each employee to decide which format they prefer.

Peter Marchesini, chief learning officer of inVentiv Health

AGE DIVERSITY IN THE WORKPLACE

To a large extent, how companies manage the differing expectations, career needs, communication styles, and learning preferences of each generation will determine how well they attract, develop, engage and retain top talent. The importance of the shift in demographics that is occurring now is so significant that it is worth diving deeper to understand the implications for 2020. The quote above from Marchesini expresses the growing importance of the latest diversity issue facing organizations today: age diversity. Whereas organizations have historically dealt with diversity in terms of race, gender, sexual orientation, and physical disabilities, they will now also need to manage extreme age diversity as members of four, soon to be five, generations work together side by side.

While a record number of Millennials (those born between 1977 and 1997) are entering the workplace, many older workers are also returning for second careers. Because of the economic meltdown that began in 2008, many older workers simply cannot afford to retire. Interestingly, research from the Pew Research Center's Social and Demographic Trends project found that the key factor in whether an individual decided to delay retirement was how much money he or she had lost in the economic meltdown. Pew reports that among a sample of 2,969 working adults between the ages of 50 and 64, those who had lost 40 percent or more of their investment nest eggs in the market meltdown were roughly twice as likely as those who had not lost any money to say they would delay retirement.[1]

These older workers may either stay in their current jobs longer or enter second careers, fulfilling long-held dreams when possible. Increasingly, the federal government is one sector that appears to be hiring older, more experienced workers.

The Partnership for Public Service, a Washington, D.C.–based public service advocacy group, has launched an initiative to encourage federal agencies to recruit and hire older workers. Partnership data show that of the 68,000 employees hired in 2003 at General Service Levels 12 to 15 (the highest levels for government workers), 15 percent came from outside the federal government, and this number is increasing every year.[2] Take the example of John Emens, who retired from commercial banking in 2002 after thirty-two years with no idea of what to do next. At a board meeting in Washington, D.C., he mentioned his retirement to a colleague, who suggested he consider a career in the federal service.

Says Emens, "I was in a heavily regulated industry; and federal service and the opportunities it offered had never occurred to me." He joined the federal Export-Import Bank, where he is now senior vice president for small business.[3]

To recruit more people like Emens, the Partnership has called on agencies to launch an elite fellowship program for older Americans, modeled after the White House Fellows program. This is the type of creative solution needed to deal with the pending shortage of talent facing federal government agencies.

While the federal government deals with how to attract older workers for second careers, other companies acknowledge a different challenge: how to integrate younger Millennial workers into the workplace. Consider the heightened expectations Millennials bring with them to work. As Ron Alsop, formerly of *The Wall Street Journal* and the author of *The Trophy Kids Grow Up*, says, "Millennials have been prepping for years to excel at everything they touch, and they bring this to the workplace."[4] In his book he quotes James Danko, the business school dean of Villanova University, who shares a story of how an applicant's parents once gave him a copy of the Excel spreadsheet they had used to record their child's every accomplishment. Danko continues:

> "It's a credential-driven generation, no doubt about it. . . . I have to give them credit for their drive and ambition, but there's sometimes almost too much intensity in competing with peers. It gets to the point where they feel they need to take college courses in the summer and have double, even triple majors in college to keep their edge."[5]

What happens in the workplace when these credentials-driven Millennials are forced to work side by side with older coworkers, who may at times view them as out of touch with reality?

To successfully answer this question and the others raised by having an age-diverse workforce coexisting in the workplace, it's important to develop an understanding of each generation as well as the challenges the different generations bring to the workplace in terms of communication styles, career aspirations, and knowledge transfer. Understanding each generation is critical because employers who adapt the fastest to a multigenerational workforce will be able to attract the highest-quality employees when the war for talent is in full swing.

INTRODUCING FIVE GENERATIONS

Today employers are dealing with four generations in the workplace, but by 2020 there will be five generations, and each will bring its own values and beliefs and a different lens to the workplace.

As we can see from figure 2-1, the Bureau of Labor Statistics projects that by the year 2020 there will be five generations in the workplace, with Millennials comprising more than 50 percent of the workforce.

With these projected demographics, companies will need to create new strategies to deal with motivating, communicating with, developing, and engaging the members of each generation. Thus, understanding of the needs, expectations, and demands of each generation will be crucial to creating a workforce development plan for the coming years.

Let's examine each generation and the implications their differences will have on human resources, learning, and communications

Figure 2-1: Five Generations in the Workplace

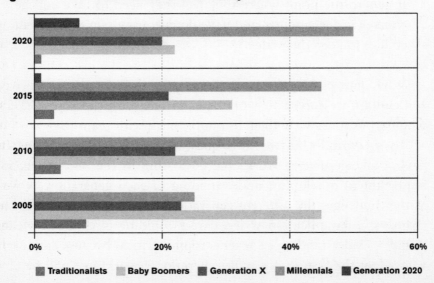

Source: Bureau of Labor Statistics Employment Projections.

Figure 2-2: U.S. Population by Generation

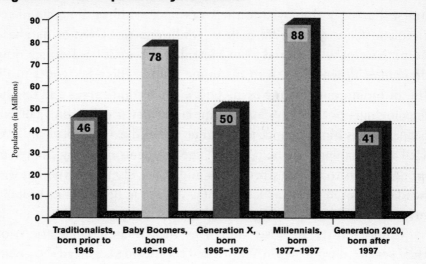

Source: U.S. Census Bureau, 2007 American Community Survey.

strategies. First, developing an understanding of the demographics is key. Figure 2-2 shows U.S. population data according to the U.S Department of Census as of 2007.

Traditionalists: Born Before 1946; 46 Million

Traditionalists are also called the Silent Generation and Veterans. As of the year 2010 they were all over the age of 64. The defining events of World War II and the Korean War changed millions of lives and shaped the hardworking, loyal, and patriotic character of the Traditionalist generation. Perhaps Tom Brokaw best captured the Traditionalists in his book entitled *The Greatest Generation* when he wrote, "They won the war; they saved the world. They came home to joyous and short-lived celebrations and immediately began the task of rebuilding their lives and the world they wanted."[6] If there are two words that describe this generation, they are "dependability" and "sacrifice." They learned at an early age to put aside their needs and wants to work toward a common goal—be it the church, the military, or the workplace.

Today, some Traditionalists have retired, but a growing number are still actively employed in the workplace with no thoughts of retirement. Consider Les Resnick, a Traditionalist IT senior database administrator who retired from Merrill Lynch in 2005. Resnick now commutes down the hall to his home office, where he works in IT for an Indian outsourcing firm. This is his second career and one he is enjoying—not only because of the flexibility it offers him but because it gives him a chance to continue to build his technical skills as well as his savings. As he puts it, "The real reason for my change in work life was to reduce stress levels and take a similar job with fewer headaches, even if it was less money. As a side benefit, I'm keeping my skills current."

Traditionalists are also known as the Greatest Generation for their service during World War II, but they have also faced the greatest amount of technological change in their home and work lives. Just think about the technological inventions that have occurred in the sixty-plus-year time span since the end of the war, from the first credit card issued in 1946 to color television in 1950, the personal computer in 1981, the first mobile phone in 1987, the emergence of the World Wide Web in 1991 and the introduction of Google in 1998, followed by a host of social media inventions ranging from MySpace to Facebook, YouTube, Second Life, and Twitter.

By 2020, the tail end of the Traditionalists will be 75 years old, and, as we have learned from the Pew Research Center, some of them will still be in the workforce. In researching this book, we encountered one 82-year-old sales representative at PPG Industries, an industrial manufacturing firm, who so thoroughly knows his products and how his clients use them that the CEO of PPG takes him along to key customer visits. Think about it: 82 years old and still working side by side with multiple generations at the company.

Baby Boomers: Born Between 1946 and 1964; 78 Million

As of 2010, Baby Boomers are between their midforties and sixties and make up a large segment of the workforce. Boomers have been called the Cold War Generation and the Growth Economy Generation.[7] But regardless of their moniker, two of the largest impacts on this generation were the television and the personal computer. In 1950 only 12 percent of U.S. households had a television, but by 1958 that number had soared to 83 percent. The rise of television shaped this generation perhaps more than anything else, and it became the most powerful communication medium available at the time.[8] As Boomers sat in front of their television sets, their generational personalities were being shaped for years to come. Events such as the Vietnam War, Watergate, the first man on the moon, and the assassinations of the Kennedy brothers were revealed through the visual medium of television, and as Boomers watched TV, their respect for and suspicion of authority was formed.

Though it was the television that had the most impact on the home lives of Boomers, it was the personal computer that directly impacted their jobs in the workplace. Consider this post from "Boomer Chronicles," a blog written by Rhea, a fifty-something journalist examining the changes in her career as a journalist:

> Over the course of my journalism career, I've seen a lot of technology come and go. When I was in high school, in the mid-1970s, I worked on the student paper. We used typewriters (remember them?) to write our news stories. Then I had to copy each story, letter by letter, onto sheets of paper covered with little squares. . . . In the late 1970s, at my first newspaper job with *The Sentinel* in East Brunswick, New Jersey, I remember we had typesetters who would type the stories into a machine, which would produce long strips of yellow paper with holes punched in it. . . . Around 1979, I remember seeing my first desktop computer while I was in journalism school. No one used it except the teacher.[9]

Many Boomers can still remember when they had to "walk to the computer," because it filled an entire room. The room had card punchers, paper-tape readers, and magnetic tape drives. Employees had limited access to "the computer." Everything changed in January 1975, when *Popular Electronics* ran a cover story called "Project Breakthrough: The World's First Minicomputer Kit to Rival Commercial Models." This article referred to the Altair, a do-it-yourself computer you could assemble at home, and led to the launch of the first commercial personal computer in 1981. The world changed dramatically after this, and Bill Gates and Paul Allen, the cofounders of Microsoft, born in 1955 and 1953, respectively, were old enough to see the potential of having one's very own computer when it first became feasible for them in their early twenties. It is not surprising that the Boomer generation points to the personal computer as the invention that most changed their work lives.

Generation X: Born Between 1965 and 1976; 50 Million

As of 2010, Generation Xers are between their thirties and early forties. In the ten years following the boom years of the 1950s, birthrates declined dramatically, and there were 15 percent fewer babies born. Enter Generation X, so named after the title of a 1991 novel, *Generation X: Tales for an Accelerated Culture,* by Douglas Coupland. In this novel, Coupland describes a generation who comes of age in the late 1980s with a burning desire to hop off the merry-go-round of status, money, and social climbing. In the workplace, they were energized by a Tom Peters manifesto titled "The Brand Called You," which first appeared in the August 1997 issue of *Fast Company* magazine when the members of Generation X were in their twenties and thirties. Peters wrote:

> Regardless of age, regardless of position, regardless of the business we happen to be in, all of us need to understand the importance of branding. We are CEOs of our own companies: Me Inc. To be in business today, our most important job is to be head marketer for the brand called You. It's that simple— and that hard. And that inescapable.[10]

Peters's call to action ignited the aspirations of Generation Xers to become free agents. This is a generation that seeks self-reliance, independence, and balance in their lives. According to "What Business Thinks," a survey of 408 Minnesota executives conducted by the authors Lynne Lancaster and David Stillman, Generation Xers are willing to pursue balance almost regardless of its impact on their finances. Free time is highly valued by this generation, and they are less likely to work for one employer, as they will go to the company that best fits their work/life needs.

Generation Xers are individualistic and idealistic. Often referred to as "latchkey kids" in their youth due to their early self-sufficiency, they are now known for thinking like entrepreneurs, thriving in situations where they can be independent thinkers, and expecting work/life balance. Starting their careers in a period of social and economic change, members of Generation X have witnessed AIDS, the Persian Gulf War, and the effect of the 1987 stock market crash on their families. Today, they are the generation that most resembles how Millennials use technology to run their personal and professional lives. Although many may be similar to Millennials in their usage of technology, they are aware that Millennials are waiting in the wings for their jobs.

The oldest of this generation are middle-aged in 2010. Expectations will be high for them to become the mentors and coaches of the next generation, the Millennials.

Millennials: Born Between 1977 and 1997; 88 Million
As of 2010, Millennials are in their twenties and early thirties. These young people have been referred to as Digital Natives, Generation Y, the Net Generation and the Google Generation. But whatever you call them, they have been living on the Web for as long as they could write their names. They are digitally confident and easily share photos, text friends, post messages on their Facebook wall, and watch YouTube videos—sometimes all at once.

When you look back over the last twenty years, one of the most significant changes affecting Millennials has been the rise of the World Wide Web and its associated host of digital technologies. Google, launched in 1998, is now so ubiquitous it is used as a verb, and it has become the go-to location to ask questions affecting one's personal and professional life. In 1983 only 7 percent of households owned a personal computer, but by 2004 that number grew to 44 percent.[11]

Today, three-quarters of U.S. teenagers between the ages of 15 and 17 have a mobile phone, and 73 percent of young people between the ages of 12 and 17 use the Internet.[12] As these young, tech-savvy people arrive in the workplace, employers will need to figure out how to manage, develop, and engage them.

To get a sense of just how hyperconnected Millennials are, consider the global survey of 862 Millennials commissioned by the Chartered Management Institute in the United Kingdom, entitled "Generation Y: Unlocking the Talent of Young Managers." A profile of Millennials emerges as a generation that is ambitious, demanding, and hyperconnected and firmly believe they can change the world. According to this survey, Millennials want to:

- Work for an organization that does something they believe in.
- Be self-directed when it comes to their learning and personal development, with 68 percent saying they want to initiate most of their own learning and development.
- Work for organizations that are supportive, empowering, and inspiring.
- Blend their home life and their work life in a fashion that allows them to work when, how, and where they want.
- Develop new skills and good career prospects with their employer.[13]

In summary, this survey paints a picture of young professionals who are in a hurry for success. They have had access to mobile phones, laptops, Facebook, MySpace, and YouTube since their adolescent years. When they did their homework in grade school, they were using Google to find answers quickly. With the latest information constantly streaming into their bedrooms, Millennials have witnessed the Oklahoma City bombings, the September 11, 2001, terrorist attacks, and the Columbine school massacre. Not surprisingly, they cite their personal safety as being of high importance to them on the job.

Though the image of Millennials is often that of an entitled generation, the reality, as demonstrated in our survey, "The Generations @ Work," and other studies, is that they are the most socially conscious generation since the 1960s. They are committed to developing new skills and want to work for organizations where they have coaches and mentors to learn from on the job. Corporate training is often cited as one of the most attractive benefits to Millennials as they seek to differentiate themselves in their careers.

PricewaterhouseCoopers (PwC) polled 4,271 new college graduates, asking them "What benefits would you value most over the next five years other than salary?" One-third chose training and development as their first-choice benefit other than salary. This was three times higher than those who chose cash bonuses as their first-choice benefit.[14] When asked how they prefer to learn on the job, they listed formal classroom training, coaches, and rotational assignments as their top delivery modes, as seen in figure 2-3.

Figure 2-3: How Much Do You Value the Following Development Opportunities?

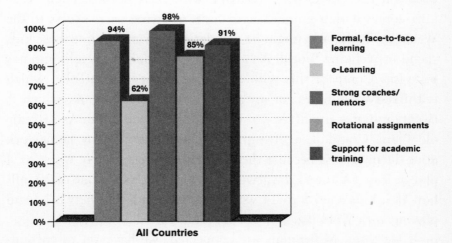

Source: PricewaterhouseCoopers, *Managing Tomorrow's People.*

Interestingly, the least preferred vehicle for training and development was traditional e-learning, pointing to the preference Millennials have for more experiential and personal learning as well as leveraging one's network of peers and mentors for development.[15] One respondent from the "Managing Tomorrow's People" survey of college graduates says it best: "Personally I find it critical to have access to coaches and mentors at my job."[16]

Generation 2020: Born After 1997; 41 Million

When it comes to hyperconnectivity, Millennials are the focus at the moment. But forward-thinking employers are starting to research and study the emerging generation, which we call Generation 2020 (Gen 2020). Members of Gen 2020 were born after 1997, making them roughly 11 years old and younger as of the writing of this book. But they will enter the workplace as college graduates in the year 2020.

As a group, they have grown up in a hyper-networked world. For many, their first exposure to social networking started before they entered school on sites such as Disney's Club Penguin. In elementary school, they learned to network on Webkinz World, a type of Second Life for kids. In this virtual world, children build profiles much like those on Facebook, while chatting with their friends. Each Webkinz comes with a unique secret code, allowing users access to the Webkinz World. You might be wondering how much time these kids spend in Webkinz World. An amazing two hours and eight minutes per visit. Compare this with an average visit on YouTube, which is thirty-two minutes, or an average visit on Facebook, which is twenty minutes and fifty-two seconds, as of April 2008. As 11-year-old Liana Crandall, a fifth-grader, says, "I get all my homework done during recess because then I can go home and play Webkinz. I play at least an hour a day, two hours tops." Liana is one of 20 million U.S. kids aged 8 to 14 who are online in social networks and playing with Webkinz.[17]

If we think Millennials are connected, we have yet to encounter Gen 2020 in the workplace. They will bring a heightened set of requirements and digital expectations with them as well as a "wish list" of what they expect of their employer. To see just how hyperconnected Gen 2020 is, CTIA—The Wireless Association, in conjunction with Harris Interactive, surveyed a nationally representative sample of 2,089 teenagers 13 to 19 years old about their mobile phone usage in a report entitled "Teenagers: A Generation Unplugged." The results show the following Gen 2020 values:

- 66 percent want the freedom to get an education anywhere on Earth, even through their phone.
- 66 percent want to have their medical records and other critical information available to rescue workers via a mobile device.
- 57 percent of smart phone users and 29 percent of regular cell phone users said they carry their cell phone because it is how they stay connected to their world.
- 59 percent want mobile access to help them organize their volunteering opportunities and corporate social responsibilities.[18]

For many of these kids, the ideal mobile phone is a fully featured multimedia device that is essentially an MP3 player, GPS, desktop/laptop computer, portable video player, text-messaging device, and phone all rolled into one.

"THE GENERATIONS @ WORK" GLOBAL SURVEY

To understand the needs, wants, and expectations of a multigenerational workforce, we polled more than 2,200 members of four generations currently in the workforce. All respondents were working professionals employed in industries ranging from administrative services to education, financial services, the government, health care, high tech and telecommunications, manufacturing, professional services, and retail. The distribution of these respondents in our survey is shown in figure 2-4. The survey explored the values, behaviors, and mind-set of each generation, along with the expectations they have of their employer.

Figure 2-4: "The Generations @ Work" Research by Industry and Region

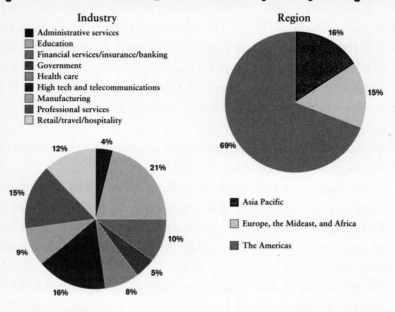

Source: Future Workplace.

The various generations have lived through vastly different world events, and each has developed generational core traits that reflect the eras in which they grew up. These experiences and traits are shown in table 2-1.

TABLE 2-1: WHO ARE THE FIVE GENERATIONS?

Generation	Major Influences	Broad Traits	Defining Invention
Traditionalists Major trait: loyalty	World War II, Cold War, Korean War, rise of suburbs	Sacrifice, loyalty, discipline, respect for authority	Fax machine
Baby Boomers Major trait: competition	Watergate, women's rights, Woodstock, JFK assassination	Competitive, sand-wiched generation, hard work, long hours	Personal computer

Generation	Major Influences	Broad Traits	Defining Invention
Generation X Major trait: self-reliance	MTV, AIDS, Gulf War, 1987 stock market crash, fall of Berlin Wall	Eclecticism, self-reliance, free agents, work/life balance, independence	Mobile phone
Millennials Major trait: immediacy	Google, Facebook, 9/11 terrorist attacks, election of Barack Obama	Community service, cyberliteracy, tolerance, diversity, confidence	Google and Facebook
Generation 2020 Major trait: hyperconnectedness	Social games, Iraq War, Great Recession	Mobility, media savvy, life online starting in pre-school, reading books on e-readers	iPhone apps

Source: Future Workplace.

FIVE KEY FINDINGS FROM "THE GENERATIONS @ WORK" SURVEY

Each generation brings a different lens to the workplace. They have differing expectations for how they want to work, learn, and communicate. The different lenses of each generation will impact the employer-employee relationship. Five findings from "The Generations @ Work" research reveal how these preferences and expectations will play out in the future workplace.

1. Traditionalists and Boomers Are as Likely to Be Web Contributors as Millennials Are

It is not only the Millennials who are active contributors on social media sites; members of all generations are engaging with and contributing to these sites. However, Traditionalists and Boomers are more likely to be active contributors to existing content, while Millennials focus on creating and publishing new content.

Figure 2-5: Social Media Usage of "The Generations @ Work"

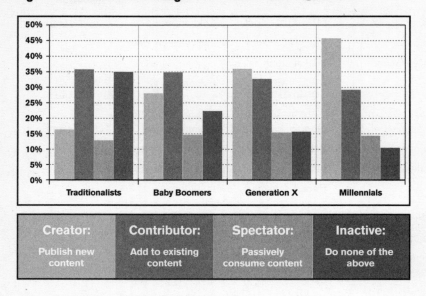

Source: "The Generations @ Work" survey, Future Workplace.

Figure 2-5 shows how the use of social media varies by generation, with contributors represented in all four generations. We were surprised to find that the contribution rate for each generation was remarkably similar, meaning that working professionals across the spectrum were active contributors of content on the Web. However, while each generation contributes to the Web, the quantity of contribution may vary, even though the ability to contribute may be similar.

Variations in the usage of social media thus may be more likely to reflect the differences of individual mind-sets than generational biases. Some Traditionalists view the latest technologies as toys they will perhaps get around to learning to use someday, while other Traditionalists view experimenting with the latest technologies as an extension of themselves and an important way to stay on top of their game. Many Boomers also fall into this category. Jean Frink, the 48-year-old owner of Frink Family Farms of Fayetteville, North Carolina, says this about how she uses Facebook: "I find myself able to rapidly communicate with a group of 'friends' on Facebook. I use

Facebook to give me feedback on new products at the farm—in fact, I think of my time on Facebook as providing me with a mini new-product test kitchen. My Facebook friends have been instrumental to helping me build my business."

2. Boomers and Generation X Look for a Work Life/Home Life Balance, While Millennials See Work as "Part of Life"

Boomers and Generation Xers place a high value on being able to blend their work and home lives, while Millennials consider work to be part of life. For Millennials, finding a balance between work life and home life seems "irrelevant," in the words of one survey respondent, because "work is part of life, not separate from it." Millennials live in weisure time, the next step in work life, where work and leisure are one and the same.

> **Friends**: On social networking sites, contacts whose profiles are linked. To "friend" an individual is to request to link his or her profile with yours.

Millennials see their work as a place to make new friends and develop work relationships that will benefit them for the rest of their lives. As Joy Thomas, a 24-year-old Millennial based in California who works as an accountant for Aera Energy LLC, says, "I do not think of work being separate from the rest of my life. I think the term 'work/life balance' is out of date and not meaningful at all. Rather, I'll stay with a company if I'm able to be challenged by the work, make new friends, learn new skills, and be fulfilled in what I do." Though Millennials want more flexibility in choosing where to work, when to work, and how to work, they still want and expect interaction with teammates on the job.

3. Millennials and Generation X Place a High Importance on Working for a Company That Develops Both Their Career and Life Skills

Millennials and Generation Xers acknowledge that establishing oneself in a career is vastly different from going to school. What's important to members of these two generations is being able to take advantage of company-funded training and development programs.

Figure 2-6: The Percentage of Respondents in Each Generation Who Placed High Importance on Developing Skills

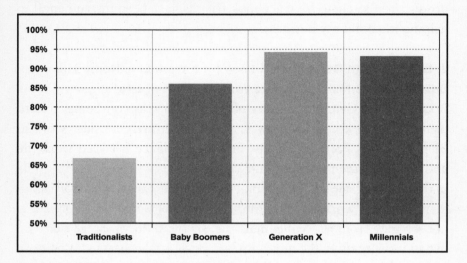

Source: "The Generations @ Work" survey, Future Workplace.

As figure 2-6 shows, members of Millennial and Generation X could also be called the Learning Generation, for the importance they place on continuous skill development on the job.

Perhaps most surprising, Millennials and Generation Xers are requesting training and development in "life skills" as well as technical skills. In fact, two-thirds of those polled in the PwC survey "Managing Tomorrow's People" would be comfortable with the idea of "employers providing more personal services to workers, such as housing, food, and regular doctor and dentist appointments."[19] Similarly, "The Generations @ Work" survey respondent Debbie Merrington, a 40-year-old executive assistant at a travel and tourism agency in Cape Town, South Africa, says, "I think employers should not only train employees in job-related skills, but they should also give employees assistance with building better life skills. By life skills, I mean training in areas such as financial literacy (i.e., buying a new car, investing in the stock market, or buying a new house), learning a new language, and health and wellness." Millennials and Generation Xers see a growing blurring of the lines between work and home life, and as they spend more of their leisure time working, they expect their employer to play a greater role in assisting them with developing their life.

4. Millennials Are Likely to Select an Employer Based on the Ability to Access the Latest Tools and Technologies at Work

Fifty-eight percent of Millennials and 52 percent of Generation Xers agreed that having access to sites such as Facebook, LinkedIn, and YouTube is a factor in selecting a new employer.[20] Figure 2-7 shows the importance of access to the latest tools and technologies at work. And what happens if employers do not allow access to these sites? A recent survey conducted by Accenture reports that Millennials will use their own technology and mobile devices at work, and one factor they will use in selecting an employer will be how accommodating the company is to their personal technology preferences. The survey polled more than four hundred students and found that they expect their employer to accommodate their IT preferences. These range from the type of computer used at the company to access to instant messaging, RSS feeds, and social networking sites.

Figure 2-7: The Importance of Having Access to Web 2.0 Technologies

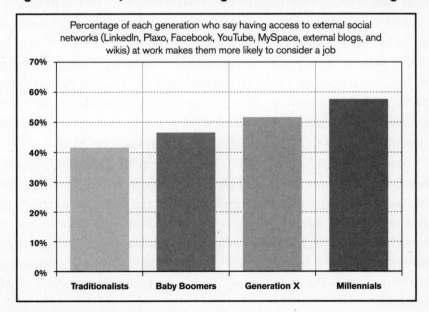

Source: "The Generations @ Work" survey, Future Workplace.

Interestingly, almost half of all Millennials surveyed who use social networks, blogs, and Twitter do so without the support of their employer's IT department (and occasionally against the IT policies of their companies). The Accenture survey argues that over time companies will have to acknowledge their employees' technology preferences, since more than half of the survey respondents said a company's usage of technology was a major factor in their selection of an employer.[21]

Brad Hargreaves, the 24-year-old founder and CEO of GXStudios, a company that creates games for corporate learning, says this: "The Millennials I hire to work in our company expect us to provide them with access to external social networking sites—we trust them to use these sites to do their jobs, and we train new hires on how to be responsible using these sites at work."

5. Both Traditionalists and Boomers Place High Importance on a Manager Who Understands Age Diversity in the Workplace

Surprisingly, Traditionalists and Boomers are the ones most concerned with working for a manager who values employees across all four generations. One might expect Millennials to be the most concerned as they enter the workforce and see established generations in front of them. But in fact the reverse is true. Why is this? It may be that Traditionalists and Boomers see the increasing focus now going to how employers integrate Millennials and Generation Xers into the workplace. Some may be saying "Not so fast, what about us?" Traditionalists and Boomers want to work for managers who value and understand how to deal with age diversity in the workplace.

Robert Burnside, a 60-year-old partner with Ketchum, a public relations firm, notes that though the average age of a Ketchum employee is 35 years, there is a great deal of age diversity in the firm. Burnside says, "Managers need to better understand the different expectations of each generation and how each approaches new work assignments. It is to everyone's benefit to surface these differences early on and learn how to use them to create a better final work product."

COMMUNICATING ACROSS GENERATIONS IN THE WORKPLACE

Once the personal needs, expectations, and desires of the generations are recognized and addressed, the next hurdle is how to best communicate with each generation in the workplace.

Deloitte Consulting and the International Association of Business Communicators (IABC) conducted a survey of 1,279 members of the IABC to identify the optimal communication style for each generation. As shown in table 2-2, the differences are sizable.

TABLE 2-2: TALKING 'BOUT MY GENERATION

The four generations represented in the current workforce have very different preferences across all aspects of communication. It is clear that communication preferences have changed and we need to adapt to engage diverse audiences.

	Traditionalists	**Baby Boomers**	**Generation X**	**Millennials**
Style	Formal	Semiformal	Not so serious; irreverent	Eye-catching; fun
Content	Detail; prose-style writing	Chunk it down but give me everything	Get to the point—what do I need to know?	If and when I need it, I'll find it online
Context	Relevance to my security; historical perspective	Relevance to the bottom line and my rewards	Relevance to what matters to me	Relevance to now, today, and my role
Attitude	Accepting and trusting of authority and hierarchy	Accept the "rules" as created by the Traditionalists	Openly question authority; often branded as cynics and skeptics	OK with authority that earns their respect

(Table continued on next page)

	Traditionalists	Baby Boomers	Generation X	Millennials
Tactics	Print; conventional mail; face-to-face dialogue or by phone; some online information/interaction	Print; conventional mail; face-to-face dialogue; online tools and resources	Online; some face-to-face meetings (if really needed); games; technological interaction	Online; wired; seamlessly connected through technology
Speed	Attainable within reasonable time frame	Available; handy	Immediate; when I need it	Five minutes ago
Frequency	In digestible amounts	As needed	Whenever	Constant

Source: Deloitte Consulting and the International Association of Business Communicators (IABC).

Whereas Traditionalists prefer digestible amounts of information delivered either in print, by mail, face-to-face, or by phone, Millennials want constant communication, ideally delivered through texting or e-mail or on internal or external social networking sites. Specifically, Millennials want:

- Shorter, more frequent updates: Millennials demand to be kept informed and plugged in. If they sense leadership is not updating them sufficiently, they will find answers elsewhere—most likely in their own online social networks. Bottom line: speed and frequency of communications are critical to them.
- Authentic communications: Marketers from MTV to eBay have bombarded Millennials for years, and in return, this generation has become a tough audience. They demand authentic communications and read each communications message with a "Why should I care?" attitude. They will disengage if they feel they are

being spoon-fed a contrived message from the "corporate brand-ing office."

- "Free-form communications" using real-world collaboration tools such as multiplayer games. Google is perhaps best associated with being a "great place to work for Millennials." In 2008, Google once again came in first in *Fortune* magazine's annual ranking of the "100 Best Companies to Work For."[22] When Google opened its New York City office in 2007, the office space was spread across four floors, placing employees from different projects in close proximity. Google's management quickly realized that the company could benefit from building stronger connections between floormates, who might not typically interact with one another on a project. The answer: an online multiplayer social game called GoCrossOffice, modeled after the game Risk, in which players collaborate with, organize, and socialize with one another and in the process strengthen their team-building and strategic thinking skills.

So what does this mean for organizations? How can you develop and engage each of the generations to work and ease the tensions that may occur when four generations find themselves in the same workplace?

First, while each generation brings a unique perspective on what it looks for in a potential employer, there are wide similarities among the generations. Business executives must first tap into generational similarities before moving toward understanding their differences.

Members of all generations want to feel valued, empowered, and en-gaged at work. This is a fundamental human need, which spans across the generations. Though Generation Xers and Millennials openly dis-cuss and even demand more flexibility in their jobs as they attempt to customize their job to the rest of their lives, Boomers and Traditional-ists have this need as well, even if they are less vocal on the subject.

In addition, members of all generations want to be trusted at work. Employees want their leaders to believe that they will perform their jobs as productively and efficiently as possible. Increasingly, this means having access to the latest tools and technologies such as Facebook, YouTube, and wikis at work. Often companies, under the excuse of inadequate bandwidth or increased security, are blocking this access. If we are honest, however, the real issue is usually one of trust.

Not long ago, there was similar hand-wringing over the use of e-mail when some business executives believed that using e-mail might expose corporate secrets to the outside world. The same argument is now being used about social media in the workplace. But by trusting their employees and providing them with guidelines for using social media, companies can create a powerful retention and productivity tool.

As Gen Xers and Millennials bring digital expectations to the workplace, they will demand changes in the types of tools and technologies they can access at work. To address these expectations, forward-thinking employers are leveraging social media tools to create communities of practice, threaded discussion boards, and open innovation jams, as well as wikis and blogs for knowledge transfer between the generations. Chapter 5, "Über-connect Your Organization," is dedicated to the innovative ways companies are using corporate social technologies to drive innovation in the workplace.

WHAT CAN YOU DO TO BETTER MANAGE AGE DIVERSITY IN THE WORKPLACE?

A handful of companies are dealing with age diversity in the workplace by creating new strategies for managing across generations. These strategies range from developing new training programs to revising performance development processes and to inventing more customized jobs and careers. L'Oréal Canada, with an age-diverse workforce made up of one-third Boomers, one-third Generation Xers, and one-third Millennials, took action by creating a training program for how to manage across the generations. According to Marjolaine Rompre, the director of learning development, "This new generation is so candid about participating and a lot freer. When we saw that, we realized we could be faced with an interesting problem.

We called it Generation Shock." To address these generational needs, L'Oréal created a training program called Valorize Generational Differences. So far, more than 500 employees have gone through the program. According to Rompre, "the Ys told us they were so happy to learn why the baby boomers were so conservative and why Gen X didn't want to share information with them."[23]

Rompre elaborates on one of the biggest impacts of the program: to showcase the values, myths, and paradoxes of each generation with a focus on Millennials. For example, Millennials at L'Oréal "really want to be autonomous, yet they also want validation. They want to be independent, but like to work in teams. They practice extensive freedom of speech and are very candid, but they lack political savvy. They want to be everywhere at the same time but have real difficulty managing priorities." Rompre continues, "When I share those things with them, they go, 'Yes.' They realize they're not that easy to manage, and this sheds light on who they are."[24]

In addition to creating new training programs, some companies are revamping their performance management processes to set career expectations in increasingly flattened organizations. Danielle Robinson, the director of diversity, talent, and organizational design for the global premium drink firm Diageo, has done just that. Robinson says the presence of Millennials in the workplace "has added a layer of complexity to an already complex work environment."[25] The answer for Diageo was to revise its performance development process and create a new section, called Big Hopes, which encourages an open career dialogue between a Millennial and his or her manager. According to Robinson, "Big Hopes can help to set Millennial expectations for career development. For example, younger employees may have unreasonable but strongly held career expectations. Having a dialogue forces the manager to explain the gap and start a conversation with the employee. The programs have been successful at Diageo because everyone walks away knowing where they stand."[26]

Finally, it seems as though everything we touch these days, from our iPods to our blue jeans, can be customized and personalized. But often our jobs and our benefits look and feel the same as last year's.

Susan Cantrell and David Smith argue in their new book, *Workforce of One*, that companies should adopt a "workforce of one approach" to human capital management, meaning applying customer-driven customization and segmentation practices to employees. After all, at the individual level, even broad generalizations about age may not hold true, as in a Boomer tech worker who may be far more social media–savvy than a Luddite Millennial. David Smith says, "Creating a workforce-of-one approach starts with segmenting employees according to various factors such as value to the organization [i.e., high potential employees,] workforce category such as mission critical areas of sales, supply chain or customer contact and finally age. Then career development, reward structures and even methods for delivering learning and development can be customized to each employee segment." Using customer segmentation strategies for employees can also lead to personalization of benefits. Rather than a standard package of health, wealth, and paid time off, companies can provide employees with a budget and a widely diverse set of options. These can range from sponsoring paid community service time overseas to allowing for credits to buy a hybrid car or even financially supporting an increased personal skill, such as learning a new language. The options are endless. How to fund this? In one survey, Millennials indicated that they are willing to make trade-offs in terms of base salary in order to have a job that fits with their values.[27]

As Millennials enter the workplace, they will begin to transform it just as they have transformed the political landscape. In the United States, those under 25 years old not only voted in record numbers in the 2008 U.S. presidential election, but they were highly involved and actively participated in providing policy suggestions to then candidate Obama's online social network, My.BarackObama.com. This online social network was responsible for raising more money, holding more events, making more fund-raising phone calls, and offering more policy suggestions than any other presidential campaign in history of American elections. If these Millennials played a key factor in deciding who won a presidential election, they will almost certainly play a larger role in a global workplace and shape how, where, and when work occurs.

Thriving in the 2020 workplace will require organizations to understand the various needs, expectations, and values of all the generations. Companies will need to start making some fundamental changes in how they design jobs, careers, learning programs, and even benefits. Increasingly, they will need to take into account the impact online consumer innovations (such as Google, Facebook, YouTube, and Twitter) will have on how, when, and where work is done. MyBarack, MySpace, and MyYahoo will lead to MyCareer, MyLearning, MyCommunityService, and MyBenefits—all powered by the latest technologies we are accustomed to in our personal lives. Though we see the heightened demands for access to these technologies from Millennials, we will soon be overwhelmed by the hyperconnected needs of Gen 2020. R U RDY?*

* R U RDY, "Are you ready?"

SUMMARY

- **Understand that the generational balance of your workplace is shifting**. Traditionalists (those born before 1946) are staying in the workplace longer, just as Millennials (those born 1977 to 1997) are entering the workplace in record numbers, and Baby Boomers (born 1946 to 1964) and Generation X (born 1965 and 1976) are reaching new levels in their careers. Members of Generation 2020 (born after 1997) are not in the workplace yet, but employers need to be preparing now for the needs and expectations this hyperconnected generation will bring to the workplace.
- **Recognize the distinct characteristics of each generation.** Each generation is defined by certain core traits. Recognizing and integrating these different generational orientations into the workplace will help allow all the generations in a company to thrive.
- **Learn to communicate in different ways to reach different employees.** Each generation communicates differently, and employers will have to learn how to negotiate their different expectations and desires. For example, whereas Traditionalists prefer information to be conveyed in a

tangible form—by print, mail, face-to-face, or phone—Millennials prefer to receive information as a constant flow of communication transmitted via new technology, i.e., text messages, instant messages, e-mail, or updates to their profile on a corporate social network.

- **Take steps to bridge the gap in managing employees of different generations.** Learn to develop and mentor employees in generationally sensitive ways. For example, research shows that Millennials prefer to learn from coaches, mentors, and in their own networks, so be prepared to expand the delivery modes of corporate learning programs.

- **Keep five themes in mind when thinking about the Millennial generation:** *politically aware, involved socially, tech-savvy, committed to learning, and driven to innovate.* Millennials, with their profound passion and commitment to using the latest technologies, will spark the development of new products, new services, new political movements, and a new set of requirements for employers. Forward-thinking companies will have to understand the needs and desires of this generation to best source, recruit, and retain them.

PART II

Practices in Action Today

CHAPTER THREE

Principles of 2020 Engagement

Andrew Levy never expected that his career would land him in the Philippines. Levy is a senior managing consultant who worked for IBM for fifteen years before being accepted to the IBM Corporate Service Corps. During those fifteen years, he gained international business experience through IBM, as well as an MBA in global management. But it was only after leading a team on emergency and disaster response for one month in the Philippines that he said, "Now I am truly a global executive. This experience of living and working in Davao City, Philippines, to improve the quality of the country's emergency response systems was life changing. The in-country experience is something no other company could offer at that time. Being able to get acquainted with other members of the IBM team via social networking groups, receiving online training and orientation on the culture and business issues facing companies in the Philippines, and taking part in an important project that made a real difference to the people of the Philippines—all of this has been a life- and career-changing experience for me. Quite frankly, it is the reason why I continue to be excited about working for IBM."

How can companies create more enthusiastic and committed employees like Andrew Levy? The factors that go into attraction, motivation, development, and retention of employees are typically called employee engagement. Most of the research on employee engagement focuses on when individuals are engaged on the job, such as when they offer to do extra assignments, speak up when they see a different way to do things, or rate their intent to stay with a company highly.[1] But, as the example of Andrew Levy of IBM underscores, it is important for companies to go beyond chronicling specific employee engagement factors. Employers must create a workplace where employees can build a personal and emotional relationship to the employer brand.

The essential ingredients used to create engaged employees are similar to those present in a satisfying personal relationship: mutual trust, authentic communication, respect, shared values, and a commitment to growing together. Consider this comment by Dorie Morgan, a Millennial document control specialist working in the manufacturing industry: "Attracting employees is like dating. For a serious relationship to work, you need to be clear and upfront from the beginning." The advice on dating is endless: just type in "What Do Men Want" in the YouTube search engine, and you will find more than 245,000 videos on the subject. But if you type in "What Do Employees Want," you will find only 2,260 YouTube videos, many of which are inappropriate for corporate consumption. Where can a company go for solid advice?

To date, there have been few holistic models for how organizations can prepare for the future by creating truly engaged employees who go on to live and breathe the employer brand while delivering exceptional service. We define the 2020 workplace as an organizational environment that provides an intensely personalized, social experience to attract, develop, and engage employees across all generations and geographies. In this chapter we present the Workplace Engagement 2020 Model (WE 2020), a set of principles any organization—large or small, multinational or local—can use to build engaged employees for now and into the future.

We propose that the underlying principles of the workplace of the future are already in action among innovative and forward-thinking organizations. These companies are living examples of how integrating the WE 2020 model gives them a competitive advantage in attracting, developing, and retaining top talent both now and in 2020.

THE WORKPLACE ENGAGEMENT 2020 MODEL

In thinking about the future, the easiest question to ask most employees is what they would like their *next* job to be like. "The Generations @ Work" survey provided a list of fifteen characteristics for respondents to indicate as criteria for selecting their next job. All four generations surveyed agreed on the top ten, as shown in table 3-1.

TABLE 3-1: TOP 10 DESIRED EMPLOYER CHARACTERISTICS BY GENERATION

	Blended Rank Order	Traditional-ists	Baby Boomers	Generation X	Millennials
Has strong values	1	1	1	2	2
Will develop my skills for the future	2	7	4	1	1
Offers flexible benefits and rewards	3	3	2	3	3
Offers the ability to blend work and life	4	2	3	4	5
Is a good employer brand	5	4	5	6	8
Offers a clear career path	6	8	8	5	4

(Table continued on next page)

	Blended Rank Order	Traditional-ists	Baby Boomers	Generation X	Millennials
Has a reputa-tion for cor-porate social responsibility	7	6	6	7	7
Will allow me to work from any location	8	5	7	8	10
Will pay for my continuing education	9	9	9	9	9
Has employees I think I could be friends with	10	10	10	10	6

Source: "The Generations @ Work" survey, Future Workplace.

Although the generations agreed on the top ten characteristics, there are some notable findings in the survey. Having a company with strong values, a strong brand, and a reputation for corporate social responsibility is of nearly the same importance across generations. Differences emerge in preparing skills for the future, as Traditionalists rank that much lower than the later generations, who might be planning to remain in the workforce for a longer time. The importance of friends in the workplace is higher for Millennials, indicating a greater need for a social environment. It is also interesting that Traditionalists rank the need for location flexibility significantly higher than Millennials rate it. Through a combination of research review, conversation with thought leaders, our surveys, and more than a hundred interviews with companies in the forefront, we have developed a model that we believe expresses the needs of all of the generations, while preparing for the workplace of 2020, shown in figure 3-1. The Workplace Engagement

2020 model covers the underlying principles that the future workplace must embody, as well as the most relevant and impactful areas in which to practice the principles within an organization.

Figure 3-1: The Workforce Engagement 2020 Model

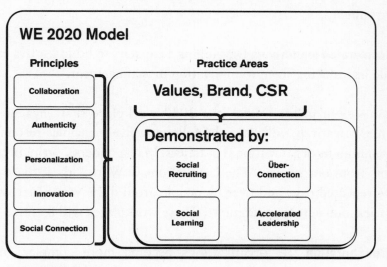

Source: Future Workplace.

These practice areas start with ensuring that strong values resonate across the generations, creating a brand that employees identify with and developing a reputation for corporate social responsibility. Although there are many areas that can contribute to an engaged workforce, we have focused on four: recruiting, connecting employees through advanced communication methods, learning, and leadership. In our model, we call these:

1. Social recruiting. A practice that leverages social and professional networks, both online and offline, from both a candidate's perspective and the hiring side, to connect to, communicate with, engage, inform, and attract future talent.

2. Über-connection. Building the organization's capability to use the social media tools already in use by many marketing departments to connect with customers and expanding their usage to the engagement of employees.

3. Social learning. Learning that is collaborative, immediate, relevant, and presented in the context of an individual's unique work environment.

4. Accelerated leadership. Developing a capacity to build leaders faster while introducing them to innovation in management.

As shown in the model, the 2020 workplace that engages employees effectively will have the following five principles resonating throughout its organizational practices. In respondents' write-in comments from our survey "The Generations @ Work," these five terms were repeated over and over by people around the world, across industries, and across generations. These workplaces will feature:

1. Collaboration. As organizations become more complex, more global, and more virtual, the need to ensure that the workplace culture reinforces collaboration across the entire enterprise becomes increasingly important. Traditionally, this has meant internal collaboration, including how people personally collaborate, as well as how the organization structures collaboration across teams. In the future, external collaboration will grow exponentially as a requirement, including working with suppliers, customers, consumers, government entities, nongovernmental organizations, and local communities. Even today, organizations are putting executives into supplier companies for temporary assignments to strengthen the total value chain to customers and provide accelerated leadership development for their own executives. Cisco's councils and boards, described in chapter 7, are an example of the 2020 workplace's collaborative environment. In thinking about what Millennials will want from the workplace of the future, Mary Greatbatch, a health care worker from Australia, said that in the future we will need to include Millennials "in major collaborative decisions."

2. Authenticity. All the generations have been shaped by recent in-cidences of corporate excess, the use of political power for personal gain, and incessant, pervasive marketing. The emerging requirements will demand that an organization harmonize its messaging across all aspects of its operations in a way that reflects its core "values in use," as Edgar Schein called them, as opposed to "professed values."[2] Authen-ticity is of primary importance in building an organization's values, brand, and reputation. A necessary component of authenticity is trans-parency, and the best companies are already pioneering in this area, frequently using social media, through the use of techniques such as open financial books, blogging from CEOs to line employees, collective wikis, and full disclosure on pay. Danielle Pearson, a Generation Xer and consultant to the energy industry, advocates using "realistic job previews as part of the retention process, provided they are authentic."

3. Personalization. The words "personal" or "personalized" showed up hundreds of times in the write-in sections of our survey. No longer will it be possible to "process" all employees in the same way with nearly identical employment offers, career paths, and benefits op-tions. Even the concept of "processing" employees as they come into an organization suggests an antiquated assembly-line view of the em-ployee relationship. We advocate banishing the word from the human resources lexicon. Crafting an employment relationship that meets the needs of every generation at each life stage while providing them with the ability to attain their personal career goals will require orga-nizations to use mass customization techniques usually reserved for consumers. As Nichole Urban, a Millennial working in the hospital-ity industry, says, "Personal attention goes a long way. Employees my age are much more likely to feel invested in the goals of the com-pany if they are ingrained in the community of the company. That is why it is important to have friends at work." Some of the examples we cover include reaching out to potential employees in their own spaces, using informal learning techniques to allow context-based customization, and freeing employees to use social media to allow them to über-connect across the organization.

4. Innovation. The power of innovation is that it enables organizational and personal sustainability. Organizations that innovate are able to compete continually in the marketplace. People who work in innovative organizations are personally learning and advancing their skill sets to the leading edges of their domain expertise. Potential employees are attracted to organizations that have a renewable and energizing source of ideas for the future, putting pressure on organizations to also offer innovative practices aligned to organizational strategy. Innovative companies take traditional practices and turn them on their head. For example, in chapter 6 we relate an example of how mentoring can be expanded using social media and can even become reverse mentoring, with Millennial line employees mentoring senior executives, as featured in chapter 7. As Darryl Greyling, an internal compliance officer based in South Africa, says, "Millennials respond better to innovative and mature management," suggesting the importance of experience in management while using progressive and up-to-the-minute techniques.

5. Social connection. The era of recognizing heroic individualism is over—at least as it relates to how we engage, recognize, and reward employees. After all, who gets the credit for a product that was developed on a wiki by dozens of people through five major iterations? Employers will need to offer fun, engaging environments—whether virtual or physical—that satisfy the basic human need to be a member of a highly regarded community. A natural extension of providing a social environment is the use of social media tools and techniques to allow employees to connect with communities that will best enable their workplace performance and support their life interests, covered in chapter 5. The presence of a vibrant, social workplace is of high importance for Millennials, as, among other things, they are seeking a workplace with employees they can connect with on and off the job. This is an image that no company evokes as strongly as Google, often referred to as "a company that feels like grad school."[3] Every company builds its brand as an extension of what its founders believe in, and at Google, Larry Page and Sergey Brin set out to create a company where they would enjoy spending time. In other words, they aimed to create an environment that has the feel of graduate school, complete with small work groups, lots of experimentation, vigorous feedback loops, and the freedom to devote 20 percent of one's time to noncore initiatives. In this way, Google continually develops new products while also being known as a place where innovation can be everyone's passion.[4]

These five principles underlie the values, brand, and reputation of a company, as well as the practice areas that can most affect the ability to engage the 2020 workforce. We considered other practice areas, such as rewards, benefits, and customized employee contracts, but the preponderance of evidence pointed us to these five areas as the most influential and practical areas on which to focus to create an engaged workforce. It is our intent to help organizations select the areas where change can be most needed and provide guidance in how to make that change happen.

THE TRIPLE BOTTOM LINE

A growing movement exists to expand the accounting practices of companies beyond the financial aspects to include human capital and sustainable environmental practices. To date, the challenge has been to reduce the subjectivity of the nonfinancial measures, so organizations are issuing separate corporate social responsibility reports as addenda to their annual reports to demonstrate good faith.

This "triple bottom line" is sometimes referred to as "TBL" or, alternatively, as "people, planet, and profits"; it refers to the concept of an organization that pays attention to values beyond those of shareholders to include those of all stakeholders. This concept is one that resonates with many Millennials as well as to those of the other generations in the aftermath of the recession that began in 2008.

People, or human capital, are a component of TBL that pertains to extending fair and equitable business practices to the people who are employed by the company and the region in which a corporation conducts its business, thus recognizing the interdependencies of all stakeholders. Planet, or natural capital, refers to the need for sustainable environmental practices. A TBL organization endeavors to leave as small an environmental footprint as possible, to try at least to do no harm. This includes managing energy consumption and reducing waste throughout the supply chain. When the entire supply chain is considered, including what it takes to grow the crops that feed the cattle that go to slaughter that are shipped to the stores that are packaged for consumers, it is estimated that the average U.S. consumer generates a ton of waste per *day*.[5] Organizations that pay attention to their environmental impact can attract a generation who were sensitized to environmental issues in kindergarten and spent their high school years volunteering in community service projects. Progressing to a workplace where they have the opportunity to play a proactive role on the issues they care about in the world will be an appealing proposition.

Profit, or financial capital, is the economic benefit paid to the owners of the organization. Of course, companies will always be measured on their financial returns, but some have speculated that the singular focus on quarterly returns was partially to blame for the 2008 economic crisis.[6] Now is the opportunity for companies to report on their triple bottom line and to use this as a way to attract the next generations of employees.

THE IMPORTANCE OF YOUR ORGANIZATION'S BRAND, VALUES, AND REPUTATION

To begin, there is one practice area so important that it must be done well, or work done in the rest of the model will not be able to compensate for its lack. First, organizations must differentiate themselves through their employer brand, creating a set of values and corresponding culture, while building a reputation as organizations committed to something more than profits. All of these were in the top ten priorities for an employee offer for each generation, as shown earlier in table 3-1.

Every company expresses its brand, values, and reputation in different ways, whether it's Google's famous "Do no evil" or Intuit's policy of allowing all employees to have three paid days off to donate their time to the cause of their choice. These principles, summarized in figure 3-1, underlie all the practices featured in this book and demonstrate how WE 2020 can be practically applied in any organization. Establishing and implementing a set of values, and reinforcing the tenets of a culture with brand and resulting reputation, may actually be the least expensive and most effective way to create a compelling workplace. Potentially, this can have the most lasting impact on encouraging employees to select and remain at a company. Social media can be used to help communicate with and reach potential employees, but, as seen in some of the following examples, it is not a necessary requirement.

Projecting a Brand

Although many factors contribute to an employer's value proposition, most employees desire a company name on their résumé that gives them a sense of pride. Talented employees from tarnished companies have experienced the heartache of having their own future employability threatened by the disgrace of their executives, as, for example, happened to some employees of Enron, who have largely given up looking for corporate jobs and started their own businesses.[7] No matter how well a company performs in the other aspects of the model, if this core is not solid, no amount of work on other areas will compensate for it.

Libby Sartain, a former head of HR at both Southwest Airlines and Yahoo!, was once asked in a job interview, "What are the things you have to do in HR, no matter what?" As she describes it, her first reaction was "Each company has its own set of priorities and challenges, which call for different solutions." But after a moment's thought, she replied, "The importance of an employee brand is so core that no matter where I worked, I would ensure we were clear on defining and implementing an employee brand based on the unique culture and values of the company."[8]

Building a solid brand is integral to the workplace of the future, but marketing that brand can no longer be done in the traditional ways of the past. In the first place, Sartain says, "Millennials are not going to believe the brand without hearing from their friends in their social networks. Additionally, there is still going to be a need to have a personal touch. The message that goes to a software engineer is likely not the same message that will go to a sales representative. We not only have to reach people through their trusted friends, but we also need to have a segmented approach." Especially for those who are accustomed to and comfortable with buying on the Web, choosing where to work becomes heavily influenced by online research. The ability to compare and contrast jobs via the Web and social media is unprecedented in the history of job searching. It is now easy to get a good sense of an organization's culture by getting information from friends on social media sites; visiting Web sites such as glassdoor .com, a site where people post their salaries and comment on working at their company; and judging the sophistication of the company's Web site. All these have become important factors in making career decisions.

A word of caution, though: a company with a great brand is not necessarily a great place to work at. The most successful companies have figured out how to integrate the internal and external brand seamlessly in a way that makes work life an authentic extension of the brand. No company better exemplifies this than Nike.

Mike Tarbell has been with Nike more than a dozen years and is now the head of talent management, which includes the development of Nike talent by having employees gain critical experiences, as well as engaging them in structured learning and development. "We have a philosophy that seventy percent of development happens on the job, twenty percent through coaching and mentoring, and ten percent through learning and development programs." How does the employer brand permeate talent management decisions? Tarbell continues, "It is important that our employment brand is as positive to employees and external candidates as our brand in the marketplace is with our consumers. Our talent strategy is integrated and holistic—which means it is designed to create accountability and ownership with the Nike employee and across the organization's functional 'talent pipelines.' It is strongly based on our values and engaging employees to realize both their individual potential as well as Nike's potential. We also build proactive and ongoing relationships with external candidates to build internal and external successors for future roles.

"As Nike has grown, we've worked very hard to maintain the qualities of our culture that make Nike unique. Our values, known as the Nike Maxims, are foundational to our culture. These maxims [such as 'We are on offense, always' and 'The consumer decides'] are designed to create a framework for decision making among all employees and how we operate as teams. Other symbols of the culture are embedded in our DNA—in sales meetings, new-employee orientation, performance reviews, on the internal Web site, broadcast on the Nike internal radio station, known as KAOS, and in the visual images of athletes at our offices and facilities. There's always a desire to stay grounded in our roots—and to be true to the Nike culture. We use words like innovation, performance, teamwork, and authenticity as the language of who we are.

"As the company has gotten bigger, it has remained very personal—much like many athletes and consumers relate to our brands. It's casual, nonhierarchical, and a collaborative environment. That drives the decisions we make, how we act, and what our culture looks like. Pregame, our new-hire orientation, emphasizes our heritage, history, and the Nike Maxims. We intentionally create an experience for employees to discover the culture and how they can bring their own diverse skills and abilities to make a contribution. Our cultural assessment [employee survey] is a way to solicit ongoing input from employees about the culture, diversity and inclusion, management practices and programs; and a way to hold ourselves accountable for continuing to improve. It goes back to the employment brand—making the employee experience on par with the consumer experience. When I have asked employees why they stay, they say, 'I love the brand. I love the product. I love the team.' No one thing has done this for us—but we try to reinforce these simple concepts. It's about staying true to who we are."

Nike is not alone in its commitment to building a strong employer brand. As Kristen Weirick, the director of talent acquisition at Whirlpool, says, "The quickest way to kill your brand is to communicate externally something that does not resonate internally. . . . Everybody goes home and tells somebody what their day was like."[9] People are drawn to organizations they believe will enhance their own personal brand and image. Having a good brand at the company you work for is personal and influences your decision of where to work and whether or not you will stay.[10] Although communicating a brand through social media can be highly effective, as it is with connecting with customers, it is first and foremost important to have a defined, authentic, engaging brand. Engagement flows from an authentic brand, not from campaigns in any media.

Living the Values

What if a company does not have an easily recognized consumer brand? What if it is a small or midsized firm? Can it still have a set of values and a culture that stand out to make a compelling employee offer? Qualcomm, a San Diego, California–based company, grew quickly after being founded in 1985. Now a Fortune 500 company with nearly 13,000 employees, it is still not a household name, even though its technologies are contained in many consumers' mobile phones. The early culture of the company was full of entertainment, entrepreneurship, and innovation. As it rapidly expanded, it became difficult to retain the unique culture that made it have a "casual, fun atmosphere that breeds innovation."[11]

One of the programs that Qualcomm used and continues to use to sustain its fun and innovative culture is a practice called "52 Weeks." For a new employee at Qualcomm, knowing the brand and culture is not as intuitive from the start as it is at Nike, so the process of successfully integrating an employee into the culture requires a more planned program.

As Tamar Elkeles, the vice president of learning and organization development, says, "Our primary goal for '52 Weeks' is to create and retain our culture. We were growing so rapidly and hiring thousands of people every year, and we wanted to keep a culture that encouraged risk taking and entrepreneurship. The way we chose to do this is to tell stories, because we wanted to give people a realistic job preview and ensure the culture continues."

All new Qualcomm employees are automatically registered online to receive a story a week for their first year. Progressing from the founding of the company to the present day, the stories describe the history of the company's technology successes and failures, as well as the rationale behind key decisions, all while conveying the company's culture in a memorable format.

The stories continue to change and morph as employees submit newer versions of them. One of the perennial favorites is a story about the dress code. Since Qualcomm is based in San Diego, it's not unusual for employees to surf or ride bikes at lunchtime, so the dress code is understandably relaxed. However, the chief technologist came in one morning and spotted an employee parading through the halls in pink bunny slippers, inspiring him to send out a memo clarifying the dress code. Called the Franklin memo, after the name of the chief technologist, the memo instructed that from that point on, "While there is no dress code at Qualcomm, no one shall knowingly wear shoes with ears."

According to Elkeles, this was an amusing way to communicate that the Qualcomm dress code, though relaxed, did in fact have limits. Other stories tell about the perseverance and risk-taking attitude that distinguished the company in its early years and how contrarian thinking led to some of the company's most important innovations.

The stories also reflect transparency as a way to encourage the type of risk taking that has been successful for Qualcomm, while discouraging the converse. In another of the "52 Weeks" stories, an overengineered project is described. "The team fell in love with the technology, and with too little input from customers, ended up spending too much money and effort on a product that did not fare well in the marketplace," says Elkeles. By telling the story of a failure, Qualcomm emphasizes its commitment to customer-requirement-driven design, bounded by sensible financial investments. It also reinforces a cultural norm of open discussion and learning from mistakes, an asset that can help a technology company remain competitive and nimble in the marketplace.

How does Qualcomm know that the "52 Weeks" stories are working? "The stories get retold. It becomes lore," says Elkeles. "You know it's working because people tell the stories to others." Story suggestions are submitted by employees, so the set of stories is constantly being updated. A story is selected if it conveys a piece of the important cultural norms of execution or innovation, has a lesson that helps people understand Qualcomm, and is memorable. Each story is tracked to determine how many people click through to read the story, with the average story yielding 3,000 click-throughs, meaning that people who are not new hires are also reading the stories. A story with fewer than average click-throughs is replaced with a new one, creating a fresh and dynamic set of "52 Weeks."

Establishing Reputation Through Corporate Social Responsibility

According to a survey by PwC, 88 percent of Millennials in the United States want to engage in some form of public service, which indicates that they would also be interested in joining an employer that has a track record of corporate social responsibility.[12] Corporate social responsibility (CSR) is a concept "whereby organizations consider the interests of society by taking responsibility for the impact of their activities on customers, suppliers, employees and stakeholders as well as the environment."[13]

As Glen Naedts, a member of the Millennial generation working in the retail, travel, and hospitality industry in Europe, says, "I believe we are a new breed on the market with higher regard for the values the company has instead of money as the sole incentive. We are more concerned about the environment and the future of the planet, monetary system, human relations, etc."

For all generations, working for a company that has a strong commitment to corporate social responsibility is one of the top ten factors that influence their selection of a future employer, as reported in "The Generations @ Work" survey. Corporate social responsibility is also important to customers, and studies show that potential customers who identify personally with the CSR activities of a company are more likely to buy from that company. Similarly, employees want to remain with a company that is working for something bigger than the company alone.[14]

For small- and medium-sized businesses, it is possible to create a sense of purpose for each employee that can be a competitive appeal to attracting Millennials and their desire to make a difference. However, large companies have the advantage of scale in creating and implementing wide-reaching, high-impact CSR possibilities that can also be appealing to the Millennial generation, as Andrew Levy of IBM noted at the opening of this chapter. While members of all four generations surveyed consider CSR as a factor in selecting an employer, it is especially key for younger employees. One possible reason for this is that many Millennials spent years in high school volunteering on community projects, sometimes as a criterion for graduation. They thus enter the workplace with this as one of their expectations for an employer.

For some organizations, this means picking specific social issues that are strongly linked to their core mission. Some companies, such as Goldman Sachs, a global investment bank with offices in all the major world financial centers, have developed CSR programs that are becoming an important lever for creating social change and attracting employees to the firm. In 2009 Goldman Sachs was one of the top ten companies in *Fortune* magazine's 100 Best Companies to Work For. The firm has received much media acclaim for its "10,000 Women" program, which is "increasing the number of underserved women receiving a business and management education . . . and improving the quality and capacity of business and management education around the world." In this five-year program, "Goldman Sachs will support partnerships with universities and development organizations that will lead to 10,000 women receiving a business and management education."[15]

While the initial partnerships fund business and management education certificates for 10,000 women in countries around the world, the program does much more than that. It opens doors for thousands of women whose financial and practical circumstances prevent them from receiving a traditional business education. Clearly, preparing brand-loyal future investors aligns with the mission of Goldman Sachs, but the $100 million investment shows a dedication to more than the potential future business those 10,000 women will bring to the company.[16]

Qualcomm's CSR program includes working with local and global partners to bring wireless technology around the world to developing communities. Its Wireless Reach program helps deliver everything from better health care to improved education and business opportunities and safer streets, all of which serve to improve quality of life.[17] Since Qualcomm products are so closely aligned with mobile phone availability, the company is able to achieve an especially well aligned set of objectives.

Intuit is another example of how a company's founder can build an employer brand to reinforce his or her own beliefs about corporate social responsibility. Intuit, recognized as one of the most admired software companies, operates under the principle "With our success comes the responsibility to give back to the community."[18] Scott Cook, the founder of Intuit and a former Bain & Company consultant, emphasizes the importance of creating a healthy company. But the underlying values he holds are reflected in his statement that it is the responsibility of a company to give back to the community, backed by a policy allowing employees three days of personal time to volunteer at the organization of their choice. "It becomes part of the watercooler talk," said Rob Lake, a former head of talent acquisition at Intuit. "People enjoy telling the stories of what they did with their time. Some people went to help out with the aftermath of Hurricane Katrina, and others donated their time after the tsunami in 2004. Personally, I used to work as a tradesman, so I donate my time to helping remodel and rebuild women's shelters. The thing at Intuit is that you know it's part of their DNA and not just a set of values up on the wall." This commitment to corporate social responsibility has become a strong part of Intuit's operating principles.

Sometimes reaching people early in their careers not only helps build a favorable impression of a company's brand but also can influence future employees and customers through a broad set of activities. Cisco is one such company, as it has cultivated a strong reputation across areas such as environmental, economic, educational, and social initiatives.[19] One example of Cisco's CSR projects is City Year, and organization that places young adults in a year of community service. A key part of the program is leadership development of the volunteers, making them much more likely to emerge as leaders in their careers when their service with City Year is complete.[20] The thousands of young adults who have gone through the City Year program will also remember the investment Cisco made in their own development.

But CSR can reach beyond recruiting to be aligned with the mission of a company's corporate learning department. Consider CIGNA University, the learning department of CIGNA, a health service company that has expanded beyond offering learning to its internal employees to providing educational programs to consumers on how the health care system works, as well as key components of the health care political debate.[21] Inspired by www.freerice.com,[22] the CIGNA University developed a program called Water for People. As people take a short online quiz answering questions about their knowledge of health and the health care system, money is donated to Water for People. Every three questions correctly answered provide a day's worth of water for children in India. Using a gaming approach and a set of interactive tools, the program helps consumers learn about making informed choices about health care, while simultaneously creating a way for them to play a part in donating clean, safe water to countries in need. Karen Kocher, the chief learning officer of Cigna, shares this insight about the value of the Water for People program: "Not only does the free training lead to better-informed consumers of health care benefits, which benefits the company overall, but it helps build a reputation as a company invested in more than its own profits."

A DIVERSITY OF PATHS LEADS TO THE 2020 WORKPLACE

Innovation in building and communicating the employer brand, values, and reputation is only the first step to ensuring an engaged workforce in the future. To achieve employee engagement, companies are using very different tactics, each unique to their own culture and brand. There is no single path to achieve an engaged workforce in 2020. We recommend creating workplaces that are collaborative, authentic, personal, innovative, and social, expressed in the unique culture of the organization. To start, build a strong brand message consistent inside and outside the organization, supported by values that resonate across generations and geographies. Then seek to innovate the HR practices, particularly in the areas of recruiting, corporate learning, usage of social media inside the company, and leadership development. Taken together, these are the building blocks of a 2020 workplace, necessary to address the forces described in chapter 1: shifting demographics, globalization, and the social Web. In the next four chapters, we will profile practices which provide the greatest opportunity to showcase value to the employees of 2020. Each of these practices, however, emanates from the core of the organization. A small yet growing group of employers has penetrated the frontiers of employee engagement. Through their stories, we will share creative, successful methods to find and engage your employees, expand beyond traditional corporate learning, and accelerate leadership so that organization success is part of everyone's job.

SUMMARY

- **Expand your definition of collaboration in the workplace.** Traditionally, collaboration has been conceived of as internal, referring to how individuals collaborate on a one-to-one basis. In the workplace of the future, external collaboration will gain in importance as companies and communication technologies expand on a global scale.
- **Be authentic in your policies and branding.** The era in which we live is saturated with information. Potential employees expect to be able to access unprecedented amounts of information about companies prior to considering working at them. Companies that do not offer this level of

transparency will be hurt by their lack of disclosure. Employers should also expect that potential employees will conduct thorough research of any claims made by the company on a variety of Web sites. Thus, honesty and transparency are key facets of authenticity that will need to be instituted.

- **Personalize the employment contract.** Employees are beginning to demand that they be treated as individuals. One-size-fits-all employment offers, career paths, and benefits options are becoming a thing of the past. The savvy HR professional will instead focus on fostering employment relationships that meet the needs of each discrete segment of employees.
- **Make innovation a core value of your company.** Organizations that innovate are able to compete continually in the marketplace and help their employees learn and advance their skill sets. Companies need to focus on innovation, not only to stay current in the market but because potential employees are attracted to organizations that have ideas for the future.
- **Encourage social interactions and connections among your employees.** In the networked world we live in, providing a social environment at the office, though necessary, is no longer enough. Instead, employers will need to foster the use of social media tools and techniques to allow employees to connect with global communities.

CHAPTER FOUR

Social Recruiting Emerges

I mean it when I say that Twitter got me my job," says Kevin Smith, currently working as a software developer at Gnoso.

About a year and a half ago, Smith was restless, and, as he wrote on the Web site Marketing Profs Daily Fix, "I was joining the ranks of people who read *Dilbert* for the empathy more than the humor. . . . I was stuck in Office Space hell, right down to the Hawaiian shirt day."

Early in Smith's job search process, he started using Twitter, a free social networking and microblogging service that allows users to send and receive text messages of 140 characters, known as tweets. Tweets are displayed on the user's profile page and delivered to other users, known as followers, who have subscribed to that person. Smith first started using Twitter as an outlet, as he says, "to whine about my current job." One early tweet read, "i'm officially the only one in the office choosing to not wear a hawaiian shirt. /sigh."

> **Microblogging**: A sibling of blogging that consists of sending short messages (140 characters or less) to a group of followers.

Not surprisingly, this was not the route to success. But what Smith did next got him his dream job. Smith decided he wanted to work in the programming language Ruby and used Twitter as a way to find a Ruby community. Inspired by the community of peers he was surrounding himself with, he started tweeting about his favorite articles, notices on upcoming conferences, and other subjects that came to him. About the same time, he made a checklist of his criteria for his ideal employer: small, local, collaborative, open to new ways of doing things, focused on quality and design, made up of a community of Mac users, and generally a place where everyone was expected to be continually learning and improving his craft each day.

Shortly after making up the list of criteria, Smith realized that one of his new Twitter followers worked at Gnoso, a company that happened to meet most of his requirements. Smith went to the company's Web site and was immediately drawn to its philosophy: "Imagination. Function. Beauty."

Smith sent in his résumé and waited a few weeks but heard no word. So he sent a message to the follower he knew was from Gnoso, and after several more tweets and some LinkedIn messages, Smith was offered an interview and, eventually, a job as a software developer at Gnoso.

Peter Waldschmidt, the founder and CEO of Gnoso, said this about the process of hiring Smith: "We were able to get a good idea of Kevin's skills and interests just by conversing over Twitter for several months. While it doesn't remove the need for interviews, it makes the interview process more like hiring a friend than hiring a stranger."[1]

Now compare Smith's job search experience with traditional networking. Often in networking, the communication is face-to-face or via e-mail. When there is a meeting, it lasts for a short amount of time, is usually over after an hour, is followed by thank-you notes and perhaps a onetime connection on LinkedIn or Facebook. That is typically the end of the process for many candidates.

But by using social recruiting in a job search, the process continues. After going off their separate ways, the two parties continue to interact through social networking tools and have an opportunity to continually make an impression. Some of the control in the recruiting relationship moves to the candidate, who can place him- or herself on people's minds each day through the use of social networks. A recent survey conducted by Jobvite of 115 human resource recruitment professionals found that 80 percent were using social media or social networking for recruitment and that this practice was increasing among 39 percent of the sample. Additionally, among those using

Social recruiting: A practice that leverages social and professional networks, both online and offline, from both a candidate's perspective and the hiring side, to connect to, communicate with, engage, inform, and attract future talent.

social networking for recruiting, LinkedIn is now used in seeking job candidates by 95 percent of recruiters, while Facebook is used by 59 percent, having gained 23 percent in a one-year period from 2008 to 2009. Twitter already ranks third, with 42 percent of respondents using the tool for recruitment purposes.[2]

RECRUITING REDEFINED: SOCIAL RECRUITING EMERGES

As we saw in chapter 1, shifting workforce demographics mean that Millennials will be the dominant segment of the workforce in 2020. Table 4-1 shows how companies are redefining the recruiting function to focus on social recruiting.

TABLE 4-1: RECRUITING REDEFINED

Challenges	Traditional Recruiting	Social Recruiting
Expanding globally	Recruiting fairs in high-growth countries	Sourcing of candidates on social networks
Finding talent	Job boards, search firms	Facebook groups, crowdsource job specs
Attracting talent	On-campus interviews	YouTube channels, employees' video contests
Building relationships	Several face-to-face interviews	Twitter groups, parents at work programs
Communicating company values	Research on company Web site	Links to company YouTube channels, Facebook groups, or Twitter posts

Source: Future Workplace.

Rather than recruiting candidates on college campuses, companies are becoming virtual talent scouts and utilizing a range of social media tools, such as Facebook, YouTube, LinkedIn, Second Life, and Twitter, to attract and engage tomorrow's workers. Recruiting heads are going where Millennials live—online—to find the people they need, many of whom may not be actively looking for a new opportunity. These social networks have become very influential in sourcing talent, establishing relationships with candidates, and beginning a conversation with a wide range of influencers. After all, prospective job candidates like Smith are proactively seeking employers that hold the same values they do: authenticity, personalization, collaboration, innovation, and a desire for a social workplace.

Second, as companies go global, the recruiting function must lead the effort to source a global talent pool as efficiently and effectively as possible. This means creating a presence on Facebook or Second Life, so your company's recruiting can reach the more than 350 million people who now have profiles on social networks.

Third, the Internet has made it possible for most knowledge workers to be located far away from their employers' physical center. Designers, call center operators, salespeople, even many in the human resource department, can work effectively wherever they wish. In this mobile world, texting and instant messaging are surpassing many other forms of communications in many counties, so recruiters must utilize these forms of communication as well.

Last, employers are recognizing how social and collaborative the world of work can be and are incorporating this into their job descriptions. For example, Best Buy recently advertised for a senior manager of emerging-media marketing, seeking job candidates with at least one year of active blogging experience, a graduate degree, and more than 250 followers on Twitter. When the job description caused a stir in the blogosphere, Best Buy's chief marketing officer, Barry Judge, went one step further—he crowdsourced the job specifications by asking everyone who was interested in the job to help write the job description. The crowdsourced job description spoke to the traits of the social media revolution we are experiencing: humor, collaboration, and authenticity. For instance, the revamped job description included a requirement that the senior manager understand a list of commonly used social media acronyms as well as fully understand all the capabilities of a smart phone. Best Buy is leading the way in using the strengths of the social Web to source and attract top talent.

Crowdsourcing: Harnessing of the skills of individuals through an open call for participation. These individuals, due to their enthusiasm, contribute content, do research, and solve problems together.

Job candidates, as well as employers, are savvier than ever before. They have access to unparalleled information about a prospective employer through the social Web and through their own social networks. As these candidates become more connected to one another and their prospective employers, we are seeing a shift from the Information Age to a Collaboration Age, in which workers value constant collaboration, communication, and connection to each other.

In the Collaboration Age, recruiting is both personal and social, so recruitment managers must be part of the social Web in order to source and attract the best talent. The importance of leveraging social recruiting is evident in a comprehensive survey conducted by PricewaterhouseCoopers (PwC), with recent college hires to the firm. The survey, entitled "Managing Tomorrow's People: Millennials at Work" polled 4,271 college graduates from forty-four countries about their work expectations. One of the central points of the survey was the role technology played in the work lives of these Millennials, as 86 percent of the respondents reported that they belong to a social networking site and expect to be able to access external social networking sites as well as text messaging and instant messaging on the job. As one participant in this study put it, "Technology will be at the center of everything we do, in ways that may now be unimaginable."[3]

The Millennials surveyed see social networking technologies as tools for increasing their productivity, rather than as tools reserved solely for interacting with friends. They believe that technology will be at the center of their lives over the course of their careers and expect employers to adopt the latest technologies and tools in the workplace so they can work faster and smarter.

As more businesses go global, so do the expectations of Millennials in the workplace. Nearly all Millennials—94 percent—expect to work across geographic boundaries. International experience is an essential requirement of their career, with more than 70 percent of Millennials wanting to learn a new language at work. This is understandably higher in countries where English is not the main language, but even in countries where English is the main language, there is an expectation that being proficient in another language will be required to be successful in the workplace of the future.[4]

Even if we assume that the Baby Boomer segment of the workforce will work until the age of 74 years or older, Millennials are the future workforce of 2020. As Millennials make up a greater percentage of professional service and information technology firms, it is these firms that are experimenting the most by using the latest tools to source Millennial talent.

Not surprisingly, the companies that perennially land on the *Business Week* list of the Best Places to Launch a Career are pushing the envelope as they recognize the ways in which the world of work is changing. These companies are leveraging the latest social networking tools for attracting and recruiting new hires. As standout examples, Deloitte is starting to recruit in middle and high school, Ernst & Young is creating groups on Facebook and Twitter, while KPMG shares videos on its highly customized YouTube channel. The goal of all this outreach is to go where Millennials congregate and build an employer brand that is fresh, authentic, and personal—just what Millennials say they want.

PRECOLLEGE EMPLOYER OUTREACH PROGRAMS

Fearing a worker shortage in the accounting and engineering fields, some companies are seeking innovative ways to build their employer brands as early as the middle and high school years. A major study performed in 2007 by Weekly Reader Research on behalf of Deloitte

LLC, entitled "Accounting and the Next Generation of Workers," found that students were already considering career possibilities by the age of 12. According to Stan Smith, the national director of Next Generation Initiatives (NGI) at Deloitte Services, a division of Deloitte LLC, students pass through various stages in making a career choice. They contemplate career possibilities as early as 10 to 12 years old, consider various types of careers at 12 to 14 years old, and focus on a few possible careers at the ages of 15 to 16. According to Smith, "Our research shows that students are most open to the widest number of possible career choices between the ages of twelve and fourteen years old. After that age, they begin to narrow their career choices. So our focus in the precollege outreach is to develop a pipeline of students in middle school who are exposed to what we do as a business."

Consider the following statistics: in 2007, there were 16.5 million students in grades nine through twelve in the United States. It is estimated that roughly 33 percent will graduate from high school, enroll in college, and graduate with a bachelor's degree within four to six years. This means that about 5.4 million college graduates will potentially come into the job market over the period 2011–2014. When the number of high school students who indicate an interest in accounting or consulting is examined, the number narrows to just 2.3 percent.[5] To avert a potential talent shortage in accounting, Deloitte LLP is creating partnerships with middle and high schools to assist students in their career exploration process. The goal: to turn them into prospective employees at as early an age as possible.

Though companies have sought to shape public school curricula before, previous efforts often focused on teaching students vocational trades or providing certificates in specialized forms of technology. Now companies are starting to tout their employer brand to students as young as 12 years old. These partnerships represent a new dimension in the business world's growing influence in public education.

Smith points to what he sees as a perfect storm in the demographics impacting the accounting profession. Quoting a survey conducted by Robert Half, a leading employment firm, Smith estimates that there will be a 26 percent increase in available accounting jobs through

2015 due to two factors: a wave of Baby Boomer accountants set to retire by 2015 as they begin to reach 70 years of age and a decline in interest in accounting as students seek higher-paid employment in fields such as consulting and information technology. These forces have combined to make the field of accounting one that will see a talent shortage in the near future.

Smith's solution is a three-pronged program, including (1) a prescriptive curricula for K–12 students entitled *Life, Inc.: The Ultimate Career Guide for Young People,* by Neale Godfrey; (2) an accompanying "virtual coaching" system that encourages students to look at their likes and dislikes though an interactive Web site found at www.nealeslifeinc.com; and finally (3) an online business simulation entitled Deloitte's Virtual Team Challenge. This online challenge showcases what it is like to work in business. Taken together, this approach will expand the talent pool by encouraging students to take a look at business as a career and, with this as a base, to consider a career in accounting or consulting at as early an age as possible. Deloitte Foundation has funded the program to date, and future expansions in 2010 include going beyond high school students to Army-family teens on bases throughout the world as well as to veterans returning from war and their families.

The importance of this can be seen in a story Godfrey and Smith relate about the life of Dunia Fernandez. She is now age 35 and works as the director of Pathways to Success at the Maricopa Community College Foundation. Fernandez grew up in East Los Angeles, California, after immigrating to the United States from Mexico at an early age. She received a full scholarship to Brown, graduated in 1998, and then went on her journey to find a career she was passionate about. Along the way she tried law school and teaching, and she now works in an executive position where she manages eight staff members. As Fernandez looks back at her career journeys, she reflects, "As I entered college, accounting was not in my horizon. If I had known about what the job of an accountant really is—using quantitative, communications, analytical, and investigative skills—I would have chosen this as a career right out of college. But I had no exposure to accountants growing up, no role models that were accountants, and no one to turn to about what the job of an accountant was really all about. However, now, after my life has taken me towards accounting, I find I love it. I now manage a budget of more than two million dollars, and I have learned accounting as an executive. There is no question that if I were exposed to what the accounting profession offers at an early age, I would have chosen it."

Building these early school partnerships is proving to be a valuable vehicle to avert a talent shortage of engineers as well as accountants. Lockheed Martin projects that by the year 2018 half of its science- and engineering-based workforce will be eligible to retire. Meanwhile, interest in engineering as a career is declining among U.S. students. In a 2007 survey of more than 270,000 college freshman conducted by the Higher Education Research Institute of UCLA, only 7.5 percent of enrolled college graduates expressed an interest in engineering as a career—the lowest level since the 1970s.[6]

This is compounded by the fact that national security restrictions preclude Lockheed Martin and other defense contractors from outsourcing their jobs overseas.[7] Today Lockheed Martin is facing a serious strategic question: how to develop the pipeline of technical workers in the areas of engineering, the natural sciences, and computer science, as these workers make up half of the current workforce. Jim Knotts, the director of corporate and community affairs at Lockheed Martin, shares his view of the importance of companies getting involved early in the career exploration process.

According to Knotts, "We decided as a company in 2007 to create partnerships with both high schools and their middle and elementary feeder schools in areas where the company has a corporate presence. So during the last eighteen months, we developed partnerships with high schools and middle schools in nine states across the U.S., including California, Colorado, Georgia, Florida, Maryland, Minnesota, New Jersey, Texas and Virginia. Our goal is to have partnerships with at least 25 states by 2012, totaling 10,000 students that will be exposed to the Lockheed Martin Engineers in the Classroom curriculum program."

The Engineers in the Classroom curriculum program was developed in partnership with the nonprofit firm Project Lead the Way and includes eight full-year engineering courses in digital electronics and civil engineering as well as five ten-week programs in beginning robotics for middle school students.

Essentially, the Engineers in the Classroom curriculum program has four components: (1) engineering coursework, (2) extra-credit engineering projects, (3) individualized projects under the supervision of Lockheed Martin engineers, and (4) Lockheed Martin Scholarships that are merit based and directed to students who have completed the engineering curriculum in high school.

The Lockheed Martin Engineers in the Classroom Curriculum program is particularly important in light of statistics from the National Academy of Sciences that estimate that the United States will graduate roughly 70,000 undergraduate engineers annually, while China graduates 600,000 and India 350,000 engineers, respectively. While the exact size and nature of the shortage of engineering talent have been disputed, there is agreement among economists and other experts that engineering as a profession provides the United States with the capacity to innovate, which is central to the growth and success of the country in the global marketplace.[8]

Deloitte's *Life, Inc.: The Ultimate Career Guide for Young People* and Lockheed Martin's Engineers in the Classroom curriculum are just two examples of how forward-looking companies are responding to potential talent shortages. These companies are committing financial and human resources to the K–12 school systems in an effort to position their respective professions as desirable at the earliest age possible. Expect to see increased levels of innovation and commitment like this as employers seek out innovative ways to source the 2020 workforce.

LEVERAGING THE POWER OF YOUTUBE FOR RECRUITING

As individuals progressively become more hyperconnected in their personal lives, spending increasing amounts of time on Facebook, sharing videos on YouTube, and tweeting on the microblogging site Twitter, companies are following in their steps. These companies want to build employer brands where their potential employees are spending their time.

To Brian Fugere, a partner in charge of Deloitte marketing and communications, the power of using social media was made clear on February 4, 2007, during Super Bowl XLI. This was not only the day the Indianapolis Colts won the Super Bowl against the Chicago Bears, it was also the day Frito-Lay changed the game in TV advertising by allowing customers to create a thirty-second advertising spot.

For Super Bowl XLI, the cost of a thirty-second spot was $2.6 million. Instead of having its advertising agency create an ad, however, Frito-Lay decided to create a Web site called Doritos Crash the Super Bowl. On this site, consumers entered their homemade video commercials for a chance to win $10,000 and an all-expenses-paid trip to Super Bowl XLI in Miami, Florida. The marketing power of consumer-generated content quickly became evident when the Doritos Crash the Super Bowl site got more than 4 million views. Five finalists were ultimately selected from a pool of more than 1,000 entries.

As Fugere watched this revolution in consumer advertising, the idea for the Deloitte Film Festival was formed; this is a competition open to all Deloitte employees, who answer the question "What's your Deloitte?" in a five-minute video. As Fugere explains, "We started out asking Deloitte employees to create a video about one of our core values, like diversity, integrity, and customer-focused value. But the reaction from Deloitte employees was very direct: 'Give me a break—that is so boring and way too corporate.'"

Fugere agreed to change the terms of the contest—but not easily. As he admits, "Letting go is a very scary thing to do in business, and especially so for a marketing and communications professional. But I realized the concept of a film festival had to be fun, engaging, and authentic, and certainly not just an exercise to see how well Deloitte employees could memorize Deloitte's core values."

With this insight came the birth of "What's Your Deloitte?," which asks teams of Deloitte employees to create a video that represents what life is like inside Deloitte. And of course, there was an incentive: the first prize was an all-expenses-paid trip to the Sundance Film Festival.

More than two thousand U.S. Deloitte employees participated in the film festival. What's more, 30,000 people viewed and voted on the intranet site over the life of the campaign. Fugere goes on to say, "We knew at that point we had won big-time. We hoped for fifty entries and were wildly pleased when we received over two thousand." The result was an unconventional and noncorporate marketing campaign that is now a key component of Deloitte's recruiting program. One video stands out among the more than 2,000 entries. It is called "The Green Dot" and has been viewed by more than 27,000 people on YouTube as well as being featured in Deloitte recruiting materials.[9]

In "The Green Dot," a Deloitte employee is shown working as a client services "superhero," complete with cape and magic powers. Throughout, a voice-over explains what it means to work at Deloitte in terms of the values, traditions, and daily work of the firm.

Though Deloitte was the first firm to create a buzz on YouTube with its "What's Your Deloitte?" contest, KPMG touts itself as the first employer to create a customized YouTube channel that disseminates career information to potential new hires about joining the firm. According to Manny Fernandez, KPMG's national managing partner of university relations and recruiting, considerable time and research was invested in a customized channel for YouTube. Fernandez says, "We did research with college students and found they used YouTube not just for watching videos but to do research on specific topics. In other words, YouTube was becoming like Google as a search engine for Millennials. So we approached YouTube with the idea of creating a college recruiting channel expressively for the video-driven Millennial generation."

As soon as you log onto the company's YouTube site, called KPMG Go, you hear the upbeat music of "Huddle Formation" by The Go! Team.[10] Then you have a chance to search for any number of online videos on such topics as global new-hire training, giving back at KPMG, and becoming a senior associate. On KPMG Go you can view real KPMG employees sharing authentic stories of why they chose KPMG and what their experiences at the firm are like. These are not promotional videos created by a marketing firm but actual KPMG employees around the world. KPMG Go also links to an online version of the KPMG magazine, as well as to a careers section on KPMG's Web site. On the careers section of the site, there is an interactive tool that matches college majors to different practices at the firm. Enter mathematics as your major, and the site informs you of possible employment areas in economics or financial risk management. Shawn Quill, the manager of campus recruiting at KPMG, says, "In our research with college students, we found that as more students play video games like World of Warcraft and have avatars on Second Life, they expect to be entertained while they are being informed."

KPMG Go has slowly built a brand on YouTube. Now, by clicking on the KPMG Go playlist, you can watch more than sixty videos narrated by KPMG employees at various levels of the firm—from interns to associates, managers, and partners—all customized to target new hires in locations around the world. This is sleuth recruiting, and it reaches out to Millennials in a way they already find comfortable and in a forum where they are already spending their time.

> **Avatar**: A graphical representation of a person in a virtual world such as Second Life. An avatar may be an accurate representation of an actual individual, or it may be a fanciful and mythical alter ego.

CREATING A FACEBOOK GROUP TO RECRUIT NEW HIRES

Ernst & Young (E&Y), the number one company in *BusinessWeek*'s 2008 rankings of the Best Places to Launch a Career, was one of the first employers to launch a group on both Facebook and Twitter. You may think of this as innovative recruiting strategy, but according to

Dan Black, the director of campus recruiting for the Americas at Ernst & Young, it is a necessity in this day and age.

E&Y hires more than 5,000 college students and recent graduates a year for internships and entry-level career opportunities in North America. How does an organization with such huge hiring needs find enough highly qualified candidates? In addition to its traditional on-campus recruiting efforts, employee referrals, and advertising on job boards and other media, E&Y was the first employer to launch a group on Facebook to be used exclusively for recruitment purposes.

So far, the response to the E&Y Careers Facebook group has been a great success, with more than 34,000 fans. "It's very easy to join this," says Black. "All you need is a profile, and you can search for Ernst & Young. Then once you are a member of the E&Y community on Facebook, you receive updates from the company, take part in polls, and, most important, interact directly with E&Y potential employees as well as E&Y recruiters."

Competition for top graduates is intense, and by connecting graduates on the Facebook platform E&Y is able to establish a more personal employer brand and a lasting connection with the best candidates. The approach can pose risks as well as rewards, however, as companies that solicit public feedback can receive negative as well as positive comments. But E&Y's Black believes that companies need to realize they are no longer in sole control of their employer brand—social networking sites such as Facebook and Twitter, along with Vault.com, the comprehensive job-search Web site, are already bringing increased transparency into the recruiting process.

Black and his team regularly monitor the E&Y Careers Facebook group and respond to queries such as how to get a job at the firm, what types of educational backgrounds E&Y is looking for, and how to get involved in corporate social responsibility programs sponsored by the firm. Black sees E&Y's commitment to using the latest social media as crucial to finding and retaining the best talent. As Black puts it, "Millennials communicate in vastly different ways from you and me. Many prefer texting and sending

IMs to e-mail and phone. The reality is that most incoming college freshmen live their lives online, so it makes sense for us to be there as well. By leveraging social networks, blogs, microblogs, and other new-media channels, we create opportunities for students to get to know the firm on a personal basis. What is really working for us is utilizing these new communication methods throughout the recruiting life cycle. For example, at our intern conference a couple years ago, participants received text messages about the upcoming agenda from several firm leaders."

Finally, Black adds, "We have learned that brochures, print media campus events, and even our Web site are no longer sufficient by themselves to get our unique employer brand message to Millennials. Millennials want to find their own answers to questions. And they often do this by going to their own social networks. So we have a presence in both places—traditional media as well as in social media."

When you read the posts in the E&Y Careers Facebook group about the International Intern Leadership Conference, you begin to see the power of going where the Millennials are. Eddie Ho, a graduate of Queen's University, class of 2008, participated in an E&Y internship in Toronto, Canada, over the summer of 2007. At the end of the internship Ho was offered a position with the firm and has been working there full-time since August 2008.

According to Ho, the intern experience was probably the most important factor in his taking the job. As he recalls, "I'd say it played eighty percent in my decision." As an intern, he went to the International Intern Leadership Conference and, as he says, "I really got to know the firm well. It's not easy to understand a firm the size of E&Y if you are just in one office . . . but when everyone comes together from different parts of the world . . . it just becomes clear where the firm was going and what might lay ahead for me should I join the organization."

Following the International Intern Leadership Conference, Ho wrote an extensive post on the E&Y Careers Facebook group recapping his impression of the International Intern Leadership Conference:

Jim Turley, E&Y CEO, is a great guy and lots of fun to be with. During his talk, he dressed up as a DJ rather than a business suit. He shared with us the extent of E&Y's international growth. For example, I learned the countries in BRIC (Brazil, Russia, India, and China), and why this is a major area for future growth. That's where I really got to understand the strategy of the firm and why I wanted to be part of it.

If you were interviewing at E&Y, who would you turn to first for information—Eddie Ho, the intern, or the official E&Y recruiting brochure? No wonder E&Y is striving to become more transparent in building its employer brand on social networks.

RECRUITING IN SECOND LIFE: DOES IT WORK?

Beyond leveraging Facebook and YouTube, companies are exploring how to use virtual worlds to attract and recruit a global employee base. Second Life, a virtual community with more than 16 million users, is home to a growing number of recruiting offices and virtual job fairs. These job fairs are beginning to provide job seekers with direct, although limited, access to recruiters at major companies. In most cases, a job applicant has to be invited in, but people looking for work can also go to a company's virtual building in Second Life and drop off their résumés. You have to become a Second Life member first, but basic membership in the program—all that is needed—is free. In May 2008, TMP Worldwide, a recruiting firm, hosted its first virtual job fair, called Network in World, on Second Life and attracted 1,800 candidates.

As more global firms target tech-savvy job candidates, one way to assess a candidates' technical skills is to see how they operate in Second Life. For example, employers can see how well candidates are able to create their Second Life account, develop a relatively professional-looking avatar, find their way to the recruiting office, and communicate with a recruiter via text chat or voice. This demonstrates a certain level of technical literacy.

Additionally, recruiting in Second Life allows an organization to interact with a geographically diverse pool of prospective employees. The firm comScore reports that 13 percent of Second Life residents are from Asia, 61 percent are from Europe and 19 percent are from North America.[11] Think about the economies of scale in reaching a global prospective population of job candidates without having to travel or incur the costs of renting meeting rooms, buying food, paying for airfare and hotel rooms for speakers, and providing the raffle prizes typically given out at a traditional event. Making the onetime investment in Second Life in-world assets (meeting spaces, presentation screens, and so on) is significantly less than conducting comparable events in person. When you consider that global companies often recruit in thirty to forty countries, creating one "virtual recruiting office" means that cost savings quickly add up.

Polly Pearson, the vice president of employment branding at EMC, shares her perspective about how the recruiting world has changed in the last few years: "I was entertained recently when a new college graduate told me how much time he put into his résumé and cover letter and how upset he was that the company he sent it to didn't respond as he might expect. Did he really think that's how it worked?"

Instead, Pearson sees more companies using virtual contact in areas such as Second Life to attract job candidates. In October 2007, EMC held its first career fair in Second Life, where job candidates interviewed for EMC positions in marketing, technology, and sales. The EMC career fair lasted three evenings over the course of two weeks.

To date, there have been 3,780 hits on EMC's Second Life recruiting headquarters, as shown in figure 4-1. This has translated into 307 candidates applying to EMC, with 23 actual interviews conducted in Second Life. Of those interviewed in Second Life, 80 percent were asked for second-round face-to-face interviews. Two were hired by the company, and they are still employed after one year.[12]

In addition to building a pipeline and database of job candidates in Second Life, there are huge benefits to creating a recruiting presence there. One of the biggest and most obvious benefits is cost savings, as

Figure 4-1: EMC on Second Life

Source: EMC.

a onetime expense today can be used at literally any time. Pearson explains how these savings are calculated: "We estimate that an average career fair in a single city costs about $10,000, but along with setting up the career fair you have to attract candidates from that city who have the time and inclination to meet with you. With Second Life, once a company creates a presence in-world and procures the branding materials that go along with this, there is really no further cost."

Another benefit is the ability to reach a global audience in record time. While EMC advertised its Second Life career fair only in the United States, the candidates who arrived were from places as far flung as the United Kingdom, the Netherlands, and Japan. Recruiting in Second Life is a relationship accelerator. Pearson notes, "The full immersion of Second Life makes the experience of getting to know the job candidate happen much faster than what could have been accomplished on the phone, on Facebook, or on LinkedIn. The recruiter gets to know candidates better, sees their initiative and interactive skills, and observes what they laugh at, how they interact, and what they are wearing for the interview. In Second Life it may still be 'dress for success,' but the focus is on 'impress for success.' "

You may be wondering what it is really like to go through a job interview in Second Life. Does this mean you never meet your prospective employer face to face? Simone Brunozzi, a 30-year-old technical professional from Italy, shared his Second Life recruiting experience on his blog, "Thoughts of a Technology Evangelist."

> It was an ordinary day in Italy on November 28th, 2007, when I logged in to Second Life. I had planned to visit the Luxembourg Virtual Job Fair to report my impressions on my Second Life blog. Tired of being a disposable system administrator at the University for Foreigners in Perugia, without any good career opportunity ahead, I was looking for a new job, and the fair was therefore a chance for me to look around.
>
> I landed on the island with my avatar, almost half an hour before the end of the fair. With surprise, I noticed that banks and financial companies weren't the only companies attending: there was also . . . Amazon.com! Wait a minute, I thought, what brings the great Amazon.com in a tiny place like Luxembourg. You have to know that working in a company like Amazon, Google, Ebay or Yahoo has been my dream since my studying experience in California in late 2003; no doubt I decided in less than zero seconds to check it out.[13]

Brunozzi then recounts in his blog how he participated in a series of in-world, phone, and face-to-face interviews. He finally landed his "dream job" at Amazon.com six months after his first interview in Second Life. During the six-month interview process, Amazon and Brunozzi were learning about each other while using an arsenal of social media tools. So although recruiting in Second Life did not replace in-person interviewing, it did allow for Amazon to cost-effectively prequalify Brunozzi with regard to his technological, communication, and networking skills, while Brunozzi, as a prospective employee, had the opportunity to showcase his digital literacy skills to sell himself.

Are companies outside information technology using Second Life to attract and recruit new hires? The answer is yes. Canada's Vancouver Police Department (VPD) is the first organization of its kind to use Second Life to recruit tech-savvy job candidates. The VPD started offering recruitment seminars inside Second Life in order to attract police candidates from around the globe. Kevin McQuiggin, who is in charge of the department's tech crimes division, notes that almost every major crime these days has a technological aspect to it. As he explains, "Any new media that comes out, any new form of communication, crime is going to migrate there. . . . As we move into the future, we're going to need people who understand technology—those who are conversant with it, are Web-savvy, that understand the impact of it, and understand how to use it."[14]

Even given the prevalence of identity theft and various cyber-crimes that continue to challenge police departments, McQuiggin notes, "Many police departments are not prepared to use technology to solve crimes. Internet- and technology-related crimes, from fraud to harassment, are becoming increasingly common, and almost every major crime involves technology in some way, shape, or form. So recruiting in Second Life allows VPD to see a job candidate's Web skills as well as their investigative and analytical skills—something that can be observed as they are interviewing in the virtual world."

Recruiting in Second Life makes business sense as companies seek employees with digital literacy skills who are comfortable with new technologies and able to network on a global scale. What seems like a fad now will become mainstream in 2020 as organizations realize the business benefits of sourcing global talent in virtual worlds.

USING TWITTER TO RECRUIT EMPLOYEES

Twitter had a huge growth spurt in 2008–2009, during which it grew a staggering 1,382 percent.[15] Part of the appeal of Twitter is what the technology writer Clive Thompson calls "ambient awareness." By following quick, abbreviated status reports from members of your extended social network, you get a strangely satisfying glimpse of their daily routines.

Additionally, according to a survey by the employment portal Job-Hunt, more than fifty companies are using Twitter to recruit new employees. The firms using Twitter for recruitment include the ones you would expect, such as Deloitte at @joindeloitteUSA and Ernst & Young at @Ernst_and_Young. But there are also traditional firms, such as Hershey Company at @Hershey Company, and even the U.S. Department of State at @DOScareers.

Interestingly, the story behind how and why the Department of State came to use Twitter is a good example of how organizations are beginning to migrate from Facebook and LinkedIn to Twitter in their recruitment strategies. According to Rachel Friedland, a recruitment marketing consultant with the Department of State, Twitter has been used as part of the department's recruitment efforts since 2006 as a way to build employer brand awareness, communicate specific details about career opportunities, and connect candidates directly with diplomats in residence located throughout the United States. Friedland says, "In our efforts to reach potential job candidates with the right diversity (inclusive of diverse languages, skills, cultural and educational backgrounds, geographic locations, perspectives, ethnicities, thoughts, etc.), experience, and knowledge, we need to communicate on their terms and on their turf. We believe having a presence on Twitter is of central importance to sourcing the next generation of diplomats (Foreign Service generalists and specialists) and civil service professionals. In recruitment and outreach, we continuously have to answer the questions 'What does a Foreign Service Officer in the Economic career track do?' or 'What does a Foreign Service Security Engineering Officer work on?' or 'What's a day in the life of a diplomat like?' Using Twitter allows us to answer these questions in short bursts and in the process communicate the positive day-to-day realities of a range of careers at the U.S. Department of State."

The Department of State also uses Twitter to announce networking events it hosts across the country to recruit new hires for the

U.S. Foreign Service (most are quickly sold out). Using Twitter to post links to articles on topics such as what the job of a head of a U.S. embassy is all about helps inform potential recruits. Candidates can also follow Twitter links to interviews, including one with Luis Arreaga, the director of recruitment for the Department of State, explaining how employees at the Department of State work around the world. By using Twitter for recruitment, employers can readily view not only an individual's tweets but all the messages from prospective job candidates. Open, transparent. and authentic, Twitter provides all of this in recruiting job candidates.

EXTENDING RECRUITING TO THE PARENTS OF EMPLOYEES

Though the recruiting process may start in middle school or high school, it is also extending externally to include the parents of Millennial employees. Imagine being a typical new hire, 23 years old, whose company is hosting the annual Take Your Child to Work Day. If you have no children, you may still want to share what you do at work with your family. If you work for Ogilvy Public Relations Worldwide, you can invite your mom and dad to the Take Your Parents to Work Day. It has become part of the recruiting story for Ogilvy Public Relations Worldwide.

As related by Kate Cronin, the managing director of Ogilvy's New York office, "Last year, we conducted an employee survey to find out what we could do to create an environment that is friendlier to all of our employees, including our Millennial employees, and can be used as a way to keep them excited about working for Ogilvy. We formed a panel of Millennial Ogilvy employees to brainstorm how to create a more engaging workplace, and Take Your Parents to Work Day came out as a suggestion. This team identified a need among Millennials to share their accomplishments with their family just as older employees do with their children."

To her surprise, during the first Take Your Parents to Work Day, more than 30 employees brought their parents to the office to learn about the PR business and its client base, participate in a brainstorming session, and then conclude with a cocktail reception. "When I was their age," says Cronin, "I certainly would not have wanted my parents anywhere near my office. But life has changed for this generation of Millennials and their 'helicopter parents.' These young professionals often speak to their parents daily, and many consider their parents their closest advisers. So we thought: why not?"

What Cronin did not realize was that she was tapping into a global phenomenon. Patricia Somers, an education professor at University of Texas, estimates that, according to a study of parental involvement at fifteen universities, 40 to 60 percent of parents from all socioeconomic groups are helicopter parents.[16] So it is no surprise that most colleges now offer a freshman orientation workshop for both the new incoming students and their parents. Somers says this parental involvement starts long before Millennials reach college. It begins in secondary school, when parents use online programs to track their kids' test scores, help them write their résumés, use their own networks to land them an internship, and even attend their college interviews. It does not stop there. Nearly 10 percent of employers report that parents help their children negotiate salary and benefits, and 15 percent hear complaints from parents if their kids do not earn enough money.[17]

Look at what is happening in India. Companies there have found that keeping parents involved in their employees' lives leads to greater productivity and job satisfaction. A recent research study by Towers Watson & Company indicates that companies in India are increasingly involving parents as a way to engage the entire family unit. India has the highest percentage of highly engaged workers in Asia, with 78 percent of engaged employees as compared to 58 percent in China and 39 percent in Japan.[18]

Cronin and staff expanded the vision of Take Your Parents to Work Day to include an ongoing panel of the employees' mothers to talk about how they are dealing with osteoporosis. Ogilvy PR has a client that produces one of the leading drugs in this area, and Cronin felt that as long as it was hosting a group of Boomers, it might as well engage them in a subject of interest to both parties. This panel of "Ogilvy Moms" has become an ongoing community, regularly e-mailing their suggestions to their children and requesting updates on what Ogilvy is doing in this area. What started as a tool for engaging Millennials has now developed into a competitive advantage to recruit new hires and keep their families engaged with what happens to them on the job.

As companies reach out and involve parents, they are finding myriad ways to build relationships with employees' families. According to author and consultant Tammy Erickson, they can, among other things:

- Distribute information designed for parents to students at job fairs.
- Hold a career fair in your community designed specifically for parents.
- Create special FAQ material on the company Web site directed at parents' likely questions and concerns—retirement, health benefits, 401(k) plans, educational opportunities.
- Hold parent orientation sessions like those held at universities for incoming freshmen.
- Provide incentives for parents to refer their children for employment at the firm.[19]

Other ways to build these relationships might include offering discounts on university tuition for the entire family of the new hire, hosting a Take Your Parents to Work Day, and creating online panels of parents.

EXTEND SOCIAL NETWORKS TO FORMER EMPLOYEES

It used to be that when employees left a company, managers would wish them well and both parties would simply move on. Today, even as the era of cradle-to-grave employment has disappeared, it has been replaced by a shortage of talent in key areas such as engineering, accounting, and computer science. A growing number of organizations are finding that yesterday's employees can be a fruitful referral source for tomorrow's new hires.

Companies such as J.P. Morgan, Accenture, McKinsey, Bain & Company, and Sapient, to name just a few, are creating the corporate equivalent of university alumni. In fact, many university alumni associations could learn from what the corporate alumni networks have done to nurture and build better long-term relationships. The benefits of these corporate social networks range from building a sense of community among alumni to recruiting former employees, referring potential new employees, and, of course, developing business.

While alumni networks were first implemented in professional service firms such as Accenture and McKinsey, now financial service institutions are joining this group. Take the experience of J.P. Morgan. Catherine Coluzzi, the firm's executive director of the alumni network, has this to say about its development and evolution: "We started our initiative in the investment bank in April 2008 and by the end of October 2009 we had over 10,000 registered users. While we offer the typical benefits of any alumni network, such as accessing news about J.P. Morgan, attending alumni events, downloading current research, and viewing recent job postings, our newest offering is the most exciting—affinity groups. For example, starting in 2010 we will be holding regular meetings for former J.P. Morgan women who also serve on corporate boards. This niche group of alumni will be able to discuss and debate what it means to be a successful board member. This is just one example of how we are segmenting our alumni audience and offering them exceptional access to their peers."

In a study entitled "HR Executive's Guide to Web 2.0" conducted among 537 organizations by Aberdeen Group, 40 percent of organizations were using social networking to stay in touch with former employees and another 29 percent of organizations plan to implement some type of corporate alumni networking within the next twelve months.

These alumni social networks are moving from having one online presence to having well-established groups on LinkedIn, Facebook, and Second Life, where they announce face-to-face events and extend the community to the places where alumni spend their time.

The business impact of creating these alumni networks is substantial. In a study titled "Corporate Social Networking: Increasing the Density of Workplace Performance to Power Business Performance," conducted with sixty global organizations, SelectMinds, Inc., found that rehires (also known as "boomerang" employees) who are active on a corporate social alumni network can become fully productive 49 percent faster than other experienced hires and that they remain with the organization twice as long as other experienced hires.[20] These boomerang employees have specialized expertise and inside knowledge of an organization that enables them to make a contribution immediately.[21] If conducted in the right manner, these corporate alumni networks can be central to building a lifelong corporate affiliation and keeping high-performing individuals engaged with an employer's brand.

As companies transition from their traditional recruiting functions to social ones, they are using as many methods as possible—in person, on the phone, online in external social networks such as Facebook, YouTube, Twitter, and Second Life, and by creating alumni social networks. This new social recruiting is transforming the process into a series of interactive, engaging, and at times 3-D experiences. Forward-thinking companies are redefining recruiting to be social, personal, transparent, and collaborative as a way to attract the 2020 workforce.

SUMMARY

- **Use social recruiting tactics.** Recruiting heads at Deloitte, E&Y, KPMG, and EMC are all building their employer brand online, using the latest social media tools, such as Facebook, YouTube, Twitter, and Second Life. Why? Because this is where candidates live, so recruiters need to build a presence in order to source top talent.

- **Build a business case for leveraging social networks.** Before going online with your employer brand, do what EMC did: build your business case and demonstrate economies of scale in sourcing a global talent pool. Remember, your business case comes before piloting the latest technologies and tools.

- **Start recruiting as early as middle and high school.** It's never too early to start recruiting. Companies should consider following the example of Lockheed Martin and Deloitte by reaching out to potential candidates as early as ages 12 to 14, when research indicates they are beginning to choose career paths.
- **Extend relationship building to parents of employees and even to former employees.** Follow the lead of companies such as Ogilvy PR by involving the parents of Millennials in the recruiting and retention process, as they are valued advisers to the Millennial generation, and explore creating social networks of former employees as a way to tap referral sources.
- **Factor in the changing recruitment landscape.** Understand that the recruiting process is becoming increasingly social and transparent. Today's candidates value their own social networks as much as, if not more than, the official recruiting messages of employers. Remember, today's new hires are smart job candidates who do their own research. Be visible on various social networks, and make it easy for candidates to learn about your employer brand.

CHAPTER FIVE

Über-connect Your Organization

Thomas Sanchez, a 28-year-old software engineer at Cerner Corporation, brings his social networking habits with him to work. He has member profiles on LinkedIn, Twitter, Facebook, MySpace, and The A List, a local Kansas City social networking site, as well as uCern, the company's corporate social network. Sanchez says, "I'm there partly to network with friends and colleagues, but it's become the most efficient way to get work done. I no longer need to get buried in e-mails or voice mails in order to receive an answer to a question. Now, through using a combination of Twitter, Facebook and uCern, I can easily see who the experts on any number of topics are, just by viewing their profiles and reading their discussion threads. So in a matter of minutes I can identify an expert and quickly resolve an issue on the spot, often without having to send an e-mail or voice mail."

THE CASE FOR BECOMING ÜBER-CONNECTED

This is the new world of work. The Pew Internet & American Life Project estimates that as of 2008, one third of all U.S. adult Internet users had a profile on a social network site, four times as many as in 2006.[1] While media coverage and policy attention usually focus on the growing usage of social network sites used by teenagers, adults make up the bulk of users, and their usage is increasing rapidly. In the one-year period ending in 2007, the percentage of Boomers consuming social media grew from 46 percent for young Boomers (ages 43 to 52) and 39 percent for older Boomers (ages 53 to 62) to 67 percent and 62 percent, respectively.[2] What's more, Boomers are contributors of content rather than passive lurkers online. The proportion of Boomers adding new content on social networking sites doubled from 15 percent in 2007 to 34 percent in 2008.[3]

Content contributors: Individuals who add comments and a point of view to an online discussion or blog. **Lurkers**: Individuals who follow discussions occurring in chat rooms, message boards, or blogs but do not post comments or otherwise interact themselves.

The statistics for Facebook tell the story of how social networking has penetrated beyond Millennials. The user base of Facebook is now larger than the population of the United States: more than 350 million. These users have uploaded more than 15 billion photos, making Facebook the world's largest photo-sharing service.

The fastest-growing demographic on Facebook is 35- to 49-year-olds, who make up 24 million users.[4] From December 2007 through December 2008, Facebook added twice as many 50- to 64-year-olds (13.6 million) as users under 18 years old (7.3 million).[5] With more than 350 million users on Facebook, 50 million users on LinkedIn, and 44.5 million users on Twitter as of August 2009, social networks have become ubiquitous as most of us rely on them to live, work, and communicate with one another.

In the report "Global Faces and Networked Places," Nielsen Online reported social networks and blogs to be more popular than e-mail as a form of communication.[6] Two-thirds of the entire global Internet population is a member of an online social network, and this makes social networking the world's fourth most popular online activity after searching, accessing portals, and using personal computer applications. What's more, the time spent on social networks is growing at three times the overall Internet rate and accounts for roughly 10 percent of all time spent on the Internet.[7]

DID YOU KNOW?

- Every minute, **13 hours** of video is uploaded to YouTube.
- More video has been uploaded to YouTube in the last **2 months** than all the footage aired by ABC, CBS, and NBC since 1948.
- It would take **412.3 years** to view every video on YouTube.
- There are **13,000,000 articles** available on Wikipedia in more than two hundred languages.
- The average teenager sends **2,272 text messages** each month.
- More than **1,000,000,000 pieces of content** (Web links, news, blog posts) are shared each week on Facebook.
- Among large U.S. companies **17 percent** have disciplined an employee for violating blog or message board policies.[8]

Source: Brand Infiltration and Did You Know 4.0.

Companies are starting to take note of this transformation in how we live, work, and communicate with one another, by providing similar tools inside the enterprise. Our prediction for the 2020 workplace: usage of the social Web will become the premier way to attract, engage, and retain the best talent. Just examine the statistics in the sidebar "Did You Know?" to see how usage of the social Web is altering the way we all communicate with each other.

INNOVATIVE COMPANIES USE SOCIAL MEDIA TO BUILD CONSUMER BRANDS

Chances are you are already a member of a social network or using one of the tools of the social media. You may have seen a viral video on YouTube, contributed a comment on a blog, found a new musician on MySpace, or been requested to friend a former boyfriend or girlfriend on Facebook.

Companies are finding that social networking is fast becoming the way people communicate, collaborate, and find new business. This is creating an interest in launching social networks behind

Social media: Social media is a range of Web 2.0 tools such as blogs, wikis, and RSS feeds by means of which people create and disseminate content.

company firewalls to bring this spirit of innovation inside the company so employees can collaborate with one another and customers to cocreate new products and services. Before we cover how companies are using social networking internally, we'll first examine how companies are adopting an external social media strategy to deliver improved business results.

Threadless: An Online Social Network for T-Shirt Enthusiasts

Have you ever had the perfect idea for something to put on a T-shirt? Then you should know about Threadless, an online social network where members collaborate with one another to create and rate new designs for T-shirts. Eric von Hippel, a professor and the head of the Innovation and Entrepreneurship Group at the MIT Sloan School of Management, as well as the author of *Democratizing Innovation*, has called Threadless a perfect example of a new way of thinking about innovation. Threadless members solicit advice on their designs from one another, post links to blogs, MySpace, and Facebook, and ask friends to vote on their design. Once a design is submitted, the community votes, and the most popular designs are manufactured and then sold on the Threadless Web site. Winning submission designers receive both a cash prize and store credit.[9] Founded in 2000 by Jake Nickell and Jacob DeHart, the company now has sales of more than $30 million and a user base that has expanded more than tenfold in five years, from 70,000 to more than 800,000 members.[10]

Many entrepreneurs know intuitively that users of products are often the best equipped to innovate, and a growing body of research supports this. A study published in the *Strategic Entrepreneurship Journal* suggests that a large number of companies are founded by user-entrepreneurs, people who go into business to improve a product they use every day. Though many thought the wisdom of crowds could create only software businesses like Wikipedia and YouTube,

Threadless has proven otherwise. Jeff Lieberman, a board member of Threadless and managing director of Insight Venture Partners, comments, "To say Threadless is just a T-shirt company is absurd. I look at Threadless as a community company that happens to use T-shirts as its canvas."[11] The success of Threadless points to a future where communities of enthusiastic users collectively create new products and services.

John Fluevog Boots & Shoes: Open-Source Footwear

At the heart of a successful consumer-facing social network is the belief that creativity comes from simplicity. With only sixty full-time employees, John Fluevog Boots & Shoes encourages its consumers to design new shoes through its Open Source Footwear Social Network. It allows anyone to participate by submitting a design for his or her ideal shoe. No fancy form or complicated submissions process is required.

Once a consumer submits a design for new shoes, it is posted online for a community vote. The most popular sketches are made into official Fluevog shoes and sold online and in retail stores across the country. Though the designer does not receive compensation, he or she does get a free pair of shoes along with public recognition. Celebrities such as Madonna and Scarlett Johansson now wear some of the shoes designed by John Fluevog consumers.

With this idea, Fluevog allows consumers who are already passionate about the company to contribute their ideas for new shoes. As Bill Taylor, the author of *Mavericks at Work* and cofounder of *Fast Company*, writes, "Few of us are in a position to hire lots of new talent or devote big budgets to product development. But all of us have customers who are passionate about what we do, filled with great ideas, and are eager to be more connected. So why not invite them to share their creativity with your company—and turn the best ideas into actual products!"[12] Fluevog's open-source footwear program proves that innovation can come from anyone—inside or outside the company. The new job of a company's leadership is to unleash this innovation. Winning shoe designs have come from such unlikely sources as a screenwriter in Moscow and a children's book illustrator in Utah.[13]

In the case of Carrie Kozlowski of Kitchener, Ontario, Canada, the designer of the Hi Choice Vanny shoe, the experience of submitting a new shoe design actually led to a new career. Kozlowski says, "I've always been as crazy about Fluevog's off-the-wall participative marketing as I am about [their] fabulous footwear. . . . About a year ago, I decided that it was time to get out of the über-boring insurance industry where I had been working (in marketing) for too long. I spiffed up my resume by adding 'shoe designer' for Fluevog, and ended up getting a job in an architectural practice!"[14]

Starbucks: My Starbucks Idea

It's not just small innovators who are leveraging the power of social networks to create new products. Starbucks, with 172,000 employees in forty-nine countries, has a social network called My Starbucks Idea, found at http://mystarbucksidea.force.com, which allows consumers to share ideas and suggestions for how to make the Starbucks experience better.[15]

When a Starbucks consumer suggests an idea for a product or service, others vote on the idea, rank it, and share comments on it. Starbucks managers respond to the ideas and report back on what actions the company will take to implement the most promising ideas. The Ideas in Action blog, found at http://blogs.starbucks.com, is a companion to the My Starbucks Idea social networking site. It provides feedback on which ideas are selected for implementation and why.[16]

The results of My Starbucks Idea and the companion blog are indeed impressive. In one year, My Starbucks Idea received 70,000 ideas. Samples include:

- **Starbucks Gold Card.** A rewards card for frequent customers with which, for an annual $25 fee, customers receive 10 percent off most Starbucks products.
- **Birthday Brew.** Starbucks Gold Club members get a free drink on their birthday.[17]

Starbucks also engages consumers on its Twitter page with news and announcements. As of January 2010, Starbucks' Twitter page had 728,517 followers.[18] Looking at the page of a competitor, Dunkin' Donuts, you see a difference in style, which may account for why Dunkin' Donuts has only 42,192 followers.[19] Finally, Starbucks has a presence on YouTube, as well as on Facebook, where the company shares its latest commercials and information about coffee blends, as well as examples of corporate social responsibility projects around the world. The Starbucks experience shows how the company uses social networks and a range of social media to drive innovation by involving consumers to propose new product ideas.

ÜBER-CONNECT YOUR ORGANIZATION

Imagine if a company could create a simple way for employees to have conversations with one another, share their knowledge, get involved in cocreating new products and services, and contribute these ideas to the organization. Threadless, Fluevog, and Starbucks are doing this externally with their customers. But it can also be done internally as companies tap into the energy and enthusiasm of their employees to drive greater business growth.

Many companies are now becoming über-connected, meaning they are using a range of Web 2.0 tools associated with the social Web. Working behind the company firewall, companies are able to connect employees, enable mass collaboration, and improve the company's capability to innovate in the global marketplace. These companies are discovering that using social media is not just about implementing these tools; rather, it is about creating, nurturing, and energizing communities of employees, and in some cases customers and suppliers, to come together and propose new products and services.

Table 5-1 illustrates how companies are embarking on this journey to **accelerate** how they find and capture knowledge, **broadcast** and share the knowledge of employees, **collaborate** with virtual teams of employees, **design** new products, and finally **engage employees** more

TABLE 5-1: THE STAGES OF ÜBER-CONNECTION

	Accelerate	Broadcast	Collaborate	Design	Engage Employees
Goal	Find/ capture information	Dissemi- nate news/ thought leadership	Collaborate across an enterprise	Unleash creativity	Connect communities
Issue	Dispersing content	Locating experts	Increasing collabora- tion among the global workforce	Solving problems and propos- ing ideas	Increasing innovation
Tools	Forums, blogs, RSS feeds, widgets	Blogs, blog hubs, video hubs	Commu- nities of practice, wikis, virtual worlds	Innovation jams	Corpo- rate social networks

Source: Future Workplace.

fully in the workplace. Über-connection is transforming how companies manage complex information, unleash innovation, accelerate
speed to market, and gain alignment throughout the enterprise.

This is not meant to imply that a company moves through
every stage along the way. Rather, a company must understand its
unique culture, how comfortable it is opening up the enterprise,
and what changes in the internal processes and company policies
it needs to make to become über-connected. We recommend that
a company start this process by identifying the business priorities
that require greater communication, connection, and collaboration. These priorities can include decreasing the cycle time for innovation and new product/service launches, providing a vehicle
to disseminate new knowledge, and allowing dispersed employees
around the globe to create ideas for new products and services. The

result: über-connected organizations accelerate employee engagement, increase employee productivity, and improve communications throughout the company.

Examples of über-connected companies range from large established firms, such as the 120-year-old IBM, with its 398,455 employees,[20] and Bell Canada, 129 years old with 54,434 employees,[21] to smaller firms such as the 30-year-old Cerner Corporation, with 7,800 employees,[22] and 10-year-old JetBlue, with 10,795 employees.[23] What will propel more companies to create a comprehensive strategy for becoming über-connected and leveraging the power of social media? The answer: five generations of employees will be in the workplace in 2020, and they will bring with them a set of digital expectations so they can communicate and innovate on the job with the same tools of the social Web they use every day to connect with their friends and family.

THE STAGES OF ÜBER-CONNECTION

Stage 1: Accelerate the Capture of New Knowledge

JetBlue began its journey by using social media in the internal communications department. The company created the Happy Jetting campaign to address some negative consumer perceptions of flying. Before extending the campaign to the pubic, JetBlue leveraged the power of social media to create a YouTube-style Web site, JetBlueTube.com. JetBlue then selected 125 employees to be brand ambassadors for this site.

These ambassadors were given a Flip camera to create videos of themselves and other employees narrating what Happy Jetting meant to them. The result was 369 videos posted to the company intranet and a deeper understanding of the new campaign.

Fast-forward to JetBlue University (JBU), JetBlue's internal training department, with two hundred trainers responsible for training flight crews, operations, technical crews, reservationists, and customer service representatives. Murray Christensen, JBU's director of learning technologies, saw an opportunity to use social media at JBU to find and capture knowledge and best practices across the training community. Christensen explains the reasons behind becoming über-connected: "We wanted to create a way to increase communication among our own staff. I still remember the old adage about the Xerox repairmen—the really important information about how to repair Xerox machines happened in the lunchroom or at the watercooler. So I felt it was important to give our faculty a way to easily share names of training vendors, come up with ideas to increase collaboration either in a classroom or on a webcast, and suggest ways to improve our training programs."

The first tool implemented was a JetBlue University blog in which Christensen and Chief Learning Officer Mike Barger posted simple questions. For example, Christensen asked how the company could create portable learning transcripts, which automatically record all of a participant's training courses, as well as his or her external degrees, certificates, honors, and awards. After only seven months, half of the JetBlue training faculty had become contributors to the blog.

Christensen foresees expanding the focus of the blog beyond capturing new information and best practices to mass collaboration on how to improve the training department. Christensen says, "Online participation in blogs and other types of social media will be an expectation of working in the twenty-first century. This needs to be clearly communicated and built into everyone's performance goals. In a perfect world, employees will come to understand the importance of socializing their knowledge."

Stage 2: Broadcast Thought Leadership

As companies expand around the globe, their employees need to disseminate knowledge and learn best practices from one another. They need to be able to find experts who can help them do their job. Nokia, with 124,292 employees spread across 218 countries, describes itself as having a culture that encourages employees to speak out and say what is on their minds, with the belief that good ideas will result.[24]

In 2005 Nokia developed an Expert Directory. "Think of it as a 'Dial an Expert,'" says Matthew Hanwell, the senior manager for

Web experiences at Nokia. "Twelve years ago the phone book was a physical book. This evolved online to include your name, physical coordinates, organizations belonged to, what you are currently working on, and your skills and competencies, all pulled from the HR information system."

Hanwell continues, "The directory reveals individuals' online status to let you know if they're available. It's not Facebook, but it is the most used application on the Nokia intranet."

Initially, there was resistance to creating the Expert Directory. First, Hanwell was told that company policy precluded posting pictures and revealing the organization's structure, but he probed and found that this was company lore rather than policy.

Blogosphere: A term used to describe the entire interconnected world of blogs and bloggers.

Then he was asked, "Won't headhunters find our best people?" But he reasoned, "Well, shouldn't we be able to find them first?"

After the Expert Directory was launched, Nokia's R&D community began experimenting with setting up blogs as a support tool for discussing new projects. Over time, Nokia created a Blog Hub. This aggregates all Nokia employee blogs so they are searchable and ranked as to the most active, identifying the leading bloggers and what they are talking about.

Hanwell continues on why the Blog Hub was so important in the evolution of implementing social media. "Since blogging came in under the radar," he said, "it was hard to find where people's blogs were. You had to know where to find them. But by going to the Blog Hub, you could see what's going on the blogosphere inside Nokia. This has driven participation and given information on who is the most read."

With some successes under its belt, Nokia then created Video Hub, an internal video-sharing site modeled after YouTube, where any employee can record and publish a video to the site. Finally, Hanwell reveals, "We also learned that as we use these social networking tools, we have to train people. This is especially the case with making and posting videos. Everyone loves them, they show our culture and values in action, so we want to be sure all our employees know how to make a five-minute video using a Flip camera." As Mary T. McDowell, the executive vice president of corporate strategy, says, "Nokia's role is to keep the skids greased."[25]

Stage 3: Collaborate Across the Enterprise

One of the most extensive corporationwide applications of mass collaboration is IBM's internal social network, Social Blue (formerly called IBM Beehive in its research prototype). As David Millen, the manager of social software research, points out, the organization's business focus, size, and global footprint facilitated its early adoption: "IBM employees are used to working collaboratively, and being a technology company, we have a proclivity to use these tools, as well as a technical comfort level. Moreover, as one of the most global companies in the world—we operate in 170 countries and two-thirds of our workers are outside of the U.S.—we realize the importance of learning from each other."

Social Blue, launched in 2007, sits behind the corporate firewall and is designed to be a place where IBMers share and discuss both professional and personal topics. Social Blue members friend their colleagues on the site and share photos, lists, and events. One of the drivers to create Social Blue was the vision of promoting communication and collaboration among IBMers with different skill sets and expertise. There are nearly 60,000 IBM employees who are members of Social Blue, out of an employee population of roughly 400,000, thus about 15 percent of the company. There are approximately 10,000 to 15,000 unique visitors each month, and 50 percent of visitors add new content. Members let one another know what projects they are working on, as well as rate and comment on their colleagues' content.

Social Blue's success is driven in large part by two innovations; one is called "Hive Fives," and the other is known as "honey." Both were created to increase the quality of content as well as the level of collaboration among members. Hive Fives are a way for members to post five things—either personal or professional—that are important to them. Samples include lists of "Five Reasons My Project Is on Target," "Five Projects I Am Working on Now," and "Five Marathons I Have Run."

David Millen describes the power of Hive Fives: "At IBM we work with team members that are often physically halfway around the world, yet we must develop a shared vision and work together. Hive Fives allows us the opportunity to disclose important aspects of our lives, have some fun, and share projects we are working on to create better end solutions."

What drives usage and motivates IBMers to contribute to Social Blue when they are most likely on several social networks outside of IBM? Millen addresses this by saying "If your manager is on Social Blue, you need to be there as well, so we drive usage by blending bottom-up and top-down participation. More important, Social Blue has created a content promotion system to recognize and reward IBM employees for sharing knowledge."

The content promotion system is called "honey," and figure 5-1 shows how this works for IBM employees.

Each week, a group of fifty IBMers selects content from Social Blue

Figure 5-1: IBM Beehive Content Promotion Process

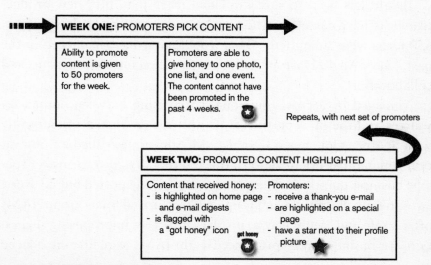

Source: IBM's Honey Content Promotion.

that they deem to be unique and interesting. They anoint this content as having honey, and it is subsequently displayed on the Social Blue home page, in the e-mail digest, and on dedicated Web pages listing the current content with honey.[26]

Content that displays the honey icon can easily be filtered and read by IBMers, and this is used to make new connections across the organization and promote greater communication and collaboration. IBM is finding that as employees form more personal networks throughout the company, they perform at higher levels and learn the value of becoming searchable.[27]

Stage 4: Design Ways to Increase Innovation

Bell Canada wanted to create a way for employees to propose new ideas to the appropriate managers and improve the speed of decision making. Inspired by *American Idol*, the hit TV show in which the audience votes for winners, Rex Lee, a former director of collaboration services, decided to build an online tool giving employees the chance to vote on new ideas. The new tool, called ID-ah!, allows anyone in the company to submit ideas he or she thinks are valuable. Employees then view, comment, and vote on them.[28] ID-ah! is similar to the Starbucks Idea Exchange described earlier.

ID-ah! has been so successful that more than fifty new productive ideas have come from nonmanagement employees. In one year, 550 ideas were submitted. "This would never have happened in the past," says Angie Harrop, Bell Canada's director of leadership and collaboration.

Managed by a cross-functional partnership between human resources and the IT department, ID-ah! was developed concurrently with another tool, called ID-ah! JAM. Sometimes called an innovation jam in other organizations, this is a tool designed to answer specific business questions. The question is typically posted online over a two- to four-day period and is much like a virtual focus group. JAMs offer a safe and secure way to involve employees in proposing suggestions for business problems. Since ID-ah! JAMs were first introduced

Figure 5-2: Bell Canada's Web 2.0 Tools: ID-ah! JAM

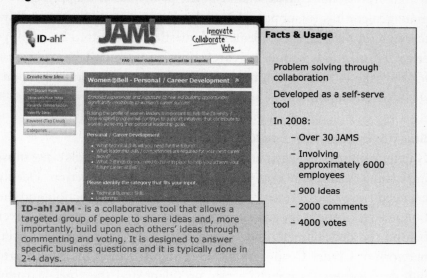

Source: Bell Canada, ID-ah! JAM.

at Bell Canada, there have been thirty JAMs reaching six thousand employees, who have proposed nine hundred ideas and added two thousand comments.

ID-ah! JAMs target business issues ranging from how to increase sales of a particular product to how to increase customer satisfaction and allow a large cross section of Bell Canada employees to share their ideas and suggestions. One ID-ah! JAM probed how to increase customer satisfaction, involved more than a thousand employees, including a large number of customer call center operators, and resulted in 360 new ideas to increase customer satisfaction.

The power of the ID-ah! tool is not only in generating new ideas but also in helping to change the culture of the company, providing a means for employees to connect and communicate and encouraging employees to become more personally invested in the company and accountable for its success. Harrop notes, "The great thing about these tools is that they are available to all employees, regardless of level, location, or function. What's important to consider, however, is that traditional change management principles still apply. Senior management has to support this and make a commitment to follow through on the feedback, ideas, and questions submitted by employees. Organizations should be careful not to push collaboration just for the sake of collaboration. It still requires careful planning, sponsorship, and support to be successful."

Stage 5: Engage with Employees

Greater employee engagement in solving business problems is the most important reason why companies embrace über-connection. Deeply engaged employees stretch beyond the walls of their function and the boundaries of the company to engage customers. This was the driver behind the development and launch of uCern, the corporate social network of Cerner Corporation, a leading IT firm in the health care industry. Robert Campbell, a vice president and the chief learning officer at Cerner, describes how uCern got started: "I was presented with a business problem from my chief operating officer, Mo Zayed, who asked, 'How can Cerner dramatically decrease the cycle time from discovery to adoption of new products and services?'" Senior executives from marketing, IT, human resources, corporate learning, and internal communications were pulled together into a task force to address this question. Rather than tweaking a current solution, this team decided to create an entirely new way to work at Cerner and recommended the development of an enterprisewide social collaboration platform.

Cerner, like many organizations, had an environment where knowledge was created in a single-threaded fashion, often by a single expert. As Campbell explains, "In this environment much of our current knowledge was locked behind password-protected Web sites, guarded in organizational silos, lost in e-mail inboxes, or stored on individual laptops. We decided to change the way we collaborated on projects. We saw a need to create more of an open culture and dramatically accelerate the cycle time of innovation throughout our company and our client base. Our vision was to create a culture where it would be as easy to collaborate on new business ideas as it is to share photos on Facebook. The tag line of uCern succinctly communicates the vision: 'To put what we learn today into use tomorrow.' "

Campbell points to a number of critical success factors Cerner put into place to encourage employees' participation in uCern. First, uCern was built into the workflow of each Cerner associate and is the customizable home page a Cerner associate logs onto after joining uCern. "Too often internal social networks are separate from one's mainstream work. This is why they fail: because they are just another to-do on an already overcrowded list of deliverables," says Campbell. So uCern was created to be a collaborative platform where Cerner associates could e-mail, share expertise, post a comment on a blog, access needed documents, and check relevant learning programs. For example, Cerner's engineers use blogs and wikis as core tools for reporting on the progress of their work. Managers routinely scan them for project updates. As the progress of a project becomes more transparent, managers can reallocate resources where needed.

The second success factor behind uCern is the active involvement of Cerner senior executives. uCern is not an IT, marketing, or HR initiative. It is a new way to work at Cerner, one that allows for heightened transparency, accessibility, and collaboration so Cerner associates have an easy way to search for and find answers to work-related questions. Campbell notes, "We realized that the transformation to a bottom-up culture needed to start at the top—with our senior executives leading the way in a new leadership approach, one that encourages transparency." For example, most Cerner senior executives have their own blogs, and associates are expected to contribute quality comments on a regular basis. It's easy to identify the most insightful contributors, as blogs are aggregated into a blog hub, highlighting which blogs are most active, who's commenting, who the leading bloggers are, and what they are saying.

In addition, Cerner encourages all associates to make uCern a success. Campbell provides an example: "The 'help' space in uCern is completely user-generated by Cerner associates. For example, when an associate asks a question on a discussion board, other associates post answers and each answer is rated in terms of its usefulness. The associate who asks the question assigns one point for a helpful answer and two points for correct and thoughtful answers. Associates then have their point totals included as input into their overall performance ratings with their manager, creating an incentive to post frequently."

To manage uCern, Campbell created an entirely new class of roles that he calls "Community Gardeners," to ensure adoption of uCern across the enterprise. Campbell adds, "Community Gardeners are professionals in the Corporate Learning Department who act as moderators for each community on the corporate social network. It is their job to generate interest in the community, post new knowledge, monitor growth, and solve problems that can derail adoption within the community. These Community Gardeners become the go-to people for each community, and their peers recognize them as thought leaders. They are trained in how to use all the tools in the community (RSS feeds, wikis, and blogs), and they encourage involvement by helping participants see what's in it for them to share knowledge with their peers."

uCern was launched to Cerner's internal population in 2009, and plans are under way to extend it to Cerner's customers and suppliers in 2010. The goal, says Campbell, "is to create a networked company, where we link employees to customers and suppliers with the goal of achieving a host of business benefits, such as reduced cycle time for innovation, greater ability to share knowledge across the enterprise, improved access to knowledge experts, and decreased time to market for new products, resulting in improved customer satisfaction."

Campbell believes that a common reason for failed participation in corporate social networks is fear among employees of not knowing what to contribute and fear of repercussions if they contribute content that is later deemed proprietary or inappropriate. Campbell recommends working through these issues with the HR, legal, and IT departments to create policies and guidelines for the usage of social media so that it becomes part of the culture.

SOCIAL MEDIA IS HAPPENING IN THE U.S. ARMY

You may be thinking that social media usage is only for high-tech companies like IBM, Cerner, or Bell Canada. However, the U.S. Army is inviting all personnel—from privates to generals—to go online and collaboratively rewrite the field manuals using the same software Wikipedia uses. The introduction of wikis is part of a larger revamping of the Army's field manual system, which currently includes more than five hundred field guides on topics ranging from counterterrorism to how to stay warm during cold-weather operations. Of the total of five hundred guides, only about fifty are not open to collaborative editing on a wiki.[29] "The goal," says Jake Pennington, the head of the Lifelong Learning Center at the Command and General Staff College in Fort Leavenworth, Kansas, "is to tap the battle-tested experience of all those in the army to write and revise these field manuals rather than just rely on a handful of specialists in the Army's array of research centers." This vision has support at its highest levels. Lieutenant General William B. Caldwell, the former commander of the Combined Arms Center at Fort Leavenworth, who is now working in Afghanistan as commander, Combined Security Transition Command/North Atlantic Treaty Organization Training Mission, wrote on the Combined Arms Center blog on July 1, 2009, "by embracing technology, the Army can save money, break down barriers, streamline processes and build a bright future."[30]

In addition to using wikis, the Army also makes extensive use of blogs. Lieutenant General Caldwell is a visionary in this, as he supports the use of both wikis and blogs to communicate and share lessons learned. On July 13, 2009, one year following the death of nine soldiers in Afghanistan, Lieutenant General Caldwell wrote the following blog post on how others could learn from the sacrifice of those nine soldiers:

LEARNING FROM THE SACRIFICE OF OTHERS
One year ago today, nine American Soldiers gave their lives for the future of Afghanistan and a better world. A contingent of

43 U.S. and 24 Afghan National Army Soldiers fought more than 200 militants in a pitched battle at Wanat, located in Afghanistan's Waigal valley. Before dawn, insurgents armed with rocket propelled grenades and automatic weapons hit the small outpost with an integrated and coordinated attack.

C Company, 2d Battalion, 503d Infantry Regiment held on through four hours of intense combat. Courageous soldiers repeatedly sprinted across the patrol base under fire to re-supply forward positions and evacuate wounded. In the face of injuries and overwhelming odds, U.S. soldiers and coalition troops refused to give ground.

Combat was particularly intense at OP Top Side, an observation post located east of the main position. Two waves of reinforcements bolstered Top Side, but not without losses. The first wave was led by the outpost platoon leader, 1LT Jonathan Brostrom. He was killed upon arrival, but his example and drive inspired his Soldiers to persist in the fight. Although the several hours witnessed combat at close quarters, it was the insurgents who broke and withdrew from the battlefield. For his actions that day, Lieutenant Brostrom was awarded the Silver Star. Eight other valiant Soldiers died with him.[31]

Lieutenant General Caldwell goes on to write in his blog post that it is our duty as a nation to remember and reflect upon the sacrifices made by our soldiers serving in Afghanistan. The Combined Arms Center and the Combat Studies Institute have taken the lessons from the Battle of Wanat and distilled them into a special case study. In addition, the Center for Army Lessons Learned recently published a handbook on Afghanistan that captures the best practices in small unit operations throughout Afghanistan.

Lieutenant General Caldwell's blog generated a number of comments, one noting how important it was to capture the accomplishments and lessons of junior officers, like First Lieutenant Jonathan Brostrom, as well as the more experienced generals. As one commenter said, "Jonathon Brostrom is a prime example of great Soldier early in his military career that demonstrated the confidence and traits we expect from our leaders."

The Command and General Staff College's associate dean of academics, James Martin, calls the Army's use of social media tools such as blogs and wikis "learning at teachable moments." If the U.S. Army can embrace collaboration, why do corporations believe these tools are too dangerous to use? Is it time for you and your company to develop a strategy for using social media in the workplace?

DEVELOPING A STRATEGY FOR USING SOCIAL MEDIA

Too often, the buzz around implementing social media starts with the technology platform and the specific bells and whistles that need to be embedded into the network, such as blogs, podcasts, video, wikis, or discussion forums. But the real starting point is to identify why you are embarking on this journey, ask yourself what business goals you are trying to accomplish, and, most important, understand this is a cultural change initiative. The example from the U.S. Army shows how culture can change in order to accomplish a greater goal: improved communication and the creation of a repository of critical knowledge. Christopher R. Paparone, an associate professor in the Army Command and General Staff College's Department of Logistics and Resource Operations at Fort Lee, Virginia, says this: "My view (not an official view) is that we have been much too rigid in our doctrine. By using a wiki, we begin to challenge dogmatic thinking."[32]

How can you start this journey? As we have worked with organizations, we have witnessed seven key steps in how they have crafted a strategy and implementation plan for becoming über-connected. These are shown in figure 5-3.

Let's walk through these steps to better understand how your organization can become über-connected.

Business Drivers

Decide why the organization wants to use social media. Identify specific business results you expect, such as increasing speed of

Figure 5-3: Developing a Social Media Strategy

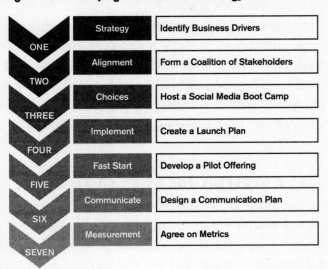

ONE	Strategy	Identify Business Drivers
TWO	Alignment	Form a Coalition of Stakeholders
THREE	Choices	Host a Social Media Boot Camp
FOUR	Implement	Create a Launch Plan
FIVE	Fast Start	Develop a Pilot Offering
SIX	Communicate	Design a Communication Plan
SEVEN	Measurement	Agree on Metrics

Source: Future Workplace.

innovation, improving decision making, streamlining processes that affect customer experience, decreasing communication costs, increasing employee engagement, reducing the time it takes to get to market with new products and services, unleashing greater creativity across the enterprise, and positioning your company as one attractive to Millennials. Next, agree on the scope of the initiative. Will this be directed to internal employees, or will it target customers and suppliers as well as employees? Finally, determine the mix of tools you will use, such as blogs, wikis, a corporate social network, and innovation jams, and agree on how these will interface (if at all) with other technologies your organization has, such as an enterprise resource planning system or a human resources information system. As you embark on this journey, remember the importance of viewing this as a business initiative rather than just an HR or learning one.

Coalition of Stakeholders

Ask yourself what discipline areas and skill sets need to be part of your effort to integrate social media into your organization and/or department. A cross-functional collaboration encompassing the corporate learning, HR, IT, legal, and internal communications departments is crucial to integrating social media into the organization. Early on, the team must create a shared vision statement to describe the strategic intent and agree on a disciplined approach to launch this in the enterprise. Assess the environmental readiness of the organization to accept more open forms of communication. The team also needs to be clear about what blend of skills is critical. Some to consider: project management, social media usage, internal communications, information architecture, and marketing. Finally, recognize that becoming über-connected will change the way work is done within the company.

Social Media Boot Camp

Provide an opportunity for cross-functional team members to experience various types of social media and discuss, debate, and brainstorm if and how these can be introduced into the organization. One of the best ways to build momentum is to create a learning experience in which the team actually uses various types of social media to create and publish ideas and network with one another. They can use this experience to propose where the organization should enter the über-connection journey and identify the specific business objectives they hope to impact.

Launch Plan

Once the vision is crafted and the team has been assembled and exposed to the power of social media, the next step is to develop a plan for how this new initiative will be introduced to the organization. Start with the business drivers you want to impact in the organization and how you will measure success. Then propose what new roles and responsibilities need to be created to properly launch and manage this new initiative. Typically, three roles are crucial: community moderators, community administrators, and internal marketing and communications experts. The community moderators are the facilitators and guides. They may be your employees, work for a third party, or be experienced members of the community. In all cases, they are the go-to people who are responsible for keeping the community alive and

Community moderator:
Someone who keeps the momentum going in an online group or forum. Community moderators often introduce subjects for discussion and then work to keep people on topic in their follow-up comments.

thriving. The community administrators have the most technical role and need to know all aspects operating the online tools. They will need to create and maintain an easy-to-use environment that will function well and support all stakeholders, while ensuring usage metrics are easy to track. Finally, internal marketing and communications professionals will be responsible for sharing the vision of the organization, as well as planning and managing all communications, including the rollout and ongoing management of the social network.

Pilot Offering

Often, becoming über-connected starts small, with a proof of concept. This may mean using one department as the pioneer, as was the case with the JetBlue University blog, or taking one business challenge, as Bell Canada did to increase customer satisfaction and create an Innovation Jam. Whatever direction you pursue, remember that this is a cultural change and will require senior management support and participation. It is both a top-down and a viral effort. Designate a group of social media pioneers in the organization—these are the enthusiasts who are avid users of social media in their personal lives and see the business advantages of being über-connected. You can think of these enthusiasts as your ambassadors. Be sure to recruit them early and encourage them to report back on their usage. Finally, adopt an iterative approach to development; your system may go through a long beta stage as you continually improve and enhance it based on comments from users.

Communication

The implementation of social media blurs the line among marketing, internal communications, and corporate learning. A new key alliance partner will be the internal marketing and communications department, which will develop a set of social media rules of engagement as well as a communications plan to integrate social media solutions across the organization. One of the most important keys to the marketing and communications plan is dispelling the common myths and concerns surrounding the usage of social media at work, such as "It's only the Millennials that will gravitate to using this at work," "If we build it, will they come and participate?," "Employees will end up sharing company secrets," "It's a security risk for the enterprise," "It's still too new and just a fad," or "It will lead to decreased productivity as employees spend their days networking online." A successful marketing and communications campaign will anticipate these concerns and build a strategy to address them.

Measurement

Finally, it's important to monitor usage and gather feedback on how employees use social media, along with their suggestions and enhancements. But social media measurement is one of those topics on which everyone has an opinion while few can agree on the solution. The key is to identify both qualitative and quantitative metrics before you launch your social media plan. McKinsey's global survey of 1,700 business executives from around the world entitled "How Companies Are Benefiting from Web 2.0" provides one view on the types of hard business results companies are experiencing as a result of implementing social media inside the enterprise. These are broken down into three categories: internal processes, customer-related processes, and external partners and suppliers.[33]

Once these business metrics are articulated and agreed to, they can be tracked and monitored as your organization becomes überconnected. As the authors of "How Companies Are Benefiting from Web 2.0" point out, "Successful companies not only tightly integrate Web 2.0 technologies with the work flows of their employees, they also create a 'networked company,' linking themselves with customers and supplies through use of Web 2.0 tools."[34] These business benefits not only accrue inside the company but also extend externally as companies use the social Web to distribute product information more easily, to encourage greater participation by their customers, to provide feedback, and to enhance products and services in real time.

The key lesson here is to think holistically about the business benefits of using the social Web—this is not just a human resources or learning initiative but one that can change the way work gets done and deliver sizable business results.

IS THERE A DARK SIDE TO CORPORATE SOCIAL NETWORKS?

Consider the recent experiences of Virgin Atlantic and British Airways. As reported in the *Economist*, Virgin Atlantic had a public relations nightmare when some of its cabin crew posted derogatory comments about the airline and some passengers on a Facebook forum.[35] Among other things, crew members joked about how they felt Virgin customers were "chavs," a disparaging British term for people with flashy bad taste. The following week British Airways experienced similar problems when some employees described British Airways passengers as "annoying" and "smelly" on Facebook postings.

Many companies have a love-hate relationship with social networking and the social Web. On the one hand, employers want their employees to use the latest tools and encourage innovative thinking inside the company. But they also worry about losing secrets to rivals or damaging the employer brand, as in the case of Virgin Atlantic and British Airways. And when companies decide to bring the tools of the social Web inside the enterprise, they find they must provide employees with clear, concise guidelines for what they can share about the company both externally and internally. In addition, companies are finding that they need to monitor all this online activity—some are hiring firms such as Cyveillance to troll social networks for confidential or damaging leaks; others are simply signing up for Google Alerts to get updates each time someone includes certain words, such as a company name, in a post. While there is much to decide before launching an internal social network, the payoff is substantial: a searchable and digital archive of the conversations and institutional knowledge inside a company.

As a way of countering possible abuses, a growing number of companies—including IBM, Sun Microsystems, and Intel—are creating instructions on how to use the tools of the social Web without violating company policies. This applies to both external social networks, such as Facebook, and internal corporate social networks. The Intel Social Media Rules of Engagement provide a set of comprehensive guidelines for how Intel employees can participate in social media while adhering to the company communications policy.

INTEL SOCIAL MEDIA RULES OF ENGAGEMENT

• **Be transparent.** Your honesty—or dishonesty—will be quickly noticed in the social media environment. If you are blogging about your work at Intel, use your real name, identify that you work for Intel, and be clear about your role. If you have a vested interest in something you are discussing, be the first to point it out. Transparency is about your identity and relationship to Intel. You still need to keep confidentiality around proprietary information and content.

• **Be judicious.** Make sure your efforts to be transparent don't violate Intel's privacy, confidentiality, and legal guidelines for external commercial speech. Ask permission to publish or report on conversations that are meant to be private or internal to Intel. All statements must be true and not misleading and all claims must be substantiated and approved. Product benchmarks must be approved for external posting by the appropriate product benchmarking team. Please never comment on anything related to legal matters, litigation, or any parties we are in litigation with without the appropriate approval. If you want to write about the competition, make sure you know what you are talking about and that you have the appropriate permission. Also be smart about protecting yourself, your privacy, and Intel confidential information. What you publish is widely accessible and will be around for a long time, so consider the content carefully.

• **Write what you know.** Make sure you write and post about your areas of expertise, especially as related to Intel and our technology. If you are writing about a topic that Intel is involved with but you are not the Intel expert on the topic, you should make this clear to your readers. And write in the first person. If you publish to a website outside Intel, please use a disclaimer something like this: "The postings on this site are my own and don't necessarily represent Intel's positions, strategies, or opinions." Also, please respect brand, trademark, copyright, fair use, trade secrets (including our processes and methodologies), confidentiality, and financial disclosure laws. If you have any questions about these, see your Intel legal representative. Remember, you may be personally responsible for your content.

• **Perception is reality.** In online social networks, the lines between public and private, personal and professional are blurred. Just by identifying yourself as an Intel employee, you are creating perceptions about your expertise and about Intel by our shareholders, customers, and the general public—and perceptions about you by your colleagues and managers. Do us all proud. Be sure that all content associated with you is consistent with your work and with Intel's values and professional standards.

• **It's a conversation.** Talk to your readers like you would talk to real people in professional situations. In other words, avoid overly pedantic or "composed" language. Don't be afraid to bring in your own personality and say what's on your mind. Consider content that's open-ended and invites response. Encourage comments. You can also broaden the conversation by citing others who are blogging about the same topic and allowing your content to be shared or syndicated.

• **Are you adding value?** There are millions of words out there. The best way to get yours read is to write things that people will value. Social communication from Intel should help our customers, partners, and coworkers. It should be thought-provoking and build a sense of community. If it helps people improve knowledge or skills, build their businesses, do their jobs, solve problems, or understand Intel better—then it's adding value.

• **Your responsibility:** What you write is ultimately your responsibility. Participation in social computing on behalf of Intel is not a right but an opportunity, so please treat it seriously and with respect. If you want to participate on behalf of Intel, take the Digital IQ training and contact the Social Media Center of Excellence. Please know and follow the Intel Code of Conduct. Failure to abide by these guidelines and the Intel Code of Conduct could put your participation at risk. Contact social.media@intel.com for more information. Please also follow the terms and conditions for any third-party sites.

• **Create some excitement.** As a business and as a corporate citizen, Intel is making important contributions to the world, to the future of technology, and to public dialogue on a broad range of issues. Our business activities are increasingly focused on high-value innovation. Let's share with the world the exciting things we're learning and doing—and open up the channels to learn from others.

• **Be a leader.** There can be a fine line between healthy debate and incendiary reaction. Do not denigrate our competitors or Intel. Nor do you need to respond to every criticism or barb. Try to frame what you write to invite differing points of view without inflaming others. Some topics—like politics or religion—slide more easily into sensitive territory. So be careful and considerate. Once the words are out there, you can't really get them back. And once an inflammatory discussion gets going, it's hard to stop.

• **Did you screw up?** If you make a mistake, admit it. Be upfront and be quick with your correction. If you're posting to a blog, you may choose to modify an earlier post—just make it clear that you have done so.

• **If it gives you pause, pause.** If you're about to publish something that makes you even the slightest bit uncomfortable, don't shrug it off and hit "send." Take a minute to review these guidelines and try to figure out what's bothering you, then fix it. If you're still unsure, you might want to discuss it with your manager or legal representative. Ultimately, what you publish is yours—as is the responsibility. So be sure.

Source: Intel Social Media Guidelines.[36]

CRITICAL SUCCESS FACTORS IN BECOMING AN ÜBER-CONNECTED ORGANIZATION

As you embark on your journey, be aware of key success factors that have helped others:

- **Start with business goals and integrate usage of social media into work flows.** Identify the goals you are trying to accomplish by using social media inside the enterprise and agree on specific metrics. Also, be aware that usage is heavily dependent on integrating social media into each and every employee's work flow, as well as ensuring that senior leaders role-model and champion the usage of social media in how they communicate with their teams.

- **Recognize that the biggest hurdle is your culture and internal processes, rather than the technology behind the creation of the social media tools.** Focus your efforts on finding ambassadors, and make it easy for them to share and participate in your social media pilot. Involve senior executives; they must buy in, or this will not have lasting value. Focus on building a culture of cocreation so employees at all levels have a voice and see the power of "we." Recognize that in the Web community, status is built upon making meaningful contributions, so be sure to include ratings by peers in your design. Finally, examine how you can integrate the expectations for social media usage in your company's performance management practices so the quality of one's online contributions is part of the overall performance management system.

- **Understand how being an über-connected company can enhance your ability to recruit top talent.** Survey your new hires. Understand their digital expectations when joining the organization? Becoming über-connected also creates the need to develop a new set of digital literacy skills for your employees. And these will be increasingly in demand as we head into the 2020 workplace.

- **Remember to jump into the social media world yourself.** Join several major social networks, such as Facebook, Twitter, LinkedIn, and YouTube. Conduct a search for how your competitors are using these social networks, and report back to your team. Learn the language of social media by reading the glossary of key social media terms at the end of this book. Once you have created your own profile, start looking for friends and topics you want to keep abreast of—jump in by following thought leaders in your industry on Twitter, connecting with colleagues on LinkedIn, and adding new friends on Facebook. You must be a user of social media in order to understand the potential for adopting this as a tool to transform your business.

- **Create guidelines and policies for employees' usage of social media.** Becoming über-connected has the potential to create improved business results, such as increases in collaboration, innovation cycles, and attraction of Millennial prospective new hires to your company. But it also requires you to create a set of guidelines, polices, and maybe even new roles and responsibilities as you begin to educate your workforce and monitor usage. It's not too late to jump in, but before your organization does, be sure you are clear on your business drivers and the rules of engagement for using social media on the job.

BECOMING ÜBER-CONNECTED: THE KEY TO CREATING AN EMPLOYER BRAND

In today's marketplace, it's not enough for companies to be connected to employees and customers via a Web site, e-mail, blogs, or instant messenging. Rather, companies need to become über-connected and provide employees with access to the same social Web tools they use in their everyday lives to communicate, collaborate, and connect with one another. Ultimately, creating an über-connected organization has the potential of developing a more engaged workforce, creating a stronger employer brand, and making the workforce more agile.

SUMMARY

- **Give those who use the products a chance to be involved in the creation process.** Users of products are often the best equipped to drive their innovation, as they are the ones who interact with them in the real world on a daily basis. Any company in the business of selling a product needs to learn how to harness the power of customers who are passionate about their products by inviting them to share their enthusiasm and creativity.

- **Consider where your organization is on the journey to becoming über-connected.** Using social media is becoming an important way to share knowledge, collaborate with team members around the world, and allow employees to contribute new ideas in the workplace. Blogs, wikis, and corporate social networks are all becoming important ways for the members of a globally dispersed workforce to interact with one another on a personal level, have discussions in online forums, and contribute their knowledge.

- **Understand that transparency is necessary to your success.** Using social media works best for companies if it is done in an open, authentic manner. Let feedback from your employees guide you in shaping your network, and be responsive to the needs and desires of the community.

- **Recognize that creating internal social networks can also be about having a one-to-many relationship.** For some companies, establishing a social network can be a way of connecting the company to customers outside the company. This works to enhance the company's brand and to expand its reach while increasing collaboration and community building.

- **Finally, make sure you focus on the business needs you hope to impact before looking into any specific flashy technologies.** Too often, the discussion surrounding the implementation of corporate social networks starts with what technologies should be used. But the better starting point is to identify the business needs for launching a corporate social network and the specific business results you hope to create.

CHAPTER SIX

The Social Learning Ecosystem

Victor Restrepo's daily commute is not unusual for anyone who lives in central New Jersey and works in New York City. After a five-minute drive to the local park and ride, he waits for the bus and takes the New Jersey Turnpike into the city. Depending on how bad the traffic is through the Lincoln Tunnel, the trip can take sixty to ninety minutes each way. What is unusual about Restrepo's commute is that on his way to work, he completes mobile sales training on his iPod Touch and then prepares for the day's sales presentations by reviewing how some of his peers have made successful sales to their accounts.

A customer-dedicated technical sales professional, Restrepo represents the entire suite of Sun Microsystems products to his customer, a global business information provider. He might be selling software one day, servers the next, and storage the day after. In selling complex products, he needs quick access to information as the customer's need develops. That is where Sun's Social Learning eXchange (SLX) steps in.

Analogous to a corporate YouTube, SLX allows Sun employees to record and post any type of content, from documents to videos, which can be viewed on anything from a desktop computer to Restrepo's iPod. Although he can access content whenever he has access to a wireless network, he tends to download it the night before so that he can view it while on the bus.

Restrepo got hooked on SLX when he saw how it would save him time preparing for the next day of customer visits—time he could now spend with his family. All he has to do in the evening is search for a few presentations and learning modules to load onto his iPod, and then he's free. When Sun came out with a new product that combined a server with storage, he downloaded the standard marketing product presentation and then searched for the highest-rated video from other people who had sold it. "In the past I had to flip through about a hundred slides of a marketing presentation to learn about a new product or service. Now I just download the highest rated ten-to-fifteen-minute-long videos from salespeople who actually sold the product," he says.

Then, on the way to work, he reviews the most relevant videos several times until he feels he has absorbed enough information to make a good presentation to his customer. One occasion provided a great outcome: his customer ordered an evaluation unit from a product Restrepo had just studied on the way in and shortly thereafter substituted it for a competitor's products in its data center. His success has motivated him enough to help contribute to SLX himself. "I'm thinking about doing a video of an 'Open Storage Technical Sales Guide for Dummies.' It's hard to find the time to become specialized in the content, so leveraging what I've learned could help others."

THE ADVENT OF SOCIAL LEARNING

"How have you helped me learn lately?" may well be the question of the new generation of workers. The way your organization answers that question may be your competitive advantage for the future. Organizations need a way to develop people when economic conditions fluctuate and in ways that deliver skills and knowledge when they are needed. We are becoming increasingly accustomed to processing shorter and shorter chunks of information. After all, five of ten of Japan's best-selling novels in 2008 started out as text-message novels.[1]

One way to address these challenges is to rethink the role of the learning department to encompass all learning activities in an organization. We define social learning as the acquisition of knowledge and skills through methods that are collaborative, immediate, relevant, and presented in the context of an individual's unique work environment. Whereas Learning 1.0 relied heavily on classroom learning and Learning 2.0 added computer- and Web-based training, Social Learning incorporates social media, gaming, real-time feedback, and advanced on-the-job methodologies.

THE EXPERT CREATION DILEMMA

The quest to become an expert in any field has become a Sisyphean task. According to a study from the University of California at Berkeley, knowledge is now doubling every three years, and the interval for doubling appears to be getting even shorter.[2] In the medical field, knowledge from clinical studies doubles every eighteen months. The number of blogs is doubling every six months.[3] As if that weren't daunting enough, as we move into the future, an increasingly small percentage of the information required to do your job will actually be stored in your mind. The percentage of knowledge you had to store in your head to accomplish your job was 75 percent as recently as 1986, when the youngest Boomers were entering the workforce. Now you can store only about 10 percent of the knowledge you need to do your job—meaning you have to rely on a myriad of other sources to do your job.[4]

Yet an unfortunate paradox exists. As Malcolm Gladwell, the journalist and best-selling author, and others have reported, the average time it takes to become an expert in any field is ten years, regardless of the field.[5] Reaching the peak of expertise only means that the climb begins again to acquire the latest knowledge in your field.

As if the individual quest for expertise were not challenging enough, consider the market pressures an organization faces to ensure that in the firm's core competency areas, there are sufficient experts to create a competitive edge. Is training the solution? Most organizations determine their curricula offerings based upon some level of return of investment. A dilemma occurs when there are too few students to

Figure 6-1: The Expert Dilemma

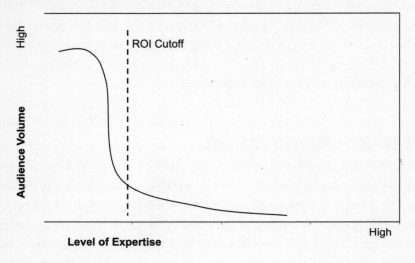

Source: Future Workplace.

justify the creation of a course, which happens frequently in nearly any subject area, as shown in figure 6-1. Scan the course catalogs of nearly any corporate learning department, and there will be plenty of programs in finance fundamentals, compliance, and communications and for new managers, new vice presidents, and so on, but far fewer programs for advanced skill sets in any field. Experts, by their very nature, are a smaller subgroup of individuals, and often they are forced to learn on their own and from others through social networks and external sources. Even then, once they are recognized as experts, with knowledge expanding so quickly it's nearly impossible for them to remain experts. The value of a strong professional social network becomes increasingly important if individuals are to remain personally competitive. Experts typically bring more value to a firm, but paradoxically they are less likely to receive training relevant to their needs. Although the impact of not investing in any one expert's further development may be minimal, the collective impact of not investing in organizational expertise creates an unsustainable situation. Yet HR and learning frequently leave it up to the individual business units to solve this dilemma on their own, which, we argue, is an abdication of a core responsibility. At a minimum, organizations should be creating platforms for experts to learn from one another while allowing their organizations to reap and share this knowledge.

THE 70/20/10 MODEL REIMAGINED

A number of studies have shown that the way people acquire professional knowledge and skills is through a blend of methods, with 70 percent involving performing the work and learning via experience.[6] Reading, using search engines, asking a question in an online forum, and trial and error all fit into the 70 percent. Another 20 percent of learning occurs through feedback from peers and mentors, and the final 10 percent of learning occurs in formal learning programs. The 70 percent has often been referred to as informal learning, while the remaining 30 percent is called formal learning. But Robert Campbell, the CLO of Cerner Corporation, says, "Traditionally we have tended to focus our people, budgets, and resources on the ten percent of formal learning and often leave the seventy percent and twenty percent to chance. This must change to recognize the growing importance of developing contextual learning. We are gradually changing this and allocating more dollars and people resources to create informal ways our associates can learn from each other."

The challenge for organizations such as Cerner is to figure out how to "formalize the informal learning" that happens in the normal course of working on the job and with one's network of colleagues. With only 10 percent of learning taking place in traditional, programmatic ways, how can an organization ensure that what employees are learning aligns with an organization's strategy, much less that this learning is productive and accurate? We have discovered that some of the most forward-thinking companies, such as Cerner, create platforms and methods to manage the entire spectrum of formal and informal learning. This is especially important, as learning budgets fluctuate over time. Rather than breathe a sigh of relief about a manageable 10 percent charter, heads of learning should expand their thinking to ensure that people are able to learn in a way that is seen from the employee's perspective as "just in time, just enough, and just for me."

The division of learning into the categories of formal and informal blurs the role an organization plays in enabling learning. Effective discussions of methods that enable effective knowledge and skill transfer at all stages of development are more difficult if the focus is on only one category. For example, in early stages of expertise development, the blend may be more like 50/30/20, whereas at the expert level it might be closer to 80/15/5. Counterintuitively, perhaps, in a learning context, informal is not the opposite of formal. Thought leaders such as Jay Cross, an author and learning industry expert, have helped get the conversations about learning to move beyond formal organizational learning alone. It is time to reimagine and reinvent the range of solutions to include all the learning occurring in organizations now.

THE SOCIAL LEARNING ECOSYSTEM

In figure 6-2, we propose a more useful way of thinking about learning in an organization. Since most organizations are resource-constrained, a common way to develop talent has been to define broad sets of competencies, sometimes by roles and sometimes for the entire organization. Feedback systems are created to assess competencies, and then training is developed that maps onto the most common needs in the organization. Our model, the Social Learning Ecosystem, has four quadrants, with competency-based learning anchoring the left side and context-based learning anchoring the right. Context-based learning is the learning that occurs on the job and during the everyday performance of work. As a result, it tends to be more personalized. There is no clear cutoff point between the quadrants, and frequently programs span quadrants because most organizations customize some level of learning to the requirements of the jobs involved.

The upper quadrants of the figure include learning that involves planned events, typically documented on an employee's development

Figure 6-2: The Social Learning Ecosystem

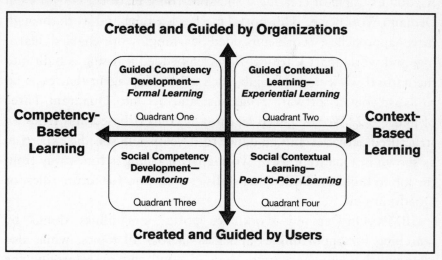

Source: Future Workplace.

plans, and is created and endorsed by the organization. The pro-grams that fall into these quadrants are generated by the organization through some formal channel and typically have been documented in an information system, such as a learning management system (LMS). The lower quadrants include the activities that happen when people learn from one another, a kind of learning frequently ignored by employee development plans. Learning in these quadrants is, by definition, both social and collaborative and can include a hidden curriculum—what is learned on the job in order to mesh in with the culture but is not often discussed publicly.

Note that the programs in Quadrants Three and Four can fre-quently be fostered via online social software to enable learning to take place successfully. For example, an organization may create a 360-degree competency-based instrument and develop a system for gathering input, but the real value of the tool is in what the par-ticipants add as content. Likewise, an organization might create a platform for enabling peer-to-peer learning, such as the one used by Victor Restrepo earlier in this chapter, but it is meaningless without the participation and contributions of a critical mass of employees.

Creating a Social Learning Platform

A good example of creating a social learning platform is IBM's On Demand Workplace.[7] This portal meshes learning and work through three approaches: work-embedded learning, work-enabled learning, and work-apart learning. Work-embedded learning is built into the natural work flow of a job, such as the help agent that pops up to assist you in software programs, and fits into Quadrant Three of figure 6-2. Work-enabled learning is context-based and relies on structured activities and guidance to develop role-specific expertise, as shown in Quadrant Two. Work-apart learning is time away from the job to build the underlying skill set necessary for future roles, or Quadrant One.

IBM's On-Demand Workplace portal streamlines things by searching for opportunities and ideas across all topics, while also allowing the company's more than 350,000 employees around the world to receive personalized content. According to one manager in the Learning Systems function of IBM, "The system provides access to many different resources besides traditional e-learning. Content is contributed to and maintained by training organizations, as well as business-unit experts and thought leaders who are in closer proximity to the urgent business needs. In this way, employees have one place to go to search for or receive guidance on their personal development."

Searching is an essential capability of the underlying platform, and IBM's portal uses its own search technology and Web 2.0 capabilities to ensure that the results of searches are relevant. Since employees store data about themselves in the system, the search engine intelligently matches the context of the employee's role to relevant search results. For example, if a manufacturing industry sales representative in Germany searches for content on lean manufacturing, the results will be served up with content specific to that representative's role, including collaborative results such as social bookmarks or the blogs of experts in the area. The results might direct the representative to embedded tools available for use on the job, formal classes, e-learning from internal and external course providers, or the names of experts from the IBM Blue Pages.

IBM uses learning experts as content moderators to build intelligence into searches. However, Web 2.0 systems that use rating and tagging can help organizations—especially those without the luxury of learning experts—to create highly effective search results. Another key element of learning on demand is that not every learning asset is stored in the learning management system (LMS). The portal instead is a mash-up of resources from a variety of systems, while the LMS stores the records for the more formal, work-apart learning.

In the remainder of this chapter, we will provide examples that demonstrate how companies are innovating in all four quadrants to develop employees. Some types of programs clearly fit into one quadrant, while some use various techniques that cut across quadrants. All of the examples demonstrate how organizations are designing platforms to enable learning beyond the formal classroom and extend learning across all four quadrants.

QUADRANT ONE: GUIDED COMPETENCY DEVELOPMENT

For an organization to develop traditional courses, which fit into quadrant one of the Social Learning Ecosystem, the topic area involved generally must have some stability, due to the high cost of new-course development. Many of the big-name consulting firms have legions of college-graduate new hires every year, so these firms can and do make large investments in extensive curriculum- and facilities-based courses to teach the same introductory material to each incoming cohort. Witness the learning facility Deloitte is scheduled to open in Westlake, Texas, in 2011.[8] Open any corporate learning catalog, and you are likely to find common courses, down to even the exact names of the course, since many organizations use the same vendors.

The challenge for classroom- or Web-based learning in the future will be to engage and motivate learners in a world where collaboration and interdependencies are a way of life, making the lone-learner model increasingly outdated. The first and second generations of e-learning courses accomplished the purpose of transferring knowledge, but frequently at the expense of utter boredom on the part of the learner, largely due to the lone-learner model. To address a generation of learners brought up on video games, organizations are now using high-quality, multiplayer, interactive learning games and weaving in links to places where Millennials congregate. As Brad Hargreaves, the 24-year-old founder of GXStudios, says, "We integrate access to social networking sites into our own training programs to try and overcome the major problem I see with most corporate training. It is like the world of encyclopedias—dry, dull, and stale. Millennials, like myself and my employees, expect training to be more like the rest of our lives: instant, fun, and social."

Edutainment

To make competency development more interesting and engaging, organizations are using creative, entertaining methods, sometimes called edutainment. The D2D Fund, for example, is a nonprofit organization whose mission is to provide access to financial services and asset-building opportunities for low-income families. However, since not many people are interested in reading textbooks about credit limits, APR, finance charges, and so on, it turned to a simulation and gaming company and to Peter Tufano, a financial management professor at Harvard, to build a financial literacy game called Celebrity Calamity, which can be found at www.celebritycalamity.com. Tufano says, "We can design the best curriculum in the world, but if nobody is willing to spend time on it, it won't work. Our goal in all of these things is to find something people will voluntarily do."[9] Players get to help their chosen celebrity manage money and handle various money crises in a game format while learning about the impact of high-interest-rate credit cards and how to develop other personal money management strategies.

The game has demonstrated results. Testers in the pilot program "showed a 15–30% increase in confidence in their financial skills, and a 55–70% improvement in knowledge of concepts like credit limits, credit vs. debit, APR, and finance charges."[10]

Nearly all organizations have a need to onboard their new hires, and some companies are finding ways to go beyond death by Power-Point. Sun Microsystems developed two versions of the same video game scenario for their new hires, which is available for play by anyone since the content informs players of Sun's products and services (figure 6-3). Originally the two games were designed to allow for computers with both low and high graphics capability. A text-based adventure, Dawn of the Shadow Specters, allows users on older machines to enjoy the interactivity of a game, while those with more graphics capability can enjoy Rise of the Shadow Specters. In both games, Ray is a Sun new hire. He shows up for his first day of work to find that the Shadow Specters have attacked and are threatening to infect the network. His first task is to help defeat the Shadow Specters.

For the more graphically intense game, a leaderboard tracks which employee has the highest score for the month, and that employee is awarded a prize. One accidental finding, according to the game's designer, Brandon Carson, was that "We didn't expect that people would select which game to play based on their age. But we found that people who were younger were more drawn to Rise because they

Figure 6-3: Two Versions of New Hire Games

Rise of the Shadow Specters:
A video-arcade quality game

Source: Sun Microsystems.   **Dawn of the Shadow Specters**: A text-based game

are comfortable with gaming navigation and interaction, whereas older people who had grown up on the original text-based games chose to play Dawn."

Virtual Worlds

Although organizations want to save travel expenses on meetings, many often use fairly low-tech teleconferencing technologies with somewhat limited voice or text interaction. But now virtual-world companies are changing this. They are entering the marketplace with enterprise solutions designed to incorporate video, presentations, and interaction in predesigned worlds (figure 6-4). As David Gardner, the CEO of the Venue Network, a virtual-world and virtual-events company, puts it, "Many of the conferencing tools have taken the worst of live meetings and training and put them on the Web. It's a drone-athon, with slides and talking heads."

Virtual worlds, predesigned and implemented on an enterprise basis, have the potential to bring people together to learn. These

Figure 6-4: A Venuegen Virtual Classroom

Source: Venuegen.

virtual worlds have a low barrier to entry and do not require a company to purchase and design islands as in Second Life.

Gardner's company has introduced a service delivered over the Web in which users can create their own customized 3-D virtual worlds and events. All a user has to do is upload a picture, which is then automatically converted to an avatar. Through simple navigation on his or her computer keyboard, the user can make the avatar express facial movements such as smiling or frowning. When a person signs in to an event, he or she is automatically placed into a seat, making even people who have never been in a virtual world able to participate. Virtual participants can easily simulate walking around an event by simply aiming their cursor at a destination and clicking, thereby moving the avatar to the desired destination.

Does this mark the demise of live meetings that require extensive travel and expensive logistics? The ability of participants to interact with one another as if they were in a live environment can provide a very powerful sense of presence. Imagine talking to the virtual person next to you as you're watching a presentation. Further, presenters can set up a virtual event in a matter of minutes by selecting an avatar and a room, then inviting people to the event. These virtual worlds are lifelike and, more important, mimic the real world. By using virtual worlds, companies can save time and money as well as create a sense of community and connection among their global employees or business partners. The applications seem limitless.

Tomorrow's Campus

Bill Pelster, a principal and the national director of talent development at Deloitte Consulting LLP, believes that as companies become more virtual, there is a greater need to create a "cultural center," a physical space where professionals can learn, connect to one another, and innovate—all geared to increasing their performance on the job. And he, along with senior leadership of the organization, is bringing this to life in the design and launch of Deloitte University, a new 700,000-square-foot facility outside Dallas, Texas. Pelster says, "At Deloitte, we see an increasing need to bring people together to collaborate and build a shared understanding of the organization's vision, direction, and purpose. Inevitably, this means rethinking the meaning of corporate classrooms." Pelster is on the front lines of creating tomorrow's campus, one that is highly collaborative and enables accelerated learning and spontaneous team building.

Perhaps the first place where the campus has begun to evolve is on traditional university campuses. Comfortable with technology and its integration with learning, university students today have seen classrooms with movable, modular furniture and walls, various interaction spaces, and designs that encourage interaction by students' looking at one another as well as the professor. According to Mark Greiner, the senior vice president of WorkSpace Futures at Steelcase, "How we work and learn has significantly changed over the years, but often the physical space has remained essentially the same. You can look at two pictures of classrooms a hundred years apart, and nothing has changed. We asked the question 'How would you design a space—a learning lab—for the classroom of the future?'"

After conducting extensive research on how people learn, Steelcase designers designed a plan that orients learners toward one another. Instead of having content that is projected in only one place, they designed a way to replicate content in different planes in the various corners of the room—not just the front of the room—so students look over one another, as shown in figure 6-5.

"It's not surprising that our research shows that grades go up in this kind of environment. The learner is central to the design, and the instructor can be anywhere in the room since they have a switcher that allows them to project content from any student or instructor laptop to any or all screens in the room. This means the instructor is not limited to just the front but can walk throughout the room to make their point," Greiner says. "Steelcase believes there is a strong correlation between learning, memory, and physical space. Our memory is in fact triggered, per neuroscientists, through the context of physical space, almost like a card catalog system in a library. This is such a new and exciting area of research that you

Figure 6-5: Traditional Classroom versus Learning 2.0 Classroom

Traditional Classroom Layout: Instructor
and Presentation at Front

Multifocal, Learning 2.0 Classroom
Layout: Instructor in Center of Room

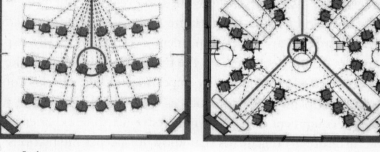

Source: Steelcase.

can now get a joint degree in architecture and neuroscience at some universities."

Of course, the Steelcase University on the Grand Rapids, Michigan, campus is designed to demonstrate some of these ideas. "Instead of working in their assigned office spaces, many employees choose to work in the university, becoming a mobile 'free agent' for the day," Greiner says. "This facilitates more collaboration as they interact with other work associates."

At Steelcase University, "we took out all the walls. It looks like café booths, and there are barlike tables in front of the booths. You can get your morning bagel and coffee and hang out with others, if you want. Adjacent to those are places to share and collaborate for up to eight people. These are high-fidelity team rooms with media:scape, a new product based on Steelcase's research into ubiquitous computing. Beyond that, if someone needs some quiet time to wrap up a project, there are individual stations available. In other words, there are a series of spaces at Steelcase University with a goal of developing social connection."

Deloitte University is also following this journey of creating open spaces in which employees can more easily work with one another on work teams. With more than 42,000 senior consultants across the United States and in India, creating a cultural center in which partners, principals, and employees can collaborate and work together is very critical.

Pelster adds, "Of course, the work of developing our professionals will continue far from the Deloitte University campus. Leading-edge teleclassrooms are being implemented to exponentially expand the numbers of our people across the organization who can take advantage of the Deloitte University experience. These teleclassrooms, currently being planned for four offices, will include innovative technology and equipment for a fully immersive learning experience and flexible furniture arrangements that allow for deeper interactions and sharing."

If there's a theme here, it's that both Deloitte University and Steelcase University are experimenting with new tools, processes, and even furniture arrangement to enable social connection. After all, learning is a social process. With the advent of social media, we are now starting to see the potential and power of connecting people so they can more effectively and efficiently solve problems and innovate on the job.

QUADRANT TWO: GUIDED CONTEXTUAL LEARNING

When a content area is unique to an organization or setting and it is important to have a shared understanding, it makes sense to consider custom solutions. Especially for executive programs focused on helping participants understand an organization's strategy and direction, programs such as custom business simulations can be helpful. Programs for high-potential employees, such as assigned mentoring, also fall into this quadrant, although mentoring can fall into more than one quadrant depending on the degree to which the organization is involved with tracking and guiding the mentoring process.

Experiential Learning

Cindy Brinkley, the senior vice president of talent development and chief diversity officer at AT&T, worked with a custom simulation company to create an experiential simulation program aimed at senior managers and developed to create a common view of the direction and strategy of the company. "We've changed dramatically, through all the acquisitions of the company," she says. "Although we've got a hundred-thirty-two-year history, essentially we're a two-year-old company."

When learners show up at the program, they are presented with a company that has a look and feel similar to that of AT&T but is about half the size. Over the course of three days, the participants get the opportunity to compete in teams against one another to run the company for a three-year period. Since teams can choose to run the company as they wish, each program ends with very different conclusions, although they are all measured by the same criteria. Each member of a team has a designated function, such as head of sales or marketing, and typically participants are asked to select a role that is not their normal day-to-day role so they will get a chance to learn outside their area of expertise.

"The overarching goal is to drive toward a single culture—what we refer to internally as 'One AT&T,'" says Brinkley. "We want people to understand what we do here. What is it like to sit at the CEO table? They get to see how decisions you make in one area of the business—like advertising—impact other areas of the business—like business sales. They also see the impact on human resources when there aren't enough people to implement all the initiatives you want to launch in the company. There are important trade-offs that need to be assessed in order to run a successful business. People walk away with a greater understanding of financial decisions that are made, and they see why their capital project may not have been funded. The experience helps them understand how and why decisions get made."

Teams competing against one another for market share are ultimately measured on how much return they create on invested capital. However, they must meet a threshold on an employee engagement measure or they are knocked down to last place, since the company philosophy is that engaged employees are essential to customer satisfaction. Like a pilot training to fly in adverse conditions, a custom simulation allows people to test various approaches to running the business and, through serious play, learn in ways they could never experience in the workplace otherwise.[11]

On-Demand Mentoring

As people become more familiar with technology, new forms of mentoring and coaching are being created, especially since this method is a top preference of Millennials. One such example is anonymous, on-demand mentoring, which matches mentees with mentors outside the organization. This process includes profiling of the mentee through psychological testing and a background review. The mentoring engagement is completely online and anonymous for both parties and lasts for six to twelve months. Here is a typical exchange:

Hey Mentor,

Tomorrow afternoon at 4 p.m. EST I am scheduled to talk to the board of directors about our Q4 forecast and I have presented to them once before but this time I am delivering some bad news and I am quite nervous. In fact, I am VERY nervous!
    Can you help?

Hey mentee,

I got your message and first you should know that I have done literally hundreds of presentations with some good and bad news and some good and bad results.
    I am putting in your locker an article from Harvard Business Review that was published just three months ago about presenting to boards with difficult news. I happened to find it through a quick search on EQresearch (Thomson-Gale database) which is in the EQ Village.
    When I have bad news, what I typically like to do is a benefit/cost analysis of the bad news. What that means is that every piece of bad new costs something, therefore to be able to quantify it is very

important. Remember that your primary focus should be to get them to some level of concrete action planning to address the bad news and I have found again that quantifying it takes away the subjectivity of the message and the messenger and allows all parties to focus on what they can do to fix it.

My other recommendation to you which I really wish someone had told me before is that you should go there with a mitigation plan. That is a set of ideas of your own or that of your team's that addresses potential solutions to the bad news. I have found that boards like to make decisions and giving them a set of options to choose from is great!

My final personal experience to share with you is that the best way to not feel nervous is to rehearse your presentations with someone. We call this a dry run, and let whoever your audience is be very critical of you. That way the real experience will be much easier.

Good luck and let me know how it went.[12]

One of the mentors contracted by the firm is Bob Wall, 64, of Connecticut. He has worked as a consultant for twenty-nine years. "My first reaction was 'You do what?' " he says. "I couldn't imagine mentoring not only online but also asynchronously and anonymously, especially on any topic based on emotional intelligence. But I went through the qualification and certification process, which included reading materials, taking a test, and then doing a simulation to qualify, and then going through training. First off, it was amazing how well matched I was to my mentee. I felt like I had a twin out there somewhere. Over time, I think I figured out that my mentee was probably male and probably pretty experienced. It turned out to be a highly intimate relationship while remaining completely anonymous. . . . We easily fell into a conversation three to four times a week about life, life goals, and motivation regarding making a career change. When the six months was up, it was like losing a dear friend."

Since Wall has had extensive mentoring engagements in the course of his career, he was able to compare the on-demand experience to traditional ones. "Most people have more than enough to do, and so getting time with people face-to-face can sometimes get in the way, especially if travel is involved. This process strips out race, gender, and culture, allowing two people to have an authentic conversation. I think the anonymity gives the mentee an incredibly safe environment to explore what they want to explore."

Joanna Sherriff, 33, the vice president of creative services at Decision Toolbox, is an example of a mentee who used online mentoring. Working from her home in Tauranga, New Zealand, two hours from Auckland, she was able to access a mentor somewhere in the United States, although she never learned her mentor's identity. "My original thought was that it would be odd, and it was awkward initially. In the long run, though, I could see why the anonymity was required. I would never have shared with my mentor some of the things I did if he or she had known my identity or that of my company. We had one crisis situation to work through at work, and having a mentor really helped me keep emotionally balanced during the crisis. My mentor has a marketing background, so now we're working on reviewing my marketing plan."

She adds, "The confidential and anonymous aspect came to be very powerful because of the crisis situation I was in—it took a lot of the emotion out of it and allowed me to disclose fully. I do also like the asynchronous online element. I work from home in a virtual environment. I enjoy writing . . . maybe even prefer a written environment because in some ways I express myself better in that format than I might in person. So this kind of mentoring really worked for me."

Mobile Access to Learning

With knowledge workers traveling, working from home, or assigned to remote temporary locations, ease of access to learning is fundamental. As learning becomes ubiquitous, mobile phones will become an increasingly important delivery device. Wachovia Bank first developed a strategy for mobile learning when its human resources team brought to light two business issues requiring deep product knowledge traditionally conveyed through a series of paper workbooks. Needless to say, these workbooks were often outdated as soon as they were published and were often left in the car or office. Enter Wachovia's mobile learning solution: all product knowledge related to selling treasury services was converted from a paper workbook to a format readable on a BlackBerry, and since the device is carried by the community bankers at all hours of the day, it ensures not only that the most recent update is used but that the information is accessible to bankers on the move.

Nokia's Matthew Hanwell, the senior manager of Web services, agrees that the evolution of learning to mobile devices is inevitable. He says, "I don't actually know when I start and stop working because of my constant access to my mobile device. I'm connected all the time. When I have a great idea or thought, I can choose to participate in work-related activities wherever or whenever I want. If you could mine e-mails to see how work is getting done at Nokia and how decisions get made, you'd see it doesn't follow organizational structure lines. Rather, it follows people and their expertise. The more we allow people the ability to share knowledge, the more productive they will become and the greater an impact they will have on their businesses."

QUADRANT THREE: SOCIAL COMPETENCY DEVELOPMENT

Most organizations have a stratified talent management approach that focuses on successors and high potentials, leaving few resources available for personalized programs for the majority of employees. However, ask any organization if it uses its succession plans 100 percent of the time or if someone designated a high potential remains forever a high potential, and you are likely to find that there is a lot more flux in the stratification of talent than is usually admitted.

As a result, it makes sense to have programs that give broad access to people who very well could accede to succession plans or be designated as high potential in the next few years. Additionally, developing many individuals in the same competencies allows an organization to ensure alignment in the system so that as people move into more highly managed talent brackets, their development as a unit has already begun.

Group Mentoring

AT&T has both mentoring programs for high potentials and platforms to allow self-organizing mentoring groups, which it calls learning circles. Using a mentoring software tool as the platform, it makes four types of programs available to its employees, which, according to Cindy Brinkley, are just one small part of its overall talent strategy.

The first category of mentoring is reserved for high-potential employees and analyzes their skill sets using mentoring software. AT&T decided to modify the competencies preloaded into the software to match their unique skill sets. More senior employees, designated as mentors, also complete a skills profile. Brinkley's team then matches pairs based on their profiles. All the instructions for getting started on mentoring are then embedded in the software, with development tools, mentoring contracts, and scheduling tools included.

The second and third categories allow for more mass mentoring by creating learning circles that function through one mentor, who is able to facilitate an online mentoring relationship with several mentees at a time. One section of the leadership circle focuses on leadership capabilities, while the other focuses on specific topics, such as sales lead generation. These second and third categories require a lower investment from an HR perspective but have the potential to yield as much development as does one-to-one mentoring. In these categories, Brinkley's group helps get the circle started by surveying for desired topics to match to circles and then monitoring the circles periodically. Since the software tool has some built-in social networking capability, people are able to connect to others with very little hands-on assistance by HR.

The fourth type of mentoring is one that is not always thought of as mentoring but does indeed help in the development of people. Leaders at AT&T are given developmental assignments to write leadership blogs, which then can be read by more junior managers. The blogs are topic-based but, once written, provide an permanent content library for new leaders to read as they encounter similar situations in their careers. The leaders also get the benefit of feedback enabled by the comments sections of the blogs.

On-Demand Microfeedback

Like microblogging, microfeedback allows users to gather instant feedback from others, with feedback limited to 140 characters. Susan Hutt, the senior vice president of services and product development at Camilion Solutions, a Toronto-based software company, realized a few years ago that work life had changed. "When I came into the workforce," she says, "I expected to learn from my managers and adapt to their way of working. But with the Millennial generation, who make up most of my workforce, I realized that we as managers were going to have to change the way we worked. The Millennials wanted constant feedback and information on their career progress. So we changed our HR practices to match the needs of the younger generation." One of the biggest challenges for Hutt in her previous job was that employees were starving for the attention they were used to receiving in school and at home, and they wanted feedback that would help them progress rapidly in their careers. To help ensure that employees were getting feedback beyond the annual reviews—which employees believed were just about making raise decisions, not about evaluating employees' performance—they instituted quarterly reviews and an on-demand feedback system.

"The online feedback tool helped make feedback relevant," Hutt adds. "Most of the younger employees here use MSN Messenger because it's more immediate and short. They don't use e-mail that much. Using online microfeedback, employees can get relevant feedback from a broad set of people, fast. They can manage their own feedback and career."

For example, one project manager at Camilion had an on-site meeting with a customer to wrap up an engagement from the prior year and plan for the next year. Afterward, he sent around an online request asking how he had done driving the conversation. The feedback helped him prepare for the next meeting.

Hutt runs an all-hands meeting at the end of the quarter and then sends requests for feedback to five people. "Was it relevant?" she might ask. "Did it cover the content you need?"

"People can be more honest and give you real feedback," Hutt said. "People have to think about their response because it's short. All the responses are organized, so I can look back at it and see trend lines from the dashboard. That helps me to adjust my messaging over time."

QUADRANT FOUR: SOCIAL CONTEXTUAL LEARNING

People's ability to share knowledge directly with each other on topics relevant to their work environment is one of the most leading-edge advances in learning. Victor Restrepo's story from the beginning of this chapter is just one example of this kind of learning. With a good basis of platforms, tools, and guidelines, there is no limit to the content that can be generated by users, who see value in sharing knowledge with one another. No organization, no matter how large and how well funded, can match the power of learners connecting with one another.

Record Your Knowledge

Joe Campbell faced a big challenge. The head of the Sales University at Sun Microsystems, he had a budget that could not begin to cover all the training topics he thought were necessary. Furthermore, the typical sales rep simply didn't have enough time to show up in a classroom. Still, he wanted to ensure that performance and results were the primary focus, while moving beyond a strictly e-learning solution.

With the help of the chief technologist in Sun Learning Services, Charles Beckham, he was able to build a YouTube–like video- and media-sharing platform with a capability to push content to smart phones. Unlike YouTube, it has built-in authoring tools and channels, so even nontechnical people can easily generate and find content. Along with rating and tagging, it encompasses a full range of Web 2.0 capabilities.

How did Campbell handle the idea that people would be learning from one another, and not necessarily through formal Sales University training? "It does not matter how people learn; as long as they pass the thresholds determined by governance boards, they can be accredited." For each level, Campbell defined three criteria: "One, the ability to pass a knowledge test; two, demonstration of behavior that confirmed they had incorporated their knowledge into real-life actions; and three, documented results, usually in the form of an accomplished sale."

For each area in the Sales University managed by Campbell, he is able to track overall impact, because he can calculate the cost of developing content versus actual sales made by reps in areas in which they had not previously made sales. Although Campbell develops online training for use by sales reps so that they can pass the first threshold of accreditation, the emphasis is on delivering results that speak for themselves. After just one content area was piloted, Campbell was able to demonstrate more than $300 million in new sales.

Peer-to-Peer Learning: Dare2Share
BT, the British telecommunications firm, has a reputation for being at the forefront of innovation and corporate learning. Creating a corporate social network to better attract Millennials was one of the business drivers in the development and launch of BT's Dare2Share corporate social network (figure 6-6). Learning beyond the classroom has been part of the DNA of BT for many years, and its enterprise learning solution, called Route2Learn, is one of the largest corporate learning management systems in Europe. Peter Butler, the head of learning at BT, shares the story behind the launch of Dare2Share. Butler explains, "In an employee survey, we found seventy-eight percent of our employees preferred to learn from their peers, but little money or attention was focused on this. So we began our journey to develop a corporate social network as a way to unlock the potential for BT employees to learn from each other." Butler worked with a consulting partner to develop a solution that met several business goals, such as capturing and storing employee knowledge, leveraging existing tools and technologies, attracting Millennials, and reducing the costs associated with corporate training.

The journey began in February 2008, when BT built a pilot

Figure 6-6: BT Dare2Share

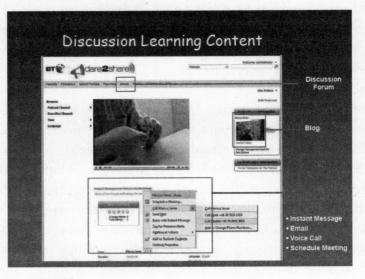

Source: BT Dare2Share.

platform for a small number of BT employees to share knowledge and best practices in numerous forms—through podcasts, discussion threads, blogs, RSS feeds, and documents and courses. BT employees could view all the content on Dare2Share either online or offline, as well as rate each learning segment according to its relevance and quality. "Learning is now more relevant, immediate, and presented in the context of one's everyday work," continues Butler. "We spend roughly a million pounds on formal learning each year, and many of the formal learning projects are too rigid, too generic, or too re-moved from the realities of work. I started on this journey to save the company money while improving the efficiency and effectiveness of the learning operation. But what I untapped along the way was an enormous amount of enthusiasm among BT employees to be in-volved in their own learning. They have contributed content in areas ranging from product overviews and leadership thoughts to general best practices in doing their jobs. And these content areas have been contributed in a variety of formats, including slide shows with audio, videos, podcasts, stories, lectures, and demonstrations. We estimate the total savings to be around eight million pounds in employee time and travel costs, but the excitement we unleashed is priceless."

BT's pilot offering of Dare2Share has demonstrated how learning can be social, personal, and, yes, fun. The learning segments are short and can be accessed on a variety of devices. What's more, the platform is integrated, so immediately after viewing a learning segment, a BT employee can easily contact the contributor and continue the dialogue. When Dare2Share is rolled out to the entire BT population, it will not replace formal learning but will augment and formalize the social learning that was already happening in the BT workplace.

Knowledge Transfer Meets Phased Retirement

Knowing that the Baby Boomer exodus will come eventually, some companies are designing programs now to ensure that the knowledge and experience that will be departing is captured and transferred to remaining employees. At American Express, a phased retirement pilot program is under way that connects retirees with the next generation of employees to ensure effective succession planning and retention of critical knowledge. Although the process, tools, and policies were created by human resources to enable the transfer, all of the content is created by the users in the business unit in the context of their work.

The program was first used by the information technology department to help solve the issue of critical software programs coded in languages no longer taught in universities. Using a process designed by a team led by Jim Rottman, the head of the Workforce Transformation initiative at American Express, an employee considering retirement has access to planning tools and information on how to plan a phased departure. After meeting with each other, the employee and his or her manager agree on a plan for phased retirement and determine how to effectively transfer knowledge over the course of a year. The impending retiree's role is deconstructed so that noncore activities are reduced and the individuals who will take over the responsibilities of the job are identified.

One format they use to understand the responsibilities of the job is a knowledge interview, which is conducted with the retiree, customers, peers, and staff to help identify critical aspects of the job. Then they begin to document the retiree's unique subject matter expertise, and, as the individual transitions to part-time work, he or she spends time with mentees in workshops, mentoring, coaching, and teaching master classes. The retiree is encouraged to hold a retrospective session after critical projects to ensure that the team working in the new space utilized all the knowledge needed for the project.

BEYOND LEARNING TO DEVELOPMENT

Though we have focused largely on learning, a full spectrum of capabilities includes job and team assignments, stretch goals, and planning for career development. Although the onus of career planning is moving more and more away from the organization and to the individual, there are important practices for companies to consider in enabling employees to build a career. Employees of all generations want to work for a company that offers them a clear career path. As shown in figure 6-7, employees across the four generations—though particularly those at earlier stages in their careers—want clear guidelines for a career path and they want extra help when it comes to how to navigate their careers.

This need has led some companies, such as Deloitte, to create a virtual coaching Web site called Coaching and Career Connections (CCC). This site provides one-on-one coaching to 10,000 Deloitte employees. Stan Smith, a principal at Deloitte, believes this site has had a direct impact on retaining from 800 to 1,000 employees, equating to a saving of between $120 million and $150 million. Other companies have evolved several methods of dealing with the challenge of defining career paths and providing career customization.

Defined Career Paths

When Charlene Allen, the senior vice president of human resources for CDM, a Cambridge, Massachusetts–based engineering consulting firm, ran an employee engagement survey in 2000, the loudest message she received was " 'career opportunities' and 'how do I

Figure 6-7: The Importance of Having a Clear Career Path

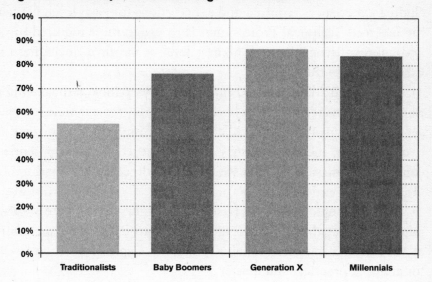

Source: "The Generations @ Work" survey, Future Workplace.

advance my career?'" she said. "People wanted to know how to get on the corporate title track and move from doing project work to working as a project manager, and so on. Also, people had some misunderstandings as to roles. They looked at client service–type sales jobs and all they could see were the perks. They didn't see the risks and responsibilities the salespeople also face.

"We needed to provide maps for people to understand so they could figure out what kind of things they needed to do in managing their own career," she continued. The workforce at CDM is made up of almost 70 percent engineers and scientists in a total global workforce of about 4,500 employees. "We had no clue where to start," she admitted. "We have so many disciplines, and then there is additional diversity within the disciplines, with multiple kinds of scientists and multiple kinds of engineers. And we had a reputation for putting out complicated programs and then not following up on them. Probably we in HR were trying to do too much. So we decided to focus on one path and really do it well, making it one of the things we rolled out that year."

Working with a consulting partner, the company took nearly two years to design a detailed description of consolidated career paths, including experiences required and expectations for each level. Named the Degreed Technical Professional Path program, it required input and approval from the very highest level of the firm, including the CTO as well as the CEO.

"We looked at it in a broad enough fashion to look at the common elements. You have to have a bachelor's degree, for example, to even get your foot in the door," Allen said. "We interviewed dozens of people across these disciplines to look at common capabilities, common milestones. Usually we interviewed people who had ten or more years of experience."

After the interviews, five business capability areas were synthesized—core capabilities that everyone had to have to be successful at CDM. Each business capability area was split into three levels: foundation, practice, and mastery.

"This is the road map which provides a way for someone to practically coach you in your own career path and goals," Allen adds. "We have 131 offices worldwide, some with only five people, so this stimulates a meaningful discussion with their manager or technical mentor. We built training tracks to match the road map. People can look at the sales road map and see what it really looks like now, and determine if it's really as glitzy as they thought it might have been when all they could see were the perks. It also helps us push people gently toward a career path."

The employee engagement survey results vouch for the effectiveness of the program, with some of the career path items increasing by as much as thirty points. It has also improved the offer-to-acceptance ratio among new college hires, especially in the highly competitive environmental space. "When we show this to students on campus, the one thing we heard for certain is that the students said they had never seen anything like this from other recruiting companies. It's really clear what you have to do. Courses are mapped to the career maps, and so the student feels confident that their career as a whole will be considered at CDM."

Paradoxically, other companies are throwing away career ladders and job titles altogether, allowing more dynamic career progression and freedom for employees to navigate their own way.[13] Google is famous for its find-your-own-way career path, and at the design firm IDEO, careers are discussed in terms of accomplishing degrees of credibility. As we have said before, there is no one right way to create an appealing proposition for the 2020 workplace; various paths are possible based on an organization's strategy, location, and workforce mix.

OPPORTUNITIES FOR LEARNING AND DEVELOPMENT

The reshaping of the economy may provide the biggest boost to alternative methods of learning and development in organizations. The risk and cost of acquiring new employees will provide an incentive to consider retooling existing employee learning using more engaging and cost-effective means. These new methods will increasingly include technology-enabled, interactive, mobile solutions that connect people with one another, not just with static knowledge or training sources. The next decade will very likely see the rise of more multiplayer online games for corporate use.

As Millennials join the workforce, they will bring their language of social media to the work environment, and their preferences for mentoring will shape the kind of learning organizations offer employees. Clay Shirky, a writer, professor, and consultant who focuses on the intersection of sociology and the Internet, says, "Human beings are social creatures—not occasionally or by accident but always. Sociability is one of our core capabilities, and it shows up in almost every aspect of our lives as both cause and effect."[14] If organizations do not provide a way to connect Millennials to one another, to mentors, and to the knowledge Millennials need, they will find a way to work around it, inside or outside formally sanctioned channels. Their career success depends upon skill acquisition, and oh-so-eighties learning functions will not get in their way. How different are the ways your learning function is currently operating from how it was doing so in the 1980s and '90s? If the answer is "Not so much," the next decade will change that, whether you want it to or not.

SUMMARY

- **Recognize the potential of user-generated learning content.** In this technological age, users are generating more and more learning themselves using Web publishing and interaction tools.
- **Create organizational social media platforms to harness the power of interactive learning.** Savvy organizations are creating platforms to enable learning interaction, whether the organization formally creates the learning or users develop their own content.
- **Understand that the line between working and learning is becoming increasingly permeable.** Learning in the context of the job is becoming more and more important with the pace of knowledge creation.
- **Respond to the Millennial generation's need for development.** Provide continuous microfeedback and mentoring. Design a career plan that integrates learning and achievement milestones.

CHAPTER SEVEN

Accelerated Leadership

Bob Taccini, a 52-year-old vice president of finance at Cisco Systems, does not consider himself a trendsetter. "I'm not a management fad follower, unless I'm so far behind on the last fad that I'm considered ahead when it comes around again," he says. "I look at applications and technologies pretty skeptically. But when we cut our travel budgets, using social technologies helped meet my need for personalization with my team. Even when I had a travel budget, I could maybe only get to some of our sites once a year. Management now requires spanning distance, even though we can't span time. Certainly, as we continue to build a multigeneration work space, social technologies will become more and more the norm."

For Taccini, the last five years—marked by constantly changing market conditions, the introduction of more distributed leadership throughout Cisco, and the increased availability of virtual meeting technologies—have demanded a change in how he views his job. As he explains, "The way in which we make decisions is more iterative and two-way. It's definitely more of an inclusive environment. So the groups involved in the decisions—say, in the budget planning stages—have better buy-in. There is a closed loop of feedback."

During this time, he has also become an adept user of social technologies. Now he conducts virtual offsite meetings, using TelePresence and WebEx, with blogs, discussion groups, and online forums as needed. As shown in figure 7-1, TelePresence is richer than e-mail

Figure 7-1: A Cisco TelePresence Meeting

Source: Cisco Systems.

or voice mail. The engagement is as if it is real and physical because participants are able to see the other life-sized virtual people involved.

One of the most effective tools Taccini has used is a monthly video blog (vlog). "It has been one of the best ways to communicate, supplemented by calls with everyone in my reporting chain," he said. "Even though it's not two-way real time, I get more participation from the vlog. My team sends questions, and they also have Web spaces to create collaboration spaces."

Taccini is not alone in forging a new approach to leadership. Our goal in this chapter is not only to define what leadership and management may look like in 2020 but also to show ways in which 2020 leaders can be developed now.

DEFINING THE LEADER OF THE FUTURE

All of the principles of Workplace 2020 come together in leadership. Creating an environment that is collaborative, authentic, personalized, innovative, and social requires leaders whose management behaviors create and reinforce that environment. In the world of 2020, with information about leaders freely shared through Twitter, text messages, IMs, and hundreds of sites where employees can publicly rate their bosses, consistency and authenticity across what is said and done will become even more important. Gary Hamel, a professor and management expert, predicts that in the future, "every employee will have a leadership score" based on ratings using social media and other input. In our model of the 2020 leader we emphasize integration of leadership and management, which, when woven together, lead to consistency and trust in the workplace.

A number of leadership gurus are predicting what the leader of the future will look like. According to Marshall Goldsmith, the important characteristics that it took to be a great leader in the past, such as integrity, customer commitment, and vision, will be retained. However, he also says that "Five different qualities [will come] out as much more important for leaders of the future: global leadership, cross-cultural appreciation, technology savvy, building alliances and partnerships, and sharing leadership."[1]

The ability to reach beyond the borders of the enterprise to collaborate with government and non-government agencies will also become increasingly important. "The CEO of the future is going to have to be somebody who deals well with government," predicts David Gergen, a media and political commentator.[2] The leader who focuses solely on quarter-end results, without a view of the role of the organization in society, may win for a few quarters but cannot create a sustainable organization where employees want to work and to which they give their all.

In his call for action, *The Future of Management*, Hamel argues that the companies that succeed in the future will be those that innovate and adapt their management practices. Some of his principles for leaders include:

- Leaders are accountable to the governed.
- Everyone has a right to dissent.
- Leadership is distributed.[3]

Sounds a lot like the principles of democracy, doesn't it? Of course this is his argument. As we have democratized information through the growth of social media tools, our need for bureaucratic hierarchies has been eliminated, and self-governing, involved employees have both the information and power to be involved in the organizational governance process. Hal Varian, Google's chief economist, agrees. "In the old organization, you had to have this whole army of people digesting information to be able to feed it to the decision maker at the top. But that's not the way it works anymore: the information can be available across the ranks, to everyone in the organization. And what you need to ensure is that people have access to the data they need to make their day-to-day decisions. And this can be done much more easily than it could be done in the past. And it really empowers the knowledge workers to work more effectively."[4] Henry Mintzberg of McGill University also calls for defining leadership to be sensitive to communities. "A healthy society balances leadership, communityship, and citizenship," he says.[5]

In our research, we interviewed dozens of executives at companies to find out what they are envisioning as the leader of the future. General Electric has commissioned an internal group to study the leader of 2019, while Cisco created a council to look at the company in 2020, including leadership capabilities. So clearly the requirements of the leader of the future are on the minds of not only leadership and management thought leaders, but also executives at forward-thinking organizations.

THE 2020 LEADER MODEL

In figure 7-2, we cover five leadership areas that seem to be emerging as requirements for the leader of the future.

The process starts with selecting leaders who have demonstrated a collaborative mind-set and who work comfortably in a networked leadership. Second, we focus on leaders who see the development of people as one of their most important goals, including providing honest feedback, career guidance, and learning opportunities. Third, the leader of the future will need to be digitally confident and able

Figure 7-2: The 2020 Leader

Being This Kind of Leader . . . Requires These Management Behaviors

Collaborative Mind-set	• Inclusive decision making • Genuine solicitation of feedback
Developer of People	• Mentors and coaches team • Provides straight feedback
Digitally Confident	• Uses technology to connect to customers and employees
Global Citizen	• Has a diverse mind-set • Prioritizes social responsibility
Anticipates and Builds for the Future	• Builds accountability across levels • Champions innovation

Source: Future Workplace.

to speak the digital language of the newest generation of workers. The fourth facet of the 2020 leader is being a global citizen, in the broadest sense. This means being not only a leader who can work well across cultures but also one who realizes the value of working with governments and nongovernmental organizations in the intertwined dependencies of the future. Finally, anticipating the future and building the capability to address it are the fifth capability area required for the 2020 leader. As Hamel says, "There's little that can be said with certainty about the future except this: sometime over the next decade your company will be challenged to change in a way for which it has no precedent."[6]

Bringing the disciplines of leadership and management together into an integrated model will require a reevaluation of how we develop leaders. In the 1990s and into the twenty-first century, a popular HR practice was to identify competencies, assess them, and create development activities aimed at specific competencies. Eventually a sizable consulting industry arose around this model, making it especially enticing to be able to purchase off-the-shelf products to jump-start leadership development programs. For the leader of the future to project an authentic, genuine, and believable approach, these capabilities must work together and be integrated into a whole experience for followers. The integration of skills and knowing when to use them is far more important than measuring and commenting on each part by itself. Effective leadership needs to live in the day-to-day environment of operational execution and therefore must be integrated with management.

To use an analogy, Michael Pollan, the author of *The Omnivore's Dilemma*, has challenged the prevailing nutrient-by-nutrient approach of thinking about what food and vitamins we need—what he calls "nutritionism"—and proposes an alternative way of eating that is informed by the traditions and ecology of real, well-grown, unprocessed food. Our personal health, he argues, cannot be divorced from the health of the food chains of which we are part.[7] Likewise, our leadership and management practices must be informed by the ecology of the organizational environment in which employees reside and in which markets change constantly. Leaders do not live apart and distinct from the employees who are a part of the overall chain of an organization, and leadership skills are more useful when developed holistically, rather than in isolation.

WHAT THE GENERATIONS WANT FROM THEIR NEXT MANAGER

Recent research into the psychology of leadership suggests that the person who is seen as the leader of a group is often determined by looking at his or her followers, which means there is no single set of personality traits that would predict good leadership. Leadership involves leading from within, fitting into the group, and exerting influence, not imposing views from above.[8]

To understand what people want from their managers, we asked our survey respondents to rate the importance of a number of factors that correspond to the leadership areas in figure 7-2. In our "Workplace of the Future" survey conducted with three hundred heads of human resources, we asked these HR executives to rate managers in their companies on each of those same areas. The rank-order comparison of how important each of the attributes is, compared with HR executives' rating of their managers' overall skills, is shown in table 7-1.

TABLE 7-1: MANAGERIAL CAPABILITIES AND STRENGTHS

	Rank Order of Desired Managerial Capabilities				Rank Order of Managers' Skills
	Tradition-alists	Baby Boomers	Generation X	Millenni-als	HR Ratings
Will help me develop my career	7	7	1	1	5
Will give me straight feedback	2	1	2	2	8
Will mentor and coach me	5	6	6	3	7
Is comfort-able with virtual and flexible work schedules	3	2	3	4	6
Will sponsor learning and development opportunities	6	5	4	5	3
Is confident with new technology	4	3	5	6	1

(Table continued on next page)

	Tradition-alists	Baby Boomers	Generation X	Millenni-als	HR Ratings
Works well across generations	1	4	7	7	4
Works well across cultures and countries	8	8	8	8	2

Source: "The Generations @ Work" survey and "Workplace of the Future" survey, Future Workplace.

Some notable findings emerge here. The biggest gap is how high all generations rated the importance of a manager who would give them straight feedback, compared to how HR professionals rated the capability of their own managers. Dead last on HR professionals' rank order list of skills, giving straight feedback appears to be a skill area that, if improved, could be a differentiating managerial capability for an organization. Joseph Grenny, the best-selling author of *Crucial Conversations* and *Influencer*, says that in his work with organizations, "Creating an ability for managers to give straight feedback is not only satisfying for employees; but organizations also accrue real benefits. Our research shows that when organizations improve the ability of their employees, and especially their managers, to have honest conversations and to give straight feedback, the bottom line improves. We've seen productivity improvement, reduction in scrap and rework, earlier notification of emerging problems, and improved retention. For example—at one telecom company a 20 percent improvement in people's candor about crucial issues corresponded with a 50 percent reduction in unwanted turnover during one of the tightest labor markets in years. At a major defense contracting firm, every 1 percent improvement in survey measures of crucial conversations was accompanied by $1,500,000 in recurring productivity improvements. Not many solutions do all that while improving employee morale."[9]

Another interesting outcome from the survey was the difference in what the two older generations are looking for in a leader versus the two younger generations. Generation X and Millennials want a manager who will help them develop their career; this is viewed as high on their priority list but is low on the lists of Traditionalists and Boomers. The four generations also pair off in rating having a manager who works well across generations, with it being important to the older generations but not as important to the younger generations. When organizations are making decisions about who the next manager of a group will be, it is important to match the demographics of the employees in the group. If the group is composed of largely younger professionals, employing a manager who is good at developing careers could help ensure a good match. If the group has older employees, finding a manager who respects the experiences of the more senior employees and balances that respect across the generations might be a good fit.

Finally, we were surprised that working well across cultures and countries was rated last by every generation, especially considering that this was perceived as a strength of managers. Was it rated lowest because of the relative importance of each of the other items or because the respondents cared more about how they were treated and not as much about how managers might work well in a broader setting? Nearly every organization offers inclusion training, which may help to explain why employees don't expend much thought on their managers' skills in this area.

BUILDING THE LEADER OF THE FUTURE

Changing demographics pose difficulties for a long-term leadership development program. Millennials may be thrust into leadership roles sooner than previous generations were, as there are not nearly enough Gen X workers to fill the ranks of departing Boomers. Millennials may also be placed into leadership roles faster than any others leaders in the last thirty years. Think of it as the "Prince Charles syndrome": will the Gen X leader ascend to power late in life, or will the leadership mantle skip to the next generation?

Organizations have become accustomed to a leisurely leadership pipeline, in which an emerging candidate is allowed diverse experiences and a predictable path through an orchestrated plan. However, for most organizations, the year 2020 will bring a new sense of urgency to develop emerging managers' skills as rapidly as possible, since leaders will be promoted into positions as much as a decade earlier than previous generations. As a result, accelerating leadership development will become necessary for organizations in 2020. A few organizations are using techniques and strategies now that are likely to set the tone for the future in how we think about developing leaders.

Cisco Systems: Redefining the Practice of Leadership and Management

Cisco Systems, the world's largest provider of Internet networking and communications equipment, is leading the way in building the 2020 leader. The dot-com bust of 2001 set into motion a rethinking of the management and leadership practices at Cisco, starting with how it organizes to prepare for the future. John Chambers has been the CEO of Cisco since 1995, at a time when the average tenure of a CEO is less than seven years for large, U.S.-based companies.[10] Chambers describes himself as someone who was quite comfortable with a command-and-control style of leadership but had to shift his style to accommodate marketplace changes. "When you're a command-and-control CEO, individuals impacted by your decisions can choose not to buy in and either slow, or even stop, the process. That is especially dangerous in an industry that moves as fast as this one. In my view, the days of being vertically integrated and having everything within your control will never return. The entire leadership team, including me, had to invent a different way to operate."[11]

Brian Schipper, the senior vice president of human resources, agrees. "We're evolving from fairly traditional leadership practices to a culture that leverages collaboration for accelerating the pace of innovation and for driving execution. John developed a strong vision for the connection between technology, process, and policy to drive the changes he knew the company needed to make in order to address rapid shifts in the marketplace. If a company misses a single transition in high tech, history has shown that it's not inconceivable that even a large company can fail. The importance of having an organization that can rapidly adjust to market and technology transitions is absolutely critical. Speed of innovation and the imperative to execute is impacting more than just technology companies. It's not the products companies sell but rather the impact of technology on the way people work and live that's driving a revolution in the practice of management."

Designing Collaboration Through Councils and Boards

Chambers believes that "only those companies that build collaboration into their DNA by tapping into the collective expertise of all employees—instead of just a few select leaders at the top—will succeed, as more market transitions occur at once. . . . At Cisco, our major priorities are managed not by our top five to 10 executives but instead by cross-functional, collaborative councils and boards."[12]

The councils and boards are a relatively new form of organization structure for Cisco, according to Schipper. "There were probably a half-dozen councils in place when I joined several years ago, but they did not have a long track record of success. Councils and boards emerged from the need to address the strategic opportunities that cross organizational boundaries in a largely functional organization. If you want to develop a viable entry into a heretofore unexploited market segment, you really need to work laterally across functions to make that happen. Another way the boards and councils got started was to solve problems for customers with similar needs. A big part of our customer base now is in the service provider segment. Five years ago that customer segment was much smaller for Cisco. In order to develop solutions, we had to get all functions focused on service provider customers in new and different ways. John believes, and I share his belief, that what most companies would do when faced with that kind of market opportunity would be to reorganize on the pivot of the customer. Our belief is companies often trade off known negatives for unknown negatives. Companies lose time and, in the rapid change of the high-tech world, risk missing a market transition while focused internally on reorganization. Our view is that serial reorganization creates unnecessary business risk when responding to the pace and scale of opportunities and challenges in the marketplace."

Cisco has carefully defined what is chartered as a working group, board, or council. "Without some clear system for making distinctions based on the scale of the work, everyone naturally wants to establish or join a council," Schipper says. A council at Cisco typically develops vision and strategy for five- to eight-year opportunities that involve market adjacencies with at least $10 billion in revenue. "Councils address big, hairy strategic problems and, as such, require a solid, repeatable governance process, including conducting operational reviews. Boards address challenging issues that require coordination and collaboration across Cisco. For example, the CIO, the controller, workplace resources, and HR decided that we needed to look at the intersection of work and the employee experience. We could have each played our position, but we chose instead to form a board and be more deliberative and collaborative in our approach to harmonize the work and improve the experience for employees," he elaborates.

The Role of Human Resources

What role can HR play in pioneering such a massive change of approaching management of a large company? "One of the things that I bring to the discussion is greater deliberation about which people systems we use to drive change and the order in which we adjust them to ensure enduring culture change," says Schipper. "My experience is that one of the last places to look is the reward system, even though that's often where most people would instinctively look to create change. Evolving a culture is by its very nature complex. Rewards, in contrast, are necessarily simple. Often rewards provide only a sound bite of a metric, so it is often ineffective if the intended outcome is lasting change. One of the things we did early was change the leadership competency model. We had a model that could have fit any traditionally led organization. We changed to a model that emphasizes the importance of collaboration. Of course, the model is only as good as the implementation process behind it. We use it to select leaders from outside the company, and our 360-feedback process internally, to vet people moving up from director to VP or from VP to SVP."

The HR leadership also had to change to support collaborative management. All HR leaders spend a substantial part of their time on work that would often be viewed as nontraditional for a human resources function. Members of the HR team are coparticipants in the many boards and councils. Rather than running a traditional staff meeting, Schipper includes everyone inside or outside the function who can help contribute to the content at hand. In other words, the formal organization chart rarely determines who participates in which initiatives.

NAVIGATING CAREERS

Perhaps one of the challenges of a complex organization is how people get feedback and learn where the opportunities exist to advance a career. Schipper chairs one council, and he must contribute to their performance expectations and reviews of everyone on that council, even though they don't report to him. Are the career paths at Cisco difficult to navigate? Schipper says, "Technology jobs are not like those in companies where roles don't change much over time and the opportunity exists to define key jobs for people to rotate through to accelerate their development. In this fast-changing environment, the incumbent and his or her background often shape the job."

In any organization, Schipper insists, people's behaviors are constantly scrutinized to determine what roles they might best fill in their next assignment. "Like many companies, we have an organic social system that rides alongside the organization chart. Decision makers are always looking for the right behaviors in emerging leaders who might be able to step up and lead the next initiative." In one of Cisco's leadership development programs, the Action Learning Forum (ALF), leaders are presented with a strategic business challenge. They team with others to solve the challenge and then present their results to a leadership board. Each idea is either funded or rejected.

The teams that are funded then go on to work the cross-company idea, giving them valuable experience analogous to that of a board or council. Cisco has funded dozens of initiatives and developed strategies to address market adjacencies through the ALF program.

At Cisco, emerging leaders have the opportunity to chair a working group or board, where they can hone their skills on solving an important strategic problem for the corporation, but through an approach that allows for cross-functional support and therefore is less risky for the leader's long-term career. If the initiative is not as successful as anticipated, the leader of a working group can apply his or her learning to the next functional role or assignment, without moving downward or being brushed aside, as can happen in a traditional organization.

A Personal Journey

Adapting to a new style of leadership has required Schipper to change the way he works and behaves. "Although I'm very comfortable with setting strategy and vision, at Cisco I have to intersect what I do with how John leads. He lays out a clear model of the vision of the future, and I have to adapt and translate that to people, technologies, processes, and tools. What I've learned, working with the Cisco leadership team, is that you have to sometimes subordinate an HR-led vision in order to support a business where all leaders are expected to establish vision and strategy. At Cisco, my role is not to create an HR-led vision but rather to build the supporting people and organization systems to ensure that the business-led vision is realized and can endure.

"This collaborative model of working with other senior leaders is infinitely more fulfilling than the model where one simply hopes that others will buy into and align with an HR-led vision. What is often forgotten is that what drives company success is having leaders who have a shared understanding of the company's values; that gives me and my team the opportunity to build the supporting culture. For example, our practices employ increasingly collaborative processes to govern work at Cisco, but we all agree that an important underlying value is to continue to care about our people and show that care through our words and actions. What's deeply satisfying for me is that because we're clear about our shared values at Cisco, I have the opportunity to execute better and respond faster than those who are serially negotiating for strategic alignment with their senior leader or peers."

General Electric Sees the Future of Leadership

One company that has long been admired as a leadership development factory is General Electric. In 2008, Bob Cancalosi, the chief learning officer of General Electric Health Care (GEHC), began a special assignment to determine the skills and capabilities needed by GE leaders in 2019, as part of an assignment on cultural transformation. Several business changes drove the need to see the future. For the first time in GEHC's history, more than 50 percent of its revenues and 50 percent of its employees were from outside the United States. The accelerated market opportunity in emerging markets suggested there needs to be a shift in how GEHC defines leadership.

While on assignment for a year to help GEHC assess its current and desired state culture, Cancalosi and others talked to more than two hundred thought leaders and experts in the field of leadership and conducted interviews with key leaders in GEHC. Altogether they determined more than 125 competencies through their interviews and research. From there, using Pareto analysis, they narrowed down the themes. Though it is still a work in process, they acknowledge seven competency areas to be important. They are, according to Cancalosi:

1. **Just plain smart.** Has both book and street smarts.
2. **Results-oriented.** Has a great execution quotient.
3. **Unwavering ethics.** Leads by example and does the right thing when no one is looking.
4. **Financial acumen.** Understands the relationships of the income statement, balance sheet, and cash flow of a business.
5. **Quick study.** Has the ability to pick up data, trends, issues, opportunities, etc.
6. **Values diversity.** Team reflects a balance of strength.
7. **Passionate.** About the business, the people, and the driving purpose.

Then GEHC identified ten leadership characteristics to fit these competency areas. Although they are more detailed, these GE characteristics provided by Cancalosi closely align with our 2020 leader model. These leadership characteristics include:

1. **Cultural agility.** Leveraging the unique skills of all global cultures within the organization.
2. **Boundaryless collaboration.** Focusing on the whole, collaborating across the organization chart and not just within their own business.
3. **Legendary builder of people and teams.** Coaching and mentoring both face-to-face and virtually; challenging people to achieve more than they believed they could.
4. **External focus on excellence.** Deep knowledge of the customer, their industry, and the global regulatory forces.
5. **Generationally savvy.** Leading well across all four generational types.
6. **Digital proficiency.** Leveraging technology to accelerate speed of decision making and business impact.
7. **Harmonious blend of EQ and IQ.** Personally self-aware in order to motivate team performance.
8. **Multiple-horizon thinking.** Rationalizing the distribution of resources and effort across the present and future to balance incremental and bold moves.
9. **Innovative proliferation.** Creating a climate of ongoing invention and creative thinking.
10. **Inspirational communication.** Motivating employees in both good and bad times; communicating effectively externally with stakeholders and media.

Once the characteristics were defined, Cancalosi and team looked across GEHC to see where the biggest gap existed between the current capabilities and the ones needed for the future. The goal here was to use this to develop a curriculum strategy to match GEHC's future growth strategy. Each year the team intends to tackle a new future competency for development, so that by the time 2019 arrives, with continuous adjustment, they will be well under way in having the bench strength they need. How many companies do you know that have a three-year leadership development plan, much less a ten-year plan that is updated regularly? GE is now working on the corporationwide review of the requirements for the leader of 2020, which will be incorporated into the curriculum planning of its corporate university at Crotonville in Ossining, New York.

Zappos: Twittering Away to Profits

Sometimes failure is the best teacher. Not that anyone would describe Tony Hsieh as a failure in any way. But when asked what the biggest mistake he has ever made was, he answered, "With my first company it was not paying attention to the culture. We hired the right people with the right experience and skill sets, but we didn't know to look for a culture fit. By the time it was 100 people, I didn't want to go into the office anymore. That was a weird feeling. That's why we ended up selling the company."[13]

As the CEO of Zappos, the online shoes and clothing retailer recently acquired by Amazon.com, Hsieh focuses first and foremost on culture. Every employee at Zappos was allowed to collaborate in the process of crafting the values of the company. Collaboration requires openness and transparency, and Hsieh achieves that through creating a culture using a number of strategies, including numerous social media tools. Here's how he describes how Twitter has helped him grow personally:

For me, it comes down to these 4 things:

1. Transparency & Values: Twitter constantly reminds me of who I want to be, and what I want Zappos to stand for.
2. Reframing Reality: Twitter encourages me to search for ways to view reality in a funnier and/or more positive way.

3. Helping Others: Twitter makes me think about how to make a positive impact on other people's lives.
4. Gratitude: Twitter helps me notice and appreciate the little things in life.

. . . By embracing transparency and tweeting regularly, Twitter became my equivalent of being always on camera. Because I knew that I was going to be tweeting regularly about whatever I was doing or thinking, I was more conscious of and made more of an effort to live up to our 10 core values.[14]

Since the CEO is such a fan of Twitter, it's not surprising that nearly half of the Zappos employees also tweet.[15] With the company's $1 billion in revenue, employees' ability to get to know other employees' interests helps build the sense of family spirit that is at the core of Zappos' values and that led to Zappos being named as number 23 on *Fortune* magazine's 2009 100 Best Companies to Work For list.

Even though he describes himself as introverted, quiet, and shy, Hsieh's openness with his employees and his Twitter followers, which now number more than one million, help him create the culture that he sees as foundational to the success of Zappos.[16] Certainly the use of Twitter helps him reach customers, but his primary focus is building Zappos' employee culture.[17] "Our company culture is based on ten core values that our employees came up with," he says. "My style is to make sure we're always living by those core values and making decisions based on them. A lot of bigger companies might have what they call 'core values' or 'guiding principles,' but it's usually something lofty-sounding, like it comes out of a press release and the employees might learn about it on day one but then it's just a meaningless plaque on the wall. For us, we actually hire people based on these values, and we'll fire people based on these values even if they're doing their job perfectly fine. Part of my job is making sure that is implemented as a policy."[18]

ZAPPOS CORE VALUES

1. Deliver WOW Through Service
2. Embrace and Drive Change
3. Create Fun and a Little Weirdness
4. Be Adventurous, Creative, and Open-Minded
5. Pursue Growth and Learning
6. Build Open and Honest Relationships with Communication
7. Build a Positive Team and Family Spirit
8. Do More with Less
9. Be Passionate and Determined
10. Be Humble

Source: Zappos Core Values.[19]

By using a platform that encourages feedback and response, Hsieh opens himself to collaboration with everyone, including anyone with a relevant point of view. Since that interchange is open to the world, those who watch him also have the opportunity to learn how he conducts himself, which is one of the best ways of developing people.

Most leaders say that the higher they move in an organization chart, the less feedback they get. The use of social technologies not only opens up the possibility for a leader to communicate authentically with the people in the organization but also allows a leader to get immediate feedback on how the message is being received. Any feedback for leaders is helpful, but in this case, social technologies allow that feedback to be in real time and instantaneous.

According to Aaron Magness, who heads up business development and brand marketing, "Zappos is a more accessible and transparent leadership team than I ever imagined. Tony gives out his e-mail and personally responds. In today's world, at many companies, there are so many gatekeepers. Tony will personally respond to e-mail sent to him from anyone in the company. He doesn't have other people read his e-mail and respond. It sends a message to the rest of the company. Openness is not only welcomed, it's expected. We all feed off of it."

When hiring leaders from outside, Zappos listens carefully to what questions they ask as a clue to their management style. Magness says, "What you'll find is people will ask who they report to or what their title will be or their office space. That means they're focused on themselves. Also, people who keep work and play separate won't fit with us. As a leader, we are asked to spend twenty percent of our time with our teams outside the office. We do work outside the office. You're building trust, so you make faster decisions."

Reverse Mentoring at Burson-Marsteller

In Mark Twain's novel *The Prince and the Pauper*, Tom Canty, the youngest son of a family of beggars, trades places with the Prince of Wales, Edward VI. Each learns valuable lessons about the other's life conditions, social environment, and worldview. Edward, who will eventually become king, gets a glimpse into the injustices of the kingdom he will one day rule, which changes his perspective and approach as a ruler. Though they swap places for only a few weeks, the future king learns valuable lessons that shape him forever. In a sense, reverse mentoring in organizations accomplishes many of the same learning experiences as Tom Canty and Edward the Sixth experienced.

Burson-Marsteller, a global public relations and communications firm with offices in eighty-one countries, has implemented reverse mentoring in its U.S. division. According to Michele Chase, the managing director of worldwide human resources, Burson-Marsteller decided to pilot a program of reverse mentoring to bridge not only generational divides but also ethnicity and specialty experience, allowing each side of the mentoring relationship to appreciate their differences.

"Our whole U.S. leadership team of nineteen executives participated—all the practice heads and market leaders, as well as the U.S. CEO," Chase says. Young and/or ethnically diverse mentors across the United States volunteered and were assigned to senior team members based on where they might have had the greatest opportunity to understand another perspective. "For example, the CEO, Pat Ford, is being mentored by a director in another location. Pat conducted an 'all hands' town hall for the U.S. and spoke to his mentor to get her reaction and her general feeling of her office's reaction to the messages. The mentor gave Pat insights that he might not have otherwise heard. Letting someone else take control of what they're teaching you and telling you is the difficult part for a senior executive, when you're used to being looked to for the answers."

In order to accomplish this, the company conducts training for both mentors and mentees, establishing ground rules around confidentiality. Typically the mentoring pair is not in the same location, so when an executive is traveling, he or she will arrange a meeting. Otherwise, they rely on phone calls or Adobe Connect. "It's difficult not to slip into our traditional roles," Chase commented. "But this arrangement is building relationships. The mentors are getting access to more senior people, and they get to go behind the scenes, so to speak, to see how leaders think and offer insights. In addition, the mentee, who typically might not get feedback from a senior executive with whom they do not have a reporting relationship, is able to receive thoughts and advice from someone who differs from them in many ways."

Chase holds meetings with the mentors to ensure that the relationship is working, and the mentors give one another tips and tell stories about what's working for them. Several of the mentors have helped their mentees set up Twitter or other social networking tools. "Reverse mentoring accelerates development for mentors," according to Chase. "To have conversations with these high-level employees is development in and of itself, but the mentor also gets better known in the organization. They've built a relationship, and when the next assignment comes up, there is a natural tendency to go to someone you know. Also, some of the mentors have never managed people, so they get a chance to preview that experience." For the executive mentees, gaining more perspective on, insights into, and appreciation for differences such as age, race, and cultural practices is a great benefit and helps foster a more inclusive culture.

Team-based Learning at PricewaterhouseCoopers

Leaders often work in an environment with a high need for technical excellence, intense pressure, time constraints, and a high cost of failure. Tom Evans, the chief learning officer for Pricewaterhouse-Coopers (PwC) in the United States, began to wonder if there were ways the natural work environment could be used to accelerate learning for the next generation of leaders.

"In our world," Evans said, "the question is, how do you develop the next generation and ensure they have the capacity to act on behalf of the firm in a way that drives differentiation and excellence—levels of distinction? Our firm has spent a lot of time tackling that question, so I started a project to understand how we can help our new associates understand globalization, technology, and the complex tasks they face.

"The generations are approaching work differently. So we in turn have to look at the workplace environment as a fertile field for accelerating the development of our people, using client problems as the day-to-day means of learning and building trust and collaboration in our teams.

"From that we started to think about how to build leaders by asking ourselves if there was a way to accelerate developing leaders without taking them out of their natural work environments. That's when we hit upon the idea that training to be a doctor is done on the job. We went out and studied teaching hospitals, and we noticed differences between hospitals, how they approached training their doctors, and the results they achieved. Johns Hopkins really stood out to us, not only because of their long-standing ranking as a top teaching hospital but also because they remain profitable, despite working in the constraints of an environment where most of their funding is from government aid."

The training of doctors, Evans learned in his conversations with the administrator at Johns Hopkins, is not considered a special event or program. It's just part of what it does and who they are as a teaching hospital. The learning is integrated with work, and the dialogue that occurs between the members of the medical team is focused on practices and a style of learning that has become natural.

"We decided to call it team-based learning—TBL—when we translated the practices from the teaching hospital back to our environment," Evans says. "We realized that an underlying foundation in order for TBL to work was to be open to a philosophy of development—a basic understanding at a teaching hospital. Our senior leaders needed to realize that, like doctors, our associates have gone through a vigorous recruiting process and there is a valuable asset in front of them. But the associates need developing and shaping; the performance bar just keeps on getting higher." To help the teams get started, Evans, in partnership with Duke Corporate Education, created a launch session to build a common understanding of the process and ensure that the underlying philosophical approach required was in place.

FIVE ROUTINES OF TEAM-BASED LEARNING
1. Rounds
2. Formal observation and feedback
3. Shadowing
4. After-action reviews (AARs)
5. Team workshops

Borrowing from practices observed at Johns Hopkins, TBL relies on five routines:

1. **Rounds.** This practice requires moving work to the most junior eligible team member. "The reason for emphasizing 'eligible' is that any assignment requires a certain level of background. At Johns Hopkins, they would do three to four patients on their first day on the job and then present to others. A resident might flash an EKG to interns and then give them fifteen seconds or less to interpret and state what needs to be seen. When you get to know EKGs, you realize that there really are a few striking things that even the newest doctor should be able to recognize and interpret almost immediately, so they get that experience on the first day." At PwC, this means letting junior members of the team work directly with clients much earlier than they might have otherwise, but not solo.

2. **Formal observation and feedback.** This second routine ensures that people are given responsibility early in their tenure, have plenty of opportunity to be observed on the job, and receive feedback not only from the leader of the team but also from other team members. The observation and feedback can be either impromptu or scheduled.

3. **Shadowing.** As an associate progresses in his or her capabilities, a senior partner schedules a time to observe the associate at a client site. "It is cultural to expect feedback from multiple sources in this environment. Even though hierarchy and structure are alive in this environment, the organization structure flattens when it comes to feedback. The same thing was true at Johns Hopkins. I watched the interaction between a cardiologist with twenty-five years' experience and a resident. When it came to discussing a patient, the resident was able to point out something to the cardiologist, who I expected to bristle and react to feedback from someone so junior. But the cardiologist listened and thanked the resident for the feedback."

4. **After-action reviews (AARs).** An AAR is conducted by the management team as a way of diagnosing how a client engagement worked. "If we get it wrong, we talk about it and learn," said Evans. "If we get it right and unique, we talk about it and learn. It's very valuable to sharing when you want to bring something to the team as a new way of approaching a particular problem or client set. It also helps seal in the learning experience."

5. **Team workshops.** As a team is set to launch each new routine, it holds a workshop to ensure that everyone understands the process and that the new routine can be easily embedded into the team's forthcoming natural work. That way it helps build an integrated approach to both work and learning, in the hope that the routine will be sustained long after the formal program ends.

According to Evans, in the places where he has conducted early pilots, "the teams are showing good results, with increased competence, good business economics, and high client satisfaction."

DEMOCRATIZATION OF INFORMATION CHANGES EVERYTHING

The structures of management common to most organizations evolved in order to control and pass information from level to level in the hierarchy. New technologies have not only made that unnecessary but have also freed people from this hierarchy. The more management tries to exercise control of information, the more likely there will be a backlash. Not only does the front line get access to information, but CEOs can now hear directly from customers. Brian Dunn, the CEO of Best Buy, says, "I . . . have a program that searches the Internet anytime somebody mentions Best Buy out there. Sometimes it's really great things, sometimes it's obscenity-laden, but I have a huge appetite for it. If I see customers have problems with things, I will contact the appropriate person in our company and have them contact that customer. Sometimes I contact the customer."[20]

Because people at all levels have access to information across the corporation, engaging the minds of everyone will lead to changing our models of what we expect in leaders, how we manage, and how to accelerate the development of the next generation of leaders. We call the leaders of the future "citizen leaders." They will reinforce the principles of openness and democracy through access to information and social collaboration in order to deliver sustainability within the overall society in which the organization operates. Our connection to nearly anyone else on the planet is only a mobile device away. Citizen leaders who embrace collaboration across all levels will be those who thrive in 2020.

SUMMARY

- **Tailor your leadership styles differently for audiences of different generations.** The Traditionalists and Baby Boomers, the two older generations, desire different qualities in a leader than do the two younger generations, Generation X and the Millennials. When organizations are making decisions about managers of groups, factoring in the ages of the employees in the groups is important information in selecting a leader. If the group is made up of largely younger professionals, look for a manager who is good at developing careers. If the group is mostly older employees, find a manager who balances respect across the generations.

- **Integrate leadership and management.** Define your leadership competencies in a way that matches not only the strategy of the company now but where the organization is headed. Will your workforce mix change and require new competencies? Develop those competencies before your competition does.

- **Ensure openness, honesty, and transparency among your leaders.** Encourage leaders to use policies that open processes to feedback from, response to, and collaboration with individuals at all levels in the organization. This allows developing leaders the opportunity to learn how leaders conduct themselves, one of the best ways for them to learn these skills.

- **Understand that the timeline for leadership development is changing.** Organizations are used to the luxury of a leisurely leadership progression. Although this has not entirely disappeared, as we move into the future, growth in new technologies and increases in the speed of business will mean a need to develop skills as rapidly as possible. Accelerating leadership development will become necessary for organizations in 2020.

- **Enact team-based projects to foster collaborative learning.** Working and learning in teams allows employees to learn from one another and all to benefit from the differing perspectives and experience levels of the team members. Additionally, working in teams helps make observation and feedback facets of the regular workday.

PART III

Envisioning the 2020 Workplace

CHAPTER EIGHT

Twenty Predictions for the 2020 Workplace

We invite you to come along with us on a journey to the future workplace. As defined throughout this book, we see the 2020 workplace as one that provides an intensely personalized, social experience, to attract, develop, and engage employees across all generations and geographies. This in turn creates a competitive advantage for the organization.

The next decade will usher in new companies and business models that are unimaginable today and will dramatically change how we live, work, learn, communicate, and play. Anticipating these changes will be critical to your ability to thrive in the 2020 workplace, where transparency, collaboration, personalization, and hyperconnectivity will rule the day.

We interviewed scores of executives, conducted online research with 2,200 working professionals in four generations, participated in futurist forums, and over the course of the past year created our own interactive collaboration site to take the pulse of what types of changes might be on the horizon in the next decade. Some of the changes we predict for the next decade may surprise you: how many of us would have thought it possible to elect our leader, play video games to learn leadership skills, or earn a Jack Welch MBA? Others may seem obvious, but they require a greater sense of urgency to bring them to reality—such as ensuring that Lifelong Learning Accounts reach the broadest global market of employees in order to develop a culture of lifelong learning.

We know that the 2020 workplace will be full of surprises. The best you can do is start today to adapt to, respond to, and prepare for the wild cards that will surely be coming your way. So, to assist you, here are twenty trends we predict will occur in time for the 2020 workplace.

1. YOU WILL BE HIRED AND PROMOTED BASED UPON YOUR REPUTATION CAPITAL

Reputation capital will be the top currency in the 2020 workplace. This is the sum total of your personal brand, your expertise, and the breadth, depth, and quality of your social networks. Companies will increasingly source, recruit, and promote new employees based upon their reputation capital. This means looking for employees who have not only wide, deep, and high-quality social networks but also demonstrate a track record of turning these networks into increased business value for the organization and a stronger personal brand for themselves.

Already some companies, such as Best Buy, are listing reputation capital as a requirement, in this case for the job for the senior manager in emerging media marketing. Some of the job requirements—developed via crowdsourcing—include being aware of and active on such sites as LinkedIn, Facebook, Twitter, MySpace, Plaxo, Ning, Delicious, Slideshare, YouTube, and Digg. By 2020, hiring companies could very well make specific requirements that prospective employees have experience using these contacts to further their business agenda. And over time building one's recognizable reputation capital will be less tied to specific social networks and will become portable, meaning you can more easily become a free agent, broadcasting your skills and competences to a wide network of followers, friends, and business connections.

According to Dr. Robert Cross, a professor of management at the University of Virginia, the high performers in an organization focus on building high-quality social networks rather than large ones.[1] They may not know everyone, but the people they know, they know very well, and they invest in those relationships before they'll actually need them to get their work accomplished. Companies will increasingly take note of how well connected current and prospective employees are in their professional communities and will seek to retain and promote individuals who demonstrate an ability to grow their network and their reputation and standing in the community. Inside the company, an employee's number of links to the internal company social Web site, the feedback from hundreds of people rather than the current dozen or so used on 360-degree instruments, and the number of times people link to him or her could indicate a leadership score and set him or her up for promotion. Look for reputation capital to be a more critical factor in both hiring and promotion decisions.

2. YOUR MOBILE DEVICE WILL BECOME YOUR OFFICE, YOUR CLASSROOM, AND YOUR CONCIERGE

More than 1.2 billion mobile phones are produced each year, and they are benefiting from unprecedented innovation. Mobile phones and tablets will be the primary connection tool to the Internet for most people in the world in 2020.[2]

In the words of Michael Jones, the chief technology advocate for Google, "The mobile phone is for the next decade what the computer has been for the last two or three. The whole experience of the Internet is becoming not a desktop computer experience, but a personal experience."[3] This is already happening in Japan, as young people equipped with mobiles see no reason to own a personal computer. The mobile phone in 2020 will become our office, our classroom, and our real-time concierge, helping us manage both our personal and professional lives. With mobility and migration on the rise, employees will no longer be limited to working in one country or region. They will be able to work anywhere, including their client locations, hotel rooms, vacation destinations, and, of course, homes. As wireless network speeds rise, with twenty-five cities in the United States expected to double their 3G network speed in 2010, and device functionality improves to the point of merging netbooks, readers, and phones, the possibilities are endless.

Already being touted as the next delivery tool for corporate learning, mobile devices are being used by companies to deliver sales training, compliance training, and up-to-date product knowledge, as well as e-coaching and e-mentoring. In 2020, if not before, look for the mobile device to be an increasingly important delivery mode for a wide variety of corporate training, new-hire orientation, mentoring, coaching, and on-the-job performance support. Coupled with improved security advances, the mobile device will be used as validation for entry into locations, citizenship, travel and expense reporting, and timekeeping for project accounting.

3. THE GLOBAL TALENT SHORTAGE WILL BE ACUTE

The global competition for highly qualified workers will take shape in 2020. Despite there being five generations in the workplace, there will be a shortage of certain skills, not just workers. The U.S. Department of Labor predicts that U.S.-based employers will need 30 million new college-educated workers in the next decade, while only 23 million young adults are expected to graduate from college in that period.[4]

Fast-breaking technological breakthroughs in new products and services will create a demand for new jobs using more complex skills. Manpower's 2009 Talent Shortage Survey of 39,000 employers in thirty-three countries finds that despite high levels of unemployment in many countries, there is a mismatch between the types of individuals available for work and the specific skills employers are looking for to achieve business goals.[5] The Manpower survey identifies the top six professions that will be in demand globally, including skilled trades in specialized areas, sales representatives, technicians in engineering and maintenance, engineers, managers and senior executives, and finance and accounting professionals. These professionals all require a higher order level of skill and training, and talent shortages in these areas will spark an intense competition for talent among companies around the world. Employees who will be in demand are those who possess these skills as well as being technologically literate, globally astute across geographies and cultures, and continuous learners.

4. RECRUITING WILL START ON SOCIAL NETWORKING SITES

Recruiting for the vast majority of professional jobs will start in one of the highly trafficked social networking sites, such as Facebook, LinkedIn, YouTube, Bebo, Twitter, and Second Life. Though the early adopters profiled in chapter 4, such as Deloitte, Ernst & Young, Amazon, EMC, and even the U.S. Department of State, are already doing this, an overwhelming number of companies—we predict at least 80 percent—will begin to tap online social networks as the first stop to recruiting global talent. Prospective employees may potentially have their first interview via their avatar, followed by several video chats and reference checks on social networks. This is social recruiting, where companies leverage a range of social media and professional networks, online and offline, to acquire talent. As social recruiting spreads from a few isolated, forward-thinking companies to mainstream companies, it will be essential for both employers and employees to develop new skill sets to be successful in this endeavor.

Both employers and employees must become fluent in how to navigate online recruiting. Employers must train their recruiting staff to conduct interviews on social networking sites, to recognize key qualities in candidates during virtual interviews, and to use social networking sites to check references and select candidates for face-to-face interviews. Employees, on the other hand, must be aware of how to use social media to position themselves for success, grow a global social network, and, most important, communicate their strengths to a prospective employer. How much will the recruiting process change in 2020? Organizations that will thrive in the 2020 workplace will develop a comprehensive social recruitment strategy using their most valued social networks to source employees as well as ensuring that job candidates are capable of leveraging social media to enhance their specific business goals.

> **THE NEW QUESTIONS EMPLOYERS WILL ASK JOB CANDIDATES**
>
> - How many followers do you have on Twitter? On Facebook? On LinkedIn? How many of these followers are in your industry?
> - How many people have recommended you on LinkedIn? Can you tell me why each one recommended you based on your current and or previous business relationship with them?
> - Have you turned any of your Twitter followers, LinkedIn colleagues, or Facebook friends into new business?
> - Do you blog regularly about issues related to your job/industry? Can you share the link?
> - Have you participated in any internal employee innovation contests at your company or external innovation contests? Which ones?

5. WEB COMMUTERS WILL FORCE CORPORATE OFFICES TO REINVENT THEMSELVES

Knowledge workers will increasingly elect to work at "third places," a term invented by the sociologist Ray Oldenburg in his book *The Great Good Place*,[6] which describes the community-building role of informal public spaces such as cafés, coffee shops, hotels, and bookstores. Human resources officers use this term to describe specifically the places people work other than the first place, meaning the corporate office, or the second place, meaning the home office. The third place can be any location—coffee shop, customer site, collaboration work site, hotel, plane—where work is done. Encouraging employees to work in third places is growing. Today Gartner Dataquest estimates that one-fifth of the nation's workforce is part of the so-called Kinko's Generation, spending a significant number of hours each month working outside a traditional office. This estimate is growing by 10 percent annually as corporations attempt to save money on real estate, adopt ecofriendly policies to reduce commuting, or just acknowledge the importance of collaboration and knowledge exchange in a work space specifically designed for the purpose.[7]

Even the federal government is encouraging its workforce to telework. Government agencies usually aren't early adopters, but many are exploring this idea. Why? Because, according to the Telework Exchange, a public-private partnership that studies this phenomenon, federal workers spend more time commuting to work each day than they do on vacation each year.[8]

With the growth of corporate social tech, it will be irrelevant where employees work as long as they deliver results to the team. Companies will spend resources to reinvent the work space to increase worker productivity, improve innovation, and connect workers to one another.

6. COMPANIES WILL HIRE ENTIRE TEAMS

As teamwork becomes increasingly important in the global workplace, companies are seeing the value of hiring and training an entire team to tackle business problems. At the same time, some teams will form into guilds and move as intact teams from company to company, in order to maintain their established working relationships. Companies will in fact start to hire entire teams of college students, not just brilliant individuals.

This is already happening in India. NIIT, a global IT learning solutions company, is partnering with the Indian School of Business (ISB) to run a collegiate business plan competition. ISB students compete by forming teams to identify an entrepreneurial business opportunity important to the NIIT brand. If the idea is selected, NIIT hires the intact team, funds it, and allows it to run the business. The members select their own leader, and the team is accountable for results to NIIT leadership.

NIIT is enthusiastic about the results of hiring an intact team of ISB students to run a new business unit. Two team members turned down offers from McKinsey and Lufthansa to join NIIT so they could work on a business project they helped co-create. NIIT projects higher retention rates as team members bond with one another, making it difficult for a competitor to come in and recruit the best person away from the team.

Look for increased sourcing of intact teams, whether they are directly from school or band together as a guild and work together across projects and companies, such as is done in the motion picture industry now. As more companies see the virtue of hiring a team whose members already know one another's strengths and have a track record of success working with one another, this practice will increase.

7. JOB REQUIREMENTS FOR CEOS WILL INCLUDE BLOGGING

Keeping in touch with customers, the marketplace, and employees is an important role for CEOs. As the workforce and customers increasingly become familiar with and rely on social media, the fastest way to communicate broadly will be through tools such as blogging and Twitter. The level of authenticity and concern that can be communicated through a CEO-level blog can't be matched by press releases or blogs written by the public relations department. Currently almost three hundred senior executives and sixty CEOs are registered as bloggers, as recorded by the NewPR Wiki, and the number is growing daily.[9] Some CEOs, such as Bill Marriott, write in longhand or dictate for others to put on the site, but Marriott credits his blog for $4 million in incremental bookings since the inception of the Web site.[10] The styles of CEO blogs range from deeply personal, such as that of Matt Blumberg of Return Path, who writes about his experience as a first-time CEO, to highly opinionated, such as that of Mark Cuban, the owner of the Dallas Mavericks, to product messaging only, such as that of Bob Lutz, the vice chairman of General Motors.[11] Others combine blogging with a Twitter presence, such as Tony Hsieh, the CEO of Zappos, who had, as of January 2010, 1,679,065 followers on Twitter.[12]

Hearing the voice of the CEO through his or her own writing, when it feels authentic, helps foster trust in an organization. Since it will be a requirement of the job for the CEO to be a blogger, expect every CXO position to also have blogging as a requirement. Does your executive team know what a blog is and how it can help them compete? Do your top three competitors' CEOs have blogs?

8. THE CORPORATE CURRICULUM WILL USE VIDEO GAMES, SIMULATIONS, AND ALTERNATE REALITY GAMES AS KEY DELIVERY MODES

Corporate training as we know it today will be transformed into a nimble, social, fun, and highly collaborative experience by 2020. Companies will rely on participatory peer-to-peer learning for at least 80 percent of all corporate learning. Some of the tools that will grow in importance include video games, simulations, and alternate-reality games to develop leadership and complex critical thinking skills. Video games, such as World of Warcraft, that are part of a category of games called massively multiplayer online role-playing games (MMORPGs), have the potential to become realistic simulators for contemporary leadership development training. These games allow players to practice a diverse set of skills, such as how to manage a culturally diverse and virtual team, promote collaborative problem solving, and analyze constantly changing data. More than 11.5 million users currently subscribe to World of Warcraft, and, as these players enter the workforce, they will increasingly expect corporate training to mimic their online experiences.

In addition to video games, companies will begin to use business simulations in which learners are asked to make a series of decisions in a given scenario and in the process improve their skills in areas such as leadership, quality, and sales. Beyond business simulations, companies will use alternate-reality games (ARGs), a type of real-world game experience where corporate training mimics their experiences online. World Without Oil is one example of an online alternate-reality game that allows players to envision a world in which the United States is cut off from oil imports. Players use a variety of media—blogs, videos, e-mails, text messages, audio clips, and mobile phones—to describe how the crisis could unfold, what to do about it, and the role energy plays in our culture and our society.[13] These alternate-reality games have a huge potential for corporate training to more fully engage participants in a highly collaborative and social experience while they learn a range of complex skills in problem solving, risk management, critical thinking, and conflict resolution.

9. A 2020 MIND-SET WILL BE REQUIRED TO THRIVE IN A NETWORKED WORLD

Employees in the 2020 workplace will communicate, connect, and collaborate with one another around the globe using the latest forms of social media. As they work in virtual teams with colleagues and collaborate with their peers to solve problems and propose new ideas for businesses, they will need to develop a new mind-set to thrive. This 2020 mind-set will incorporate abilities in:

- **Social participation.** A belief that your network is the first place you go to ask questions, seek out advice, and disseminate your expertise.
- **Thinking globally.** A capacity to think globally, have a deep understanding of how world events can impact your organization, and make decisions in ways that factor in cultural differences.
- **Ubiquitous learning.** A commitment to learning new skills and, in the process, leveraging the latest technologies that are now a pervasive part of our lives, such as mobile devices; an openness to looking for new ideas in your area of expertise; and an ability to apply new knowledge to a fast-changing set of business conditions.
- **Thinking big, acting fast, and constantly improving.** A desire to see opportunities as once-in-a-lifetime moments that must be acted upon with speed and clarity while believing in the power of continually improving beta solutions.
- **Cross-cultural power.** A conviction that embracing a diverse community of employees, customers, and consumers representing

many different backgrounds, skills, countries of origin, and ideas will result in superior business outcomes.

10. HUMAN RESOURCES' FOCUS WILL MOVE FROM OUTSOURCING TO CROWDSOURCING

Outsourcing of administrative human resource functions will drive improved business results in 2020. But HR leaders who want to be in the forefront of change will also create an innovation agenda leveraging the principles of crowdsourcing. This is a term coined by Jeff Howe, a contributing editor at *Wired* magazine and author of *Crowdsourcing: Why the Power of the Crowd Is Driving the Future of Business,* to refer to how companies such as Lego, Procter & Gamble, and Boeing use the wisdom of crowds to develop solutions for R&D problems, designs for products, and new ideas for businesses. At the heart of crowdsourcing lies a simple truth: "The most efficient networks are those that link to the broadest range of information, knowledge, and experience."[14]

Crowdsourcing will be used to reinvent human resources and corporate learning. Companies are already using crowdsourcing to create new job descriptions by inviting employees and prospective job candidates to add to them. Through this process, a company learns from the "wisdom of crowds." Corporate learning departments will similarly adopt crowdsourcing techniques to embed learning into e-coaching and e-mentoring of employees. Both human resources and corporate learning departments will shift growing portions of their budget to incorporate Web 2.0 tools and social technologies into the modes of delivery in order to drive greater collaboration in the workplace and learn from the wisdom of the crowds.

11. CORPORATE SOCIAL NETWORKS WILL FLOURISH AND GROW INSIDE COMPANIES

Corporate participation in social networks may be as critical in the 2020 workplace as managing cash flow. The essence of knowledge work is conversation, and companies will increasingly see the power of social networks to extend the reach and scale of conversations.

Companies that continue to implement total lockdowns and prevent access to social networking sites will be negatively impacted in their ability to recruit top talent. Millennials and Gen 2020 will expect and demand access to external social networks as well as the ability to use internal corporate social networks on the job. Forward-looking companies will exploit the power inherent in social networking sites to attract new employees, develop new skill sets, support and enhance team knowledge sharing, drive collaboration, and improve innovation. Corporate social networking will be used not only by current employees and customers but also by former employees. Many companies will create and manage their own corporate alumni networks as vehicles to find the best talent and recruit former employees as well as develop new business. In this networked world, building and maintaining relationships will be essential to success.

12. YOU WILL ELECT YOUR LEADER

Companies that encourage employees to elect their leader will be seen as employers of choice, especially for team-oriented Millennials and Gen 2020s. Members of both generations have grown up with a collaborative mind-set through their heavy usage of social networks and highly interactive video games such as EVE Online. Some companies are taking this a step further by experimenting with giving employees more influence in electing leaders.

Consider W. L. Gore & Associates, where senior leaders do not appoint junior leaders. Rather, associates become leaders when their peers judge them to be such. A leader gains influence by demonstrating a capacity to get things done and by excelling as a team builder. The CEO of W. L. Gore, Terri Kelly, was actually voted by her peers to become their leader when Chuck Carroll, the previous CEO, polled a cross section of employees, asking "Who would you want to follow?" This "elect your leader" mentality permeates W. L. Gore. Each team ranks every member of the team on the question "Who has made the biggest impact on the enterprise?"[15] The rankings are sorted through by a group of "contribution committees," which use the rankings as a basis for compensation. The company credits this with its low turnover rate of just over 5 percent.

While electing your leader may be viewed as just one company's experimentation in citizen leadership, it may become a strong recruiting tool for companies. Ranking and polling social media tools allow an organization to see who has a followership, a necessary quality for being a leader. Millennials who have grown up learning about the merits of collaboration and teamwork place great value on them and will seek out employers that put these principles into action.

13. LIFELONG LEARNING WILL BE A BUSINESS REQUIREMENT

The 1990s and the early years of the 2000s saw the rise of in-house, corporate-sponsored universities using a formal curriculum to develop and reskill a global workforce. In 2020 and beyond, we will see another innovation—branded lifelong learning centers—to ensure ease in continually updating one's skills for both one's current job and one's next job. Already the U.S. Army is leading the way with the Lifelong Learning Center of the Command and General Staff College. This Lifelong Learning Center, as profiled in chapter 5, incorporates a wide range of social media, such as heavy usage of blogs and wikis. One innovation stands out: Reach Back. This is a section of every online course where all alumni of the course can go back to access the most recent data on that subject. It's the Army's way of building lifelong learning into every online course.

In addition to creating lifelong learning centers, companies will increase their partnering with universities, which will now offer a range of new degree and certificate programs, some of which will be branded by celebrities. Consider that in 2010, we will see the launch of the Jack Welch MBA, a new online MBA combining Welch's philosophy of leadership and human resources into a twelve-course curriculum. What will be next? A Michael Bloomberg Certificate in Public Administration? A John Madden Certificate in Leadership

Development? Look for an increase in new online degree and certificate programs from universities, which will capture a larger share of the corporate training budget due to the growing importance of lifelong learning.

To fund lifelong learning, companies will implement 401(k)-type plans to help working adults save for continuing education. These are currently known as Lifelong Learning Accounts (LiLAs). Both employers and employees are required to contribute funds, with the provision that the employee owns the account after leaving the company. Unlike 401(k)s, LiLAs currently do not have special tax advantages. However, legislation has already been introduced to expand LiLAs and offer federal tax credits and tax breaks for these accounts in a handful of states such as California, Indiana, Iowa, Illinois, Minnesota, and Washington, and federal legislation is pending.[16] Most important, LiLAs have a huge appeal for Millennials and Gen 2020s, who are intent on continuing their education in the workplace and want to prepare not just for the jobs they currently hold but also for jobs that do not exist today. LiLAs offer these young working professionals a portable learning benefit in an era when skills become obsolete, often in as short a time span as two years.

14. WORK-LIFE FLEXIBILITY WILL REPLACE WORK-LIFE BALANCE

AOL's annual Email Addiction Survey reports that in today's 24/7 global economy, 67 percent of people check their e-mail while in bed in their pajamas.[17] Given this scenario, how do you define work/life balance? Is this still a relevant goal to aspire to? Andrés Tapia, the author of *The Inclusion Paradox*, sees a shift to flexibility rather than balance. Work/life flexibility reinforces the view that there is no such thing as work time and home time. Rather, hyperconnected workers will aspire to have the flexibility to manage both work and home lives.[18]

Work/life flexibility revolves around the ability to multitask and assign work to various chunks of time so that all of a day's priorities are accomplished, including those at work, at home, and at the gym.

In a work/life-flexible world, an employee could leave the office at 3:00 p.m., go home, prepare dinner, help the children with their homework, then go back online at 9:00 p.m., after the children are in bed and the dinner dishes are done. If you can do this and still produce results for your employer, why not? Where is the office in this scenario? It is being redefined from the single place where work gets done to all the many places where people work, collaborate, and live their lives.

One company that has led the rest in creating work/life flexibility is Best Buy with its Results-Only Work Environment (ROWE). In the results-oriented work environment, employees are free to work wherever they want, whenever they want, as long as they get their work done. Since its inception in 2002 as a pilot program, ROWE has been incorporated as an official part of Best Buy's recruiting pitch as well as its orientation for new hires. The company claims that productivity has increased 35 percent for those on ROWE, and employee engagement—which measures employee satisfaction and is often a barometer of retention—is way up too, according to a Gallup Organization survey that audits corporate cultures.[19] If people can carry their office around virtually in their pockets or pocketbooks, why should it matter where and when they work if they meet or exceed their goals?

15. COMPANIES WILL DISCLOSE THEIR CORPORATE SOCIAL RESPONSIBILITY PROGRAMS TO ATTRACT AND RETAIN EMPLOYEES

The focus on people, planet, and profits, also known as the triple bottom line, will become the main way organizations attract and retain new hires. This will be critical because 79 percent of a sample of 1,800 13- to 25-year-olds want to work for a company that cares about how it impacts on and contributes to society, as the Cone 2006 Millennial Cause Study found.[20] More than half also say they would refuse to work for an irresponsible corporation. So companies will begin to move beyond corporate philanthropy by integrating corporate social responsibility into their core business strategy and by reporting quantitative goals to current employees, prospective hires, and investors.

This is already the case in Great Britain, where the law requires companies to provide information about business goals for their corporate social responsibility programs. As one example, the annual report of National Grid, an international electricity and gas company, not only includes a review of all corporate social responsibility projects but also identifies quantitative business goals, such as achieving an 80 percent reduction in greenhouse gas emissions by 2050, deriving 15 percent of its energy production from renewable sources by 2020, and defining a global inclusion charter for the organization.[21]

But imposing a legal requirement may not be the real impetus that forces companies to report corporate social responsibility programs. The Millennials and Gen 2020s will demand companies to be socially responsible or risk losing valuable talent to competitors.

16. DIVERSITY WILL BE A BUSINESS ISSUE RATHER THAN A HUMAN RESOURCE ISSUE

The shortage of multicultural talent in the workplace will be addressed as a strategic business priority rather than as a human resources mandate or to fulfill legal obligations. When organizations see their greatest growth in new workers coming from a mix of minority job candidates, women, workers across five generations, and people from other countries, they will take steps to incorporate diversity into their business agenda.

As David A. Thomas and John J. Gabarro report in their book *Breaking Through: The Making of Minority Executives in Corporate America*, minority workers will make up close to 40 percent of the U.S. workforce by 2020, yet more than 50 percent of all executive-level positions in the United States will continue to be held by white males. The situation for working women is similar. In 2007, women made up 40 percent of the 3 billion people employed worldwide but held only 24 percent of senior management positions.[22]

But companies are seeing that developing an inclusion strategy is essential to better matching of their diverse business offerings around the world. One way to address this is to develop the talent pipeline as early as possible. The National Center for Education Statistics reports that high school graduation rates for Latinos and African Americans in the United States hover around only 60 percent. Of these graduates, only half go to college, and of this group, only 40 percent graduate—yielding an overall 10 percent college graduation rate.[23] Look for more corporate K–12 partnerships such as the ones created by Lockheed Martin for aspiring engineers and Deloitte for accountants, profiled in chapter 4, to present career options and possibilities to middle and high school age students.

17. THE LINES AMONG MARKETING, COMMUNICATIONS, AND LEARNING WILL BLUR

Marketing organizations and learning departments will enter into stronger partnerships to repackage some corporate learning programs into consumer education. These new consumer communities will be created to build stronger consumer connections to a brand and hopefully to increase consumers' loyalty and brand preference.

The consumer electronics firm Sony is already doing this with its Backstage 101, a branded consumer site that has more than a hundred interactive courses and tutorials, articles, and videos in the areas of personal computing, home entertainment, digital photography, and digital video. Users of Backstage 101 rate and review all the online courses, participate in forums and individual course discussion boards, tag other users' reviews and discussion posts, and share content on social bookmarking sites. These online courses are used as corporate training for Sony sales associates as well.[24] Look for more partnerships among heads of human resources, corporate learning officers, and chief marketing officers as corporate training programs are reimagined as consumer education online offerings and become part of the marketing/communications mix to increase market share and consumer satisfaction.

18. CORPORATE APP STORES WILL OFFER WAYS TO MANAGE WORK AND PERSONAL LIFE BETTER

As employees increasingly expect to be in control of all aspects of their lives, companies will take a page from the enormously successful iPhone App Store and create corporate app stores to help employees better manage their lives at work and at home.

Today, there are more than 100,000 iPhone apps in twenty categories, including books, business, education, finance, medical, and games. Consumers have downloaded more than two billion apps, which have generated over a billion dollars in revenue for Apple and its developers.[25] There are applications for every stage of life: iSeniors, a program designed to locate the nearest senior living centers based on your GPS location; myHomework, an application designed to help students keep track of their academic responsibilities; Diagnosaurus, a reference tool that diagnoses an illness based on its symptoms; and PetMD Dog First Aid, a medical encyclopedia for dog lovers that instructs you on how to respond to your pet's medical needs and locate the nearest veterinary clinic.

Now imagine the power of customized apps offered by an employer. On the business side, these could include an expense report app, a goal-tracking app, or a microfeedback app. On the personal side, if you are a working mother, apps could focus on the locations of day care centers, after-school programs, homework helpers, and fitness centers. Or a Millennial employee may want apps that feature opportunities to work and study abroad or learn a new language or tips on applying for a first mortgage. Customization and personalization will reign as employees both access and develop applications for managing their work and personal lives. Borrowing from Apple, the new motto of HR will be "Yes, there's an app for that!"

19. SOCIAL MEDIA LITERACY WILL BE REQUIRED FOR ALL EMPLOYEES

As organizations become über-connected and embrace a range of social media, they must ensure employees know how to use this media to collaborate, connect, and innovate in the global marketplace.

This will require Chief Human Resources Officers to partner with Chief Communication Officers and Chief Learning Officers to create training and even certification to develop social media literacy. Already Telstra, an Australian telecommunications firm, has developed a comprehensive set of social media guidelines and requires all employees to be certified on how to use social media in the workplace. Telstra calls this training in the 3 Rs: responsibility, respect, and representation. Telstra employees must be clear about who they are representing, take responsibility for ensuring any references to Telstra are correct, and show respect for the individuals and communities they interact with in the process.[26]

Here in the United States, Intel develops role-based training programs and Digital IQ certifications that licenses employees to practice social media on behalf of Intel. All these programs are under the umbrella of the Intel Social Media Center of Excellence, which push social media initiatives across the organization by creating guidelines, processes, strategies, and skill-building programs for how to be responsible and respectful using social media at work. (Intel's Social Media Guidelines are provided in chapter 5.)

In the 2020 workplace, this level of investment and training in developing social media literacy will be the norm as organizations see the power of using social media to build brands, collaborate in the workplace, and drive greater innovation throughout a company's value chain.

20. BUILDING A PORTFOLIO OF CONTRACT JOBS WILL BE THE PATH TO OBTAINING PERMANENT FULL-TIME EMPLOYMENT

Top talent in specialized skill areas will have plenty of opportunities. For the rest of us, full-time, permanent employment will start with a series of projects acquired though our social networks or through contracting agencies. Today you can bid on work on sites such as oDesk, Craigslist, and Elance, and employers can test out skills on short-term projects by using people sourced through agencies or Web sites.

By 2020, prospective employees will become more comfortable

starting with a portfolio career by working on several projects for different employers at the same time. The path to full-time, permanent employment may first include an unpaid internship, then a series of project-based assignments, obtained via social networks or through search agents gleaning Web sites for work. According to Steve Rodems, a senior partner at Fast Track Internships, a company that charges a $799 fee to help an intern find an unpaid job, "Internships are no longer the province of college students. More unemployed professionals are seeking them—whether to test drive a new career or just keep themselves occupied." Rodems continues, "Ten percent of my clients today are college graduates changing professions compared to just one percent in 2008."[27]

Cautious about repeated cycles of hiring and laying off, companies will farm out more work to be done on a contingency basis and, in so doing, test potential future employees to ensure that there is not only a fit of skills but also a cultural fit. For prospective employees, building a reputation with several companies will allow them the opportunity to select a company whose brand and culture resonates with them and thus help reduce attrition for companies. Since more people will be doing work on temporary, contracted assignments and blogging about them, building brand loyalty beyond employees will be essential for companies.

SMART COMPANIES SHOULD PLAN NOW FOR POTENTIAL WILD CARDS

What if a series of global events dramatically changes the path of those working in the 2020 workplace? Are you and your organization thinking about what course of action and what changes your organization will make in how you source, attract, reward, develop, engage, and retain employees? As you ponder the 2020 workplace, consider what you will do if the following scenarios occur:

- **There is a global lost decade in the United States** that could be similar to what happened in Japan in the 1990s, when economic expansion ground to a halt. Japan went through a long recession with serious repercussions impacting job creation, innovation, and infrastructure investment.

- **There is a political upheaval in China or India** that results in a shift in offshoring manufacturing and services to countries with stable governments, such as Costa Rica. There will be new issues in sourcing talent in these locations.
- **There are disasters** such as pandemics, terrorism, and mass climate change that will create an even greater focus on teleworking, a retreat from investments in corporate real estate, and a migration to all forms of virtual work.
- **There is a breakthrough in longevity** as predictions of a life span of 100 years come true for a large percentage of the population. This will have significant implications on the workforce, as the five generations we have been writing about will stay in the workforce longer.
- **There is more emphasis on intelligence augmentation.** As technological tools become more sophisticated, they will be able to draw upon simulations and massive data sets to help us become smarter and suggest new areas in which to update our skills or target new job opportunities.

Each wild card presents a new set of challenges and opportunities for human resource leaders in how they adjust their talent management, employee engagement, reward and recognition, and learning and development practices.

The 2020 workplace will be fluid, diverse in age and ethnicity, flexible, collaborative, mobile, global, and, above all, hyperconnected. Get ready to live it. But how can you prepare? In the final chapter, we will look at some ways you can begin to implement both short-term and long-term solutions to the issues your organization will face in 2020 and beyond.

CHAPTER NINE

Get Ready for the Future Workplace

Balancing the short term with the long term is a perennial challenge in business, especially in extraordinary economic conditions. To balance the strategic with the here and now, we offer some suggestions on how to get started now to prepare for the future workplace. Did you ever leave the first day of a job or a degree program and have the sinking feeling that you were in over your head? At times we have seen that look on people we have talked to about the changes we expect they will face in the future workplace. So we would like to make a few suggestions on how you can begin to define, invent, and prepare for the future.

In the last decade, outsourcing human resources appeared to be the wave of the future. It was thought that outsourcing HR would provide efficiencies via specialized suppliers, and HR would then be free to customize benefits and perform more strategic work. Unfortunately, however, the focus moved to cost reduction, and the savings realized were quickly applied to the bottom line rather than to drive innovation. It is not unusual at HR conferences to hear people discussing a lost decade of advancement in people-related practices or at least lamenting not gaining as much forward momentum as predicted.[1] How long will it be possible to have such dramatic changes in the marketplace and remain largely stagnant in the field of HR? Product teams that fail to deliver innovation and an ability to compete end up with existing products that are milked for cash, and a vicious decline begins with no cash for reinvestment. Why should HR be any different? As long as we deliver no innovation, no way to compete more aggressively in the marketplace, and no tangible ways to distinguish the employer brand, HR may well become irrelevant.

But there is hope. Just as marketing has been reinvented by the ability to connect with customers via social media, so too can HR use this moment in time to introduce innovation and change. We believe that human resources has the potential to craft change in organizations, should its leaders choose to exercise it. We have identified some initiatives and capabilities HR can initiate, some skills individuals can develop to get ready for the 2020 Workplace, and some ideas for staff development. Of course, the capabilities any organization, function, or person needs must be suited to each individual situation, so we provide the following lists as a way to begin the dialogue and kick-start your imagination.

INITIATIVES HUMAN RESOURCES CAN SPEARHEAD
1. Adopt a global mind-set.
2. Build a reputation as being socially responsible.
3. Become über-connected.
4. Personalize the employee experience.
5. Enable customer-focused innovation.
6. Champion openness and transparency.
7. Emphasize learning agility.
8. Build citizen leadership.
9. Drive systems thinking.
10. Create an inclusive culture.

INITIATIVES HUMAN RESOURCES CAN SPEARHEAD

One of the simplest definitions of corporate culture is "the way we do things around here." People who share common beliefs and assumptions in an organization, whether stated or not, are described as fitting into the culture. To build a culture that will enable performance at the highest levels in the 2020 workplace, HR should initiate the following now in order to get ready:

1. Adopt a global mind-set.

Develop an organizational capacity to work with a geographically dispersed set of employees, customers, partners, and suppliers from diverse cultures across time, space, geographies, and organizational boundaries.

There is a difference between multinational and global; any number of companies have offices around the world and more people outside than inside their home country.[2] As the author and politician Aimé Césaire wrote, "It is a good thing to place different civilizations in contact with each other; that whatever its own particular genius may be, a civilization that withdraws into itself atrophies; that for civilizations, exchange is oxygen."[3] Likewise, a company that withdraws into itself atrophies, for cultural exchange is vital to understanding the market.

But being truly global is evidenced by developing talent in-country to lead the organization and not relying extensively on expatriate assignments. How many of your current executives live in the countries where you do business? Is the number of native executives proportional to the revenue of those countries? If your organization is like many others, far more executives live in the headquarters country and key decisions are frequently made thousands of miles away from customers. Ask yourself: How many of your senior executive team are from the countries where you are experiencing growth? One of the keys here is to consider how long it takes to build talent, especially in emerging markets, where the talent pool may be less experienced, and compare that to your organization's revenue growth plans in emerging markets.

To address these challenges, a growing number of companies are creating opportunities for individual contributors to experience working outside their home country early in their careers. A number of benefits will ensue. For example, not only will individual contributors who experience a global assignment improve their global awareness but there will be a greater probability that they will consider a localized assignment in the future. And for employees living in countries outside the HQ country, an assignment to HQ can accelerate their professional development.

At a minimum, there is an increased likelihood that global companies will be based outside the United States, as shown in chapter 1, so how well your organization prepares for this will be a critical success factor.

Get started now. Evaluate your global leadership mix; encourage early career global assignments. Ensure that promotions to executive positions reflect the global makeup of your customer and revenue base.

2. Build a reputation for being socially responsible.

Develop a commitment to stewardship and balance of people, profits, and the planet.

As discussed in chapter 3, being socially responsible is essential to building a brand that future employees will trust. Indeed, many organizations are well on the path to corporate social responsibility (CSR). Although shareholders may one day mandate a balance sheet that reports on the triple bottom line—people, profits, planet—typically it is the annual report or separate CSR report that covers an organization's commitment to being socially responsible.

The United Nations Global Compact on Corporate Accountability is a good reference document for reporting on corporate social responsibility.[4] At least two industries—the garment and electronics industries—have taken the lead in collaborating across their respective supply chains to create a common standard for reporting on corporate social responsibility. Companies can and should join forces with others in their industry and supply chain to create a standard format for how to report on corporate social responsibility.

Get started now. Issue a CSR report as an addendum to the shareholders' annual report. Ensure that your organization's commitment to CSR is clear, quantitative, and inspiring. Look for guidance from publicly traded companies in Great Britain, where there is a legal mandate to report on corporate social responsibility.

3. Become über-connected.

Develop advanced corporate communications using a range of social media, blogs, wikis, communities of practice, and online corporate social networks to connect employees, enable mass collaboration, and improve your company's capability to innovate in the global marketplace.

In chapter 5 we laid out the five stages of über-connection. But you may wonder: what is the right level of connection to match your corporate culture and business strategy? What does your workforce age diversity look like now, and what will it look like as you approach the 2020 workplace? If your organization will be hiring early-career employees, expect them to use social media, with or without your permission. If your growth plans include global expansion, look for ways to connect employees, whether through high-quality telecommunications, such as video conferencing, or by connecting with individuals via social networking. If your research funds are limited, consider using open innovation strategies to involve people passionate to your products in generating ideas. You can also start with adding one social media tool—such as a wiki for prework and follow-up in an executive development program. This was the path taken by CLO Teresa Roche and her team at Agilent Technologies when they wanted to test using social media in corporate learning.

Get started now. Conduct a social media boot camp. Find out how the marketing function is using social media to reach its customers. Use some of the platforms to enable a two-way dialogue with your employees. Hire Millennial interns to work with your organization to draft a plan for using social media to connect employees.

4. Personalize the employee experience.

Develop a systematic and automatic capability to deliver a unique, tailored experience by offering a wide range of choices so that employees can self-select benefits and services to match their unique needs.

As organizations become more globally dispersed, virtual work becomes the norm and teams are formed and dissolved rapidly. Employees' bonds to an organization become more tenuous. But companies can create a personalized employee experience as a way to retain the best talent.

Just as people can pick the applications that they want on their computers, phones, and MP3 players to match both their work and life needs, so too should HR begin to consider how to individualize the existing one-size-fits-all approach to employees. In a sense, the goal is to create solutions that can be personalized across the organization by each individual—not to require the organization to personalize to each individual. This can start with assigning a dollar value to every benefit, giving employees an allowance to spend, and then letting employees configure their plans as they wish. Although companies frequently do this now with health benefits, we advocate spreading it to a much broader set of benefits, including additional vacation time, learning allowances, coaches, productivity tools, and more.

Think of this as employee benefit consumerism. Employees will enter companies and be given a benefits credit card. Those who are willing to take a lower salary may have an option to select more vacation days or alter the mix between their base and bonus pays. At first these programs can start in a narrow range with limited risk. For example, some companies already allow people to purchase additional vacation days, and others allow individuals to donate vacation days to those who have family emergencies. Clearly, this kind of approach will require transparency as to the costs of each benefit, but it will also enable employees to understand their true total compensation— a dollar figure much higher than most employees realize now.

Just as the Web is advancing in its semantic capabilities with intelligent agents that actively seek information, an organizational mind-set that enables the collection of information geared to the specific context of an individual will become increasingly important. Even now it would be relatively easy for HR to design a questionnaire to ask employees to consider what is important to them and suggest benefits accordingly. It is technologically possible now to design computer agents to suggest options to employees, based on other options they have chosen or other factors, such as desired retirement age, dependents' status, educational goals, etc.

HR leaders have talked about customization of the employee experience for well over a decade.

Semantic Web: Also known as Web 3.0, the semantic Web refers to the evolution of intelligent computer agents that can learn and adapt content specific to the user.

Although there have been some advances in cafeteria-style benefits, largely legal concerns have limited the innovation that is possible from a technical perspective.

Get started now. Create internal directories with pictures; advance to social networking platforms to encourage further personalization. Work with the IT function to allow employees to select their own desktop equipment and tools within a range of parameters. Evaluate the facilities and office policies of the company. Instead of having space determined by level, is there a way to allow people to opt for the space they would find most productive, within a fixed budget allowance? Create a policy regarding telecommuting, including guidelines to assist employees in setting up home offices.

5. Enable customer-focused innovation.

Thinking of innovation in terms of the budget spent on research and development is an antiquated view of the world. A wealth of wisdom exists in the marketplace about your products and services. Expand the thinking of your employees to consider how to tap into the ideas of others.

What ideas and thoughts do the people who face customers every day hold in their heads that may not be transferred to those who design the products and services? What knowledge does finance or HR have about what is inhibiting innovation across the organization or even in just one area? All those in an organization can contribute to a shared pool of knowledge from which innovation can flow, if only they are given an opportunity.

Get started now.   Encourage open innovation across all functions. Hold a company Idea Jam on a specific issue, and invite everyone to attend who wants to. We shared how this worked for Bell Canada in chapter 5. Create a public space to allow your customers and others to offer ideas. Ensure that someone from product development monitors, gleans, and synthesizes the ideas.

6. Champion openness and transparency.

Develop a bias toward full disclosure of the thought process leading to decisions that matter to the organization.

The strongest message that leaders of an organization can send is through their own behavior. If it is important to them to make good decisions and to know the impact of those decisions, opening up a level of transparency about decisions is essential. Gary Hamel advocates for "permission to hack," by which he means allowing employees to identify the weak points of a decision in order to make it stronger.[5] Admittedly, employees who hack away at decisions won't always have the full picture, and they might not always be gentle in their critiques. However, if leaders have the maturity and confidence to tolerate the bad with the good and to allow people to second-guess their decisions, the quality of decisions in the organization will increase dramatically.

Best Buy found that opening up the process of revenue prediction and other key management decisions led to more accurate forecasts—a classic example of the wisdom of the crowds. Using a form of internal market called Tag Trade, all the employees at Best Buy have the opportunity to trade imaginary stocks based on answers to managers' questions, such as how well a new product would sell in its first month. The results on Tag Trade have frequently been more accurate than the company's official forecasts.[6] A more traditional mind-set might have been that even discussing revenue forecasts with more than 100,000 employees would disclose proprietary and confidential information. Yet at the time of this writing, Best Buy is one of the few retailers that appear to be weathering the economic storm that started in 2008.

Get started now. Create a forum that outlines a major decision or strategy the company is considering; allow employees to react and offer their ideas.

7. Emphasize learning agility.

Develop an ability at the organization level to acquire new knowledge and skills across functions to adapt to a changing environment.

Karl Deutsch, a twentieth-century social and political scientist, warned about the threat of dominance in society, which can hold true for organizations as well. "In simple language, to have power means not to have to give in, and to force the environment or the other person to do so. Power in this narrow sense is . . . the ability to talk instead of listen. In a sense, it is the ability to afford not to learn."[7] Learning agility is not only about intelligence; humility, curiosity, and intent are also necessary ingredients.

Think of all the changes that have occurred in your own organization over the last five years. Did the competitive landscape change? Did your customers change their buying patterns? Were there significant changes in leadership? In what ways did the overall economic landscape and regulatory environment affect your business? If yours is like most organizations, the answers to those questions will indicate that there has been dramatic change. Some organizations have been able to respond quickly to these changes; others now line the bankruptcy benches of courtrooms. Building learning agility is not an overnight fix. We have covered some of the ways to unleash learning in an organization through the creation of social networking platforms that allow the sharing of knowledge. The example of PwC in chapter 7 is an excellent one in building a set of practices to retrain leaders and intact teams on how to use the working environment as a learning laboratory.

Get started now. Insist on learning reviews after every major customer win or loss to determine causal factors and to build a common understanding for the next customer proposal. On 360-degree surveys, include a write-in question for leaders, such as: When you think of what "best in class" could be for someone doing my job, what do you think that would look like? How would it be different from what I'm doing now?

8. Build citizen leadership.

Develop a pervasive approach that reinforces the principles of openness and democracy through access to information and social collaboration in order to deliver sustainability and integrity within the society in which the organization operates.

The 2020 leader will have to move beyond the hierarchical Frederick Taylor style of management that has been the main model for more than a hundred years. The marketplace is too complex, and conditions are changing too rapidly, for organizations to rely on cumbersome and antiquated forms of leadership and management. The John Chambers and Cisco Systems transformation described in chapter 7 is an example of the first stages of changing the management structure of a business.

Journalism is facing a historic crisis with the emergence of citizen journalists, and power has shifted from media companies to these citizen reporters. In much the same way, company leadership will be transformed by citizen leaders who are vocal about what direction they believe the company should take in order to be successful.

A citizen leader will recognize that interdependencies exist at all levels, both inside and outside the organization, and that enabling the entire organization to collaborate in nontraditional ways will accelerate its market responsiveness. A citizen leader bears in mind the ways in which the organization holds a responsibility not only to profits but also to the people of the organization and stewardship of the planet. Harmony between leadership and management, with innovation needed in both, is essential to success as a citizen leader.

Get started now. Evaluate your leadership competency model and ensure that it is so unique to your organization that no other company would have that same model. Test that the leadership brand conveyed by your model has appeal across generations. Ensure that the model goes beyond leadership to integrate with your expectations for management. Prepare for the advent of citizen leaders just as the successful media companies have; embrace their technologies and style. Ensure that your leadership team is blogging, and begin opening two-way dialogues about important decisions.

9. Drive systems thinking.

Design and connect systemically across functions and bodies of knowledge, understanding their interdependencies, to gain a competitive advantage at the organizational level.

The essence of systems thinking is to understand how structures and processes work together to create specific outcomes. Thinking in this way allows for the identification of the underlying causes of recurring problems. The more complex the decision, the more likely there are interactions across functions and perhaps even companies.

One example, an electronics company, demonstrates how systems thinking can improve operations. The shipping department was measured on both on-time deliveries and truck efficiency, meaning as close to full loads as possible. Since there were no quality measures, the shipping department started loading the trucks with empty boxes, thus literally achieving the metric for truck efficiency. A systems view would have worked backward from what customers wanted, and not only would it not have included shipping empty boxes, it might have indicated a whole new model for making microshipments.

A good question to ask when faced with what may appear to be counterproductive employee behavior is this: why would a reasonable, rational person act this way?[8] By giving employees the benefit of the doubt, you can begin to work backward from that question to understand the underlying system(s) that may be rewarding their behavior.

Get started now. Require an evaluation of similar decisions in the past as part of presentations of current projects. Include one systems diagram when evaluating a complex decision. Review the objectives, goal sheets, or playbooks for each major function in the organization. Rather than thinking about the performance and expectations of each unit, step back and look at how the whole fits together. Where could objectives actually work against each other? Are people's rewards tied to overall success across a sustainable set of objectives? Fortunately, a number of courses, newsletters, and books are available on this topic. Peter Senge is the best known in this area; you can read content authored by him and others at www.solonline.org.

10. Create an inclusive culture.

Build a welcoming corporate environment and employer brand that are sensitive to culture, ethnicity, race, age, and other differences and that provide equitable access to opportunities, products, and services for employees, suppliers, and customers.

As your customers become more global and more diverse, the need to respond with products and services that match their needs will differentiate growth companies from stagnant ones. How well does the makeup of your employee base match that of your customers? Does your senior leadership team also reflect your customer base? When it comes to decision making in the organization, are diverse and divergent views encouraged or merely tolerated?

Innovation thrives on a diversity of ideas. If you want innovation, you need a diverse set of contributors whose ideas are heard. Are those voices heard now?

Get started now. Arrange to be reverse-mentored by someone as different from you as possible. At the organizational level, put some teeth into the people review process to ensure not only that diverse candidates are considered but that final decisions end up reflecting the overall employee population of the company. Sponsor organizations and events that promote diversity and inclusion.

THREE CAPABILITIES FOR HR

1. Bold innovators
2. Executive whisperers
3. Thumb tribe members

SKILLS FOR HUMAN RESOURCES LEADERS IN THE FUTURE

As Margaret Mead said, "Never doubt that a small group of thoughtful, committed individuals can change the world. Indeed, it's the only thing that ever has."[9] Beginning with you and spreading to your team and like-minded friends and colleagues, you have the power to change. To develop the leaders of the future, here are three capabilities HR can focus on:

1. Bold Innovators

Bold innovators create centers of excellence in adopting new and advanced technologies and approaches to engage employees.

In some companies, the legal department has so sensitized HR to risk that caution and risk avoidance have set the tone for policies regarding employees. We have seen employee communications in one company get to the point that nearly every letter sent to all employees included a phrase that termination would result if the policy were not followed.

We are not advocating putting a company at risk, but we are suggesting that it might be time to ask how real the risk is and whether the potential rewards of innovation might outweigh the risk. What is the greatest innovation breakthrough you have introduced in HR in the last decade? If that question is hard to answer, maybe it's time you push the envelope.

Get started now. Pick one policy that prohibits employees from some action, such as accessing external social networks or going negative on vacation balances. List the pros and cons, and for the cons, identify the likelihood of actualized risk and the costs associated with it. Is a policy in place to prevent abuse by less than 1 percent of the anticipated employee population? Remember, in the example of social networks, if someone is determined to release confidential information, they can already do so through e-mail. What productivity gains could the benefits provide?

2. Executive Whisperers

Executive whisperers encourage advanced communication and influence of skills at the executive level, obtained through a trusting partnership.

Like a horse whisperer, who has an extraordinary ability to understand the language of horses in order to train them, HR executives will need to develop a finely honed ability to listen to, understand, and guide business executives. Getting to this level requires understanding the language of business and therefore is far beyond the goal of a "seat at the table."

The development plan of any high-potential HR junior executive should include job rotation to include ownership of a line business unit. Building an advanced ability to hold critical conversations and influencing abilities are also essential to becoming an executive whisperer.[10] The language of business is essential to communicating with executives, and working in a nonstaff role will provide a way to learn it.

Horse whisperers go beyond understanding the language of horses, though. Through gentle persuasion, they retrain the horse to a specific set of behaviors or actions. Likewise, executive whisperers influence an executive to take action in a way that will increase the organization's ability to succeed through its people.

Get started now. Read *Influencer: The Power to Change Anything* by Kerry Patterson et al.[11] Keep a log during leadership meetings of key words that seem to emerge over and over. What do those tell you about the language of the leaders? How can you learn to speak that language while influencing the leaders toward a position that will help the organization succeed in the future?

3. Thumb Tribe Members

Thumb tribe members use various forms of social technologies to create and disseminate knowledge and expertise.

Anyone of any age can become literate in social media and therefore become a member of the thumb tribe. (Our own personal ongoing transformations, from Baby Boomers to members of the thumb tribe, have confirmed that it is possible to learn to think, act, and communicate in the new ways that will be necessary for 2020.) Your ability to expand your network and your reputation capital will depend entirely on your ability to build relationships in the virtual world. Learning the language is one of the best ways to adapt to life in another country. If you want to work successfully in the 2020 workplace, you must begin learning the language of social media now. The pace of innovation in social technologies is not slowing down, so the longer you delay it, the larger the challenge of adaptation will become.

If you think you don't have time to learn these skills, rethink the meaning of work/life balance. Consider what gives you energy and what depletes your energy.[12] Look for ways to contribute and stay connected that reinforce you, whether at work or through your friends or your communities. We are social beings. Use the tools available to stay connected to the people and issues that matter to you.

Get started now. Identify one online community that matters to you deeply, whether it is work-related or not. Commit to staying in touch by making daily visits to that community for at least one month. There are courses available to get up to speed on the use of social media, and YouTube has an amazing number of videos that will teach you many of the tools. To determine which tools to use in your organization, some you should be personally comfortable with are:

SOCIAL MEDIA TOOLS YOU NEED TO DEVELOP
- RSS feeds
- Personalized portals

- Blogs
- Rating/tagging
- Video uploads
- Mobile device capabilities
- Social networking
- Instant messaging

- **RSS feeds.** At a minimum, get the feeds from your favorite newspaper, columnist, or blog. The benefit of using RSS feeds is that you do not have to actively go to a variety of Web sites to ensure that you are updated. You can read these feeds on a specialized reader (also called an aggregator), in your e-mail, or online on your personalized portal.
- **Personalized portals.** Google and Yahoo! both offer the ability to personalize your home page, as do many Web sites. Select some RSS feeds, widgets for local weather, a financial portfolio tracker (include your competitors), a couple of newspapers, and some blogs of your favorite thought leaders.
- **Blogs.** To give you a sense of how pervasive blogging is, some kindergarteners are now required to create a blog in order to graduate. Go to www.howtostartablog.org for some tips on how to get started.
- **Rating/tagging.** Start reading and rating content on your favorite Web sites. Add tag words to help other people find the content.
- **Video uploads.** Create a short video about one of your favorite topics or hobbies, perhaps showing a shortcut or tip you've learned. To learn how, go to your favorite search engine and search for "how to upload video to YouTube."
- **Mobile device capabilities.** To be truly mobile, you need to understand the full potential of the computer you carry with you every day—your mobile device. If you don't have a mobile device such as a smart phone, tablet, or netbook, get one now. If you have an iPhone, download five applications for your phone and use them.[13]

- **Social networking.** Create a Facebook account. Friend at least twenty-five people. Check in to your account every day for at least three months. You'll be surprised at how much you learn about what your colleagues and friends (and maybe even your children!) are doing. If you set up a profile and don't use it daily, you won't understand how powerful social networking can be and how it can one day replace e-mail entirely.
- **Instant messaging.** Set up an instant messaging account. Your company likely already has a tool available. Find two colleagues who will agree to be online at the same time as you for one hour a day, two to three times a week. After you are comfortable with it, ask a colleague to IM with you during a vendor meeting or a teleconference call.

NEW SKILLS FOR YOUR TEAM

NEW SKILLS FOR YOUR TEAM
1. Social connector
2. Talent scout
3. Talent development agent
4. Capability planner
5. A globally savvy team

Finally, we take a look at the skills and capabilities that should be developed at the staff level in HR, including new job categories, to adapt to the workplace of the future. To achieve success in the workplace of the future, your team must include one or more of the following:

1. Social Connector
An enabler and cultivator of networks and communities within an organization.

Most of the organizations we have discussed in this book needed a boost when first establishing their social networks. Encouraging connection and collaboration can be one of the key contributions that HR makes to a business. We believe a whole new set of job titles will emerge in HR, such as:

- **Community gardener.** Like a brand manager at eBay, a person assigned to help build a vibrant online community.
- **Futurist.** A person who envisions not only where the profession is headed but where the organization is headed and the implications for the people resources of the company.
- **Places planner.** A person who integrates facilities, IT, and HR to ensure that on-site, virtual, and collaboration sites are conducive to conducting business in the new world.
- **Chief technologist.** Instead of relying on an IT business partner, this person will build a highly technical capability within HR to identify the systems and tools needed to deliver a personalized experience. This position will be supported by widget makers, who will develop gadgets for inclusion into a personalized portal.
- **People capability planner.** A person who takes a step beyond workforce planning to match the skills that will be required by the organization in the future with a plan to develop people accordingly.

Get started now. Start by building a network of HR professionals on either a public or a private tool. If it is public, even through a password-protected site such as Ning, ensure that the policies about what can be posted are clear. Appoint a high-potential individual to garden the community. Conduct an audit to determine where the most value could be derived by connecting people in other functions, and start the influencing process with the leaders of those groups.

2. Talent Scout

A professional who identifies talent before the need arises, using both virtual and real-world methods.

Like sports talent scouts, company talent scouts will develop ways to measure emerging talent at earlier and earlier stages in their careers and will begin to build relationships with identified talent long before a specific need emerges in the organization.

Talent scouts not only will look for new talent but will also be on the lookout for experienced players who are ready to make a move and free agents available for short seasons or to integrate into the team in the long term. The building of these personalized relationships will start out almost exclusively online, using virtual methods, and so will require a strong skill set in social media. Good talent scouts will be measured by the size of their networks and the speed and success of their placement.

Get started now. Ensure that your organization has a solid Web presence for candidates. Begin recruiting on social networks, especially LinkedIn, Facebook, and virtual worlds.

3. Talent Development Agent

An individual with the ability to identify and develop not only high potentials but also to provide access to development opportunities for the self-motivated.

IBM has a form all employees must complete annually on the subject of their personal business commitments. The form contains a section on what each employee commits to learning over the coming year, enabling a conversation between the manager and the employee. HR and learning created the tools and process, allowing the conversation with each employee to be personalized.

HR will also need to find ways to accelerate development of talent by encouraging stretching experiences. Millennials are not going to have as much time to get ready for leadership positions as the last two generations did, so providing both formal and informal accelerated learning opportunities will become essential.

Get started now. Use the range of tools provided by Web 2.0 media—such as podcasts, teleconferencing, and vlogs—to connect your employees with learning opportunities. Use reverse mentoring to give high potentials early access to leaders.

4. Capability Planner

An individual who takes a companywide workforce-planning view of the skills and abilities needed to compete in the marketplace, both now and in the future.

In the future, workforce planning and learning will be more concerned with helping a business determine exactly what capabilities are needed for the next tasks, jobs, or roles on a massive scale. Anticipating the future and building the skills required will create an advantage over companies that must constantly replace employees whose skills no longer match the organization's needs.

Which is cheaper: hiring people who may not fit the culture or equipping existing employees with new skills? This is where a longer-term view can justify the development of people, since the return on investment for people development typically cannot be accomplished within a single quarter.

Get started now. Identify areas of the organization that have terminated employees and hired others at about the same rate. What are the skills gaps, and what programs are in place in that function or business unit to develop current employees? Calculate the costs over a two-year period of termination, recruiting, orientation, and making them productive, along with the dropout rate of new hires. Is there a case for a stronger development program to build the skills needed now and in the future?

5. A Globally Savvy Team

All members of the HR team should have the ability to think beyond their home countries to encompass a worldwide appreciation of cultures and differences, should have a deep understanding of how world events can impact the organization, and should make decisions in ways that optimize cultural differences.

Building a global company requires having employees who are globally savvy. You may have staff members who would be willing to live on an in-country compensation package as opposed to an expensive expatriate plan, just for the experience. How many people on your direct staff and their staffs are from countries outside the headquarters' location?

Get started now. If you have the opportunity, spend some time living outside your home country or take a short-term assignment in another location, and enable as many of your staff as possible to do the same. At a minimum, travel outside your home country on vacation or by donating your time to charitable causes. Sponsor your staff members to learn another language and include it on their development plans.[14] Hold one staff meeting a year in a location where there are a number of company employees—not necessarily in a desirable vacation spot. Create assignments for your team to meet with local employees both inside and outside work as part of the agenda.

FACING IN TWO DIRECTIONS

Like the Roman god Janus, we stand in the present facing in two directions: honoring the past and anticipating the future. We understand the pressures of living in the present, but we hope that by offering some thoughts on what the future can look like, we can help you looking both into the past for lessons and into the future for hope. Preparing for the future is best accomplished by shaping it oneself. You must build a personal capability to be ready for what comes your way and help others envision the future so they start to get ready now. By doing so, we believe, you will be able to build a sustainable organization and a renewable people capability to compete in the global marketplace. You might just find it the most rewarding experience of your life.

ACKNOWLEDGMENTS

A book is a reflection of a social network. More than two years ago, while having only worked briefly together when Jeanne worked at Accenture and consulted at Sun Microsystems, we met for dinner in Boulder, Colorado. There we discovered we were both passionate about how people can use technology to connect to one another around the globe and across generations while also getting work done in more innovative ways. Having faith in each other's reputations, we decided to write a book and then faced a task that seemed at the time almost as daunting as climbing the Flatiron Mountains we could see from the restaurant.

To climb the mountain of information and stories we needed for this book required that we reach to the edges of our mutual networks. Like mountaineers who rely on agents, guides, and base camp support, we relied on this support system for our journey. The connection agents were the people whose work brought them into contact with many forward-thinking companies interviewed in this book; the guides acted as experts deep within a field who live on the edge of the social Web and gave us a glimpse into the future; and our base camp support was made up of the people who provided us with the tools we needed to make this climb.

We are indebted to the many agents who reached across their own social networks and experiences to guide us toward the companies

interviewed in this book. These include Jessica and Dan Parisi of
BTS; Kevin Alansky and Patrick Devlin of Blackboard; Doug Sharp,
Dan Miller, and Don Duquette of GP Worldwide; Susan Burnett of
Yahoo!; Mark Greiner of Workspring; Shelley Rees of JWT; Carole
France of Oliver Wyman; David Miller of Duke Corporate Edu-
cation; Ranjani Iyengar of Hewitt Associates; Izzy Justice of EQ
Mentor; Ed Lawler and John Boudreau of USC's Center for Effective
Organizations; Tony Bingham of ASTD; Kevin Oakes of i4CP; Jim
Cornehlsen; R. J. Heckman of PDI; David Stein of Rypple; Elliott
Masie; Josh Bersin; Judy Issokson; Ashish Goyal of Cisco; Paul Casa-
nova of Sun; DeAnne Aguirre of Booz & Company; Courtney Tim-
mons and Bjorn Billhardt of Enspire Learning; Chris Browning and
Randy Emelo of Triple Creek; Dr. Gale Tenen Spak of New Jersey
Institute of Technology; Karen Kocher of CIGNA; Peter Norlin of
the OD Network; Jennifer Schram of SHRM; Scott Saslow of the
Institute for Executive Development; Melyssa Nelson of Executive
Networks; Asim Talukdar and Vijay Thadani of NIIT; and dozens of
other people who gave us a lead when we asked the question "Who
do you know that is doing interesting work using the social Web in
HR and learning?"

The process of writing this book forced each of us to learn about
emerging technologies and how the world of work is going to change
over the next decade. One person we went to over and over again was
Charles Beckham, the chief technology officer of Sun Learning Services, who helped us see how the shift in consumer technologies was
already being adapted to the workplace. Hal Stern of Sun has one of the
most futuristic minds on the planet and helped to edit the opening of
chapter 1. Brandon Carson pushed us to think about how games, simulations, and the need for people to connect socially will be the future
of the workplace, while Kelly Palmer and Joe Campbell demonstrated
how successful these strategies can be while leading groups at Sun.
Rick Von Feldt, our business partner, reminded us to identify global
examples of innovation in using the social Web for human resources
and learning as well as provided valuable input in reading the first
draft of this book. Sharon Matthews of eLynx provided insight into

the minds of Baby Boomer executives wrestling with the new world of social media. Jennifer Shepherd and Leslee Guardino of Canyon Snow Consulting advise companies on CSR every day, and their thought leadership has been insightful. Diane Hessan of Communispace and Jay Bryant of Live World were both instrumental in showing us how innovations in using social media in consumer marketing were soon to happen in the fields of HR and learning. Thanks as well to the many people who were excited about the book and sent us articles, book recommendations, and links to emerging content, such as Pamela Tate of CAEL, Frank Slovenec of JBK, Jenny Dearborn of Hewlett-Packard, Pat Johnson of ePluribus, Stacy Palestrant of Katzenbach & Partners, Beat Meyer of UBS, and JoAnn Kisling of Sun.

Determined to use the tools of the social Web ourselves, we signed up at BasecampHQ.com to keep track of all critical content and then quickly created our own base camp team. This was led by Lea Deutsch, our amazingly efficient, highly knowledgeable, and hardworking Millennial research assistant. She not only was our window into the world of what Millennials want from employers but also could magically find resources on the Web within seconds. She kept us on track for all our interviews, edited content posted to BasecampHQ.com, and did all this while managing the thousands of details and tasks that go into a project this size. Oliver Dyla set up an external collaboration site for us, and Brenda Roberts assisted with creating the global panel of working professionals. Steve Messer and Curt Hutton conducted our global survey, and Jon Frye helped us analyze the results using SPSS. Terri Walker and Leah Thrush managed schedules and calls at all times of day and night. Without this support team, we would never have finished the climb.

This journey would have been over quite quickly if John Willig, our agent, had not offered solid feedback on our proposal and used his social network to connect us to an interested publisher. We want to sincerely thank our editor, Matt Inman of HarperCollins, who, as a Millennial, added enormous insight into the structure and themes of the book. His thinking had a major impact on the evolution of the book, and he is proof that great talent lives in every generation.

As always, Bob Meister read every word in the book, many times out loud, while Jeanne made changes in real time. Thank you for this and for so much more.

Finally, we started this process as collaborators with a shared vision of how the social Web is changing every aspect of our personal and professional lives. Over the course of the past two years we have used social media to learn a new way of working, learning, and collaborating. We hope you enjoy our journey and that you will visit the book Web site at www.the2020workplace.com.

GLOSSARY OF SOCIAL MEDIA TERMS

The Web 2.0 World

Affiliate **Aggregation** Asynchronous Communication Archive Avatar **Blog** Blogosphere Blogroll **Collaborative Software** Communities of Practice **Web Content** Crowdsourcing **Dashboard** Entry Forums Friends Instant Messaging Lurkers Mash-ups **Message Boards** Metadata Microblogging MMORPG Newsreader Open-Source Software **Photo Sharing** Podcast Post **Profile** RSS Feed **Social Bookmarking** Social Indexing Social Media **Social Networking** Tag Cloud **Tag Thumb Tribe** User-Generated Content **Virtual Community** Virtual World Vlog **Voice over Internet Protocol** Web 2.0 Wiki

Affiliate Partnership sites that link to one another. Affiliate sites generally share similar interests, products, or services.

Aggregation The process of collecting content from blogs and Web sites via an RSS feed. The results may be displayed by a Web site or may be downloaded directly to your computer using software designed for that purpose.

Asynchronous communication Communications that occur independently of time and place. Internet applications that allow for asynchronous communication include e-mail lists, message boards, and forums.

Archive An index page that organizes previous posts or entries by category or date.

Avatar A graphical representation of a person in a virtual world such as Second Life. An avatar may be an accurate representation of an actual individual, or it may be a fanciful and mythical alter ego.

Blog An individual or group online Web log maintained with regular entries on the subject of the contributors' choosing. Posts are usually displayed with the most current appearing first, and readers are allowed to comment on individual posts.

Blog hub An aggregated directory of blogs making it easy to search and find blogs related to a specific topic, or blogs from the same company.

Blogosphere A term used to describe the entire interconnected world of blogs and bloggers.

Blogroll A list of sites displayed in the sidebar of a blog. Blogrolls can be used to display affiliate sites, and thus often have a similar interest, product, or service.

Collaborative software Software that allows individuals in diverse physical locations to work together over the Internet on the same documents or projects in real time.

Communities of practice Forums in which professionals gather to share best practices or work together to solve problems. The new capabilities provided by social networking tools are perfectly suited to support the creation and maintenance of communities of practice, both within organizations and across industries.

Community moderator Someone who keeps the momentum going in an online group or forum. Community moderators often introduce subjects for discussion and then work to keep people on topic in their follow-up comments.

Content contributors Individuals who add comments and a point of view to an online discussion or blog.

Corporate social network A Web site behind a company's firewall that allows users to construct a profile they use to interact with others using social media tools such as messaging, journaling, photo sharing, tagging, and searching.

Crowdsourcing Harnessing of the skills of individuals through an open call for participation. These individuals, due to their enthusiasm, contribute content, do research, and solve problems together.

Dashboard An administrative area of a Web site that allows an individual to post items, monitor usage, upload files, manage comments, and more.

Entry An individual post on a blog. Each entry is actually a Web page of its own.

Forums Also known as message boards; Web sites where visitors are able to have discussions asynchronously by posting messages.

Friends On social networking sites, contacts whose profiles are linked. To "friend" an individual is to request to link his or her profile with yours.

Global citizenship Involves understanding how to conduct business in a foreign country, developing an increased cultural intelligence and a deeper appreciation of the relationship between business and society, and being able to understand complex policy environments and how to work in virtual teams with people from all over the world.

Instant messaging Chatting synchronously with another person or other people via text messages. Popular programs include AOL Instant Messenger (AIM), MSN Messenger, and Skype Chat.

Lurkers Individuals who follow discussions occurring in chat rooms, message boards, or blogs but who do not post comments or otherwise interact themselves.

Mash-up A Web application combining data or tools from more than one source into a single interface.

Massively multiplayer online role-playing game (MMORPG) A genre of role-playing game in which a large number of players interact in a virtual world. World of Warcraft is the largest and probably best-known example of an MMORPG, with more than 11 million subscribers.

Media sharing sites Web sites designed to facilitate the sharing of various text-, image-, and film-based media. Some well-known examples include YouTube and Hulu.

Message boards Also known as forums; Web sites where visitors can leave messages, start topics, and have general discussions asynchronously.

Metadata Description of a data file. Often this can include information about a file's size, type, creation date, and other data.

Microblogging A sibling of blogging that consists of sending short messages (140 characters or less) to a group of followers. The best-known example is Twitter.

Newsreader A Web site or desktop tool that collects news from Web sites, blogs, podcasts, and vlogs using RSS feeds so the content can be accessed all at once.

Open-source software Computer software whose source code is available to be modified and to be redistributed, if desired, in modified form. Open-source software is often developed collaboratively.

Photo sharing Uploading images to a Web site that organizes and displays them for you. On photo-sharing Web sites, one can add tags and offer other individuals the opportunity to view and comment on photos.

Podcast A series of audio files distributed on the Web via syndicated download. New podcast content is downloaded automatically once it is available and then can be transferred to a mobile device such as an iPod. The most common audio file format is MP3.

Post An entry on a blog, forum, or other Web 2.0 site.

Profile The information an individual provides about him- or herself on a social networking site. A profile generally includes a picture and some basic personal information.

RSS feed A Web publisher feature that allows readers to subscribe to view posts from a frequently updated Web site without visiting the site itself. RSS stands for "really simple syndication." RSS feeds collect the posts and push them to the reader through an e-mail update or an RSS reader, or to a custom portal.

Semantic Web Also known as Web 3.0; the evolution of intelligent computer agents that can learn and adapt content specific to the user.

Social bookmarking Sharing one's favorite or bookmarked Web sites on a public Web-based service. These sites often leverage a social network to allow one to find and to share these lists. A popular social bookmarking site is Delicious.

Social indexing The process of individuals' tagging, or adding keywords, to media they encounter on the Web, whether text-, photo-, video-, or audio-based.

Social learning Learning that is collaborative, immediate, relevant, and presented in the context of an individual's unique work environment.

Social media Social media is a range of Web 2.0 tools such as blogs, wikis, and RSS feeds by means of which people create and disseminate content. Using social media is often called the democratization of knowledge, since it can transform people from passive consumers of content into active contributors when they write posts, comment on others' posts, share content, and query others to create new knowledge.

Social networking The act of participating on a Web site that allows users to construct a profile to interact with others. Social networking sites allow people to connect with one another using social media tools such as blogging, messaging, journaling, photo sharing, tagging, and searching.

Social recruiting A practice that leverages social and professional networks, both online and offline, from both a candidate's perspective and the hiring side, to connect to, communicate with, engage, inform, and attract future talent.

Social Web The cluster of Web 2.0 tools, such as blogs, wikis, and social networks, that drive community building and collaboration.

Synchronous communications Communications that occur simultaneously and in real time. Internet applications that allow for synchronous communication include instant messaging and audio or video chats.

Tag cloud A visual representation of the popularity of a category. The more often a tag is used, the larger the typeface with which it is displayed.

Tag A keyword or term assigned to a piece of content by the author or reader/contributor. Tags describe the item informally and without the use of rigid categories, enabling an item to have many descriptions and thus making easier to search and find. Collaborative tagging is sometimes referred to as a folksonomy, as opposed to a rigid taxonomy.

Thumb tribe A translation of the Japanese word *oyayubizoku*; refers to people who communicate using social media tools on their mobile device.

User-generated content Text, photo, video, and audio content published by individuals on the Web.

Virtual community A group of individuals who gather in social spaces on the Web to share ideas about a common interest via e-mail, blogs, message boards, and/or chat rooms.

Virtual world An online simulated world in which an individual can create a visual representation of him- or herself, called an avatar, and can interact with others in real time.

Vlog A blog that consists of video posts rather than text posts.

Voice over Internet protocol A telecommunications system that enables individuals to make free computer-to-computer calls, including conference calls.

Web 2.0 A term used to describe Web technology combined with social interaction, such as blogs, wikis, and social networking sites. These Web sites are dynamic and interactive, as opposed to static Web 1.0 sites.

Web content Text, pictures, sound, and video posted on the Web; any of the components of materials that can be found on the Internet.

Wiki A page or collection of pages designed to allow anyone with access to contribute or modify content. Wikis are edited collaboratively. The term is derived from the Hawaiian word meaning "quick."

GLOSSARY OF WEB 2.0 RESOURCES

Timeline of Web 2.0 Resource Introduction

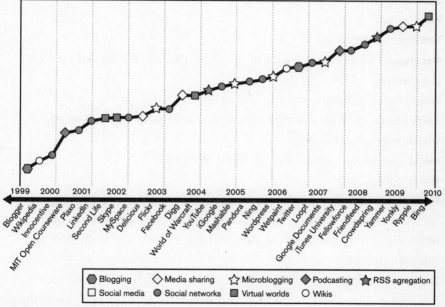

Source: Future Workplace.

Bebo The sixth largest social network in the world, according to comScore, owned by AOL and especially popular in the U.K, Ireland, and New Zealand.
www.bebo.com

Bing Microsoft's search engine.
www.bing.com

Blogger A Web site providing an online service where users can create and customize their own blogs, free of charge.
www.blogger.com

Crowdspring A Web site where individuals can get artists from around the world to contribute designs for a project.
www.crowdspring.com

Delicious A popular social bookmarking site.
www.delicious.com

Digg A social news site where users submit content that is then rated by the community. The content with the most positive ratings, or "diggs," rises to the top.
www.digg.com

eCademy An online networking service for business contacts, events, and groups.
www.ecademy.com

Facebook The largest social network in the world, according to comScore.
www.facebook.com

Fellowforce A Web site that connects talent with organizations.
www.fellowforce.com

Flickr An image- and video-sharing Web site.
www.flickr.com

Friendfeed A social media feed aggregator; allows users to aggregate services such as Twitter, Flickr, and personal blog posts on one platform. Users subscribe to one another's feeds and comment on posted content.
http://friendfeed.com

Friendster The fourth largest social network in the world, according to comScore, with 90 percent of its members from Asia.
www.friendster.com

Google Docs A Web-based office suite that allows users to collab-oratively edit documents in real time; offers word processing, spreadsheet, presentation, and other capabilities. All documents created with Google Docs are stored centrally on the Web. http://docs.google.com

Google Maps An application from Google that, in addition to point-to-point mapping and direction services, can be used to map other forms of data, such as real estate data or restaurants. http://maps.google.com

HI5 The third largest social network in the world, according to comScore, especially popular in Latin America. www.hi5.com

iGoogle A customizable start page. Allows users to add "gadgets" that range from RSS feeds of popular news outlets or blogs to weather and stock information. www.igoogle.com

iTunes University A feature present in Apple's iTunes software through which faculty at a wide variety of universities can distribute digital lessons and podcasts of their courses. www.apple.com/education/mobile-learning

Last.fm An Internet radio and music community. Keeps track of listening behavior and connects users with people who have similar tastes. www.last.fm

LinkedIn A business-oriented social network. www.linkedin.com

Loopt A mobile social mapping application that can display the current locations of a user's social network using mobile phones and mobile devices. www.loopt.com

Mashable A large Internet news blog that carries news about a variety of topics from social networking sites to emerging start-ups. http://mashable.com

MIT Open Courseware A project from the Massachusetts Institute of Technology in which the materials used in virtually all of MIT's courses are made available on the Internet, free of charge. http://ocw.mit.edu

MySpace The second largest social network in the world, according to comScore.

www.myspace.com

My Yahoo! A customizable start page. Allows users to add "gadgets" that range from RSS feeds of popular news outlets or blogs to weather and stock information.

my.yahoo.com

Ning An online service for creating, customizing, and sharing a social network.

www.ning.com

Orkut The fifth largest social network in the world, according to comScore. Owned by Google, it is especially popular in India and Brazil.

www.orkut.com

Pandora An Internet radio and music community; keeps track of your listening behavior and allows you to create radio stations tailored to your tastes.

www.pandora.com

Plaxo An online service to connect your contacts.

www.plaxo.com

QQ The most popular instant messaging program in China.

www.qq.com

Rypple A Web-based peer review tool that enables colleagues to give one another feedback.

www.rypple.com

Second Life A virtual world accessible via a free program that enables users to interact with one another through avatars.

www.secondlife.com

Skype A popular program that allows users to make free computer-to-computer phone calls and video calls over the Internet. Skype can also be used as an instant messaging service.

www.skype.com

Twitter A microblogging service through which users communicate in short messages called "tweets" that are limited to 140 characters.

www.twitter.com

Wetpaint A free wiki-hosting service.
www.wetpaint.com

Wikipedia A popular community-generated encyclopedia whose content is edited and added to by the community at large.
www.wikipedia.org

Wordpress An online service where users create and customize their own blogs, free of charge.
www.wordpress.com

World of Warcraft A massively multiplayer online role-playing game (MMORPG) with more than 11.5 million subscribers.
www.worldofwarcraft.com

Yammer A microblogging service that caters to business users; only individuals with the same e-mail address domain can join a given network.
www.yammer.com

Yonkly A microblogging service on which users can create their own customized microblogging interface.
www.yonkly.com

YouTube A video-sharing Web site where users upload, view, and share video clips. Content ranges from commercial movie and TV clips to user-generated content.
www.youtube.com

NOTES

INTRODUCTION: THE 2020 WORKPLACE
1. Michael Kanelios, "18th-Century Theory Is New Force in Computing," *CNET News*, February 18, 2003, http://news.cnet.com/2009-1001-984695.html (accessed June 12, 2009).
2. Elizabeth L. Axelrod, Helen Handfield-Jones, and Timothy A. Welsh, "The War for Talent, Part Two," *McKinsey Quarterly*, May 2001, www.mckinsey quarterly.com/The_war_for_talent_part_two_1035 (accessed May 29, 2009).
3. World Health Organization, "The World Health Report 2004—Changing History: Annex Table 4," www.who.int/whr/2004/annex/en/index.html (accessed May 29, 2009).
4. Charlene Li and Josh Bernoff, *Groundswell: Winning in a World Transformed by Social Technologies* (Boston: Harvard Business Press, 2008).
5. Marc Prensky, "Digital Natives, Digital Immigrants," *On the Horizon 9*, no. 5 (October 2001).
6. William C. Taylor and Polly LaBarr, *Mavericks at Work: Why the Most Original Minds in Business Win* (New York: HarperCollins, 2006).

CHAPTER 1: TEN FORCES SHAPING THE FUTURE WORKPLACE NOW
1. Serendipity is under development at MIT; see http://reality.media.mit.edu/ser endipity.php. Celebrity City and Cisco virtual world contacts are fictionalized, but augmented reality contacts are under development, using nanotechnology, at the University of Washington under Babak Parviz; see www.ee.washington.edu/faculty/parviz_babak.
2. "Shifting Workplace Demographics and Delayed Retirement," www.microsoft.com/enable/aging/demographics.aspx (accessed May 14, 2009).
3. Ibid.
4. Don Tapscott, *Grown Up Digital: How the Net Generation Is Changing Your World* (New York: McGraw-Hill, 2009).

5. Catherine Rampell, "As Layoffs Surge, Women May Pass Men in Job Force," *New York Times*, February 6, 2009, www.nytimes.com/2009/02/06/business/06women.html (accessed May 14, 2009).

6. Robert Rodriguez, *Latino Talent: Effective Strategies to Recruit, Retain and Develop Hispanic Professionals* (Hoboken, N.J.: John Wiley & Sons, 2008).

7. W. David Delong, *Lost Knowledge: Confronting the Threat of an Aging Workforce* (New York: Oxford University Press, 2004), 14.

8. Fareed Zakaria, *The Post-American World* (New York: W.W. Norton & Company, 2008), 196.

9. Ibid., 197.

10. Rich Morin, "Most Middle-Aged Adults Are Rethinking Retirement Plans," Pew Research Center Publications, May 28, 2009, http://pewresearch.org/pubs/1234/the-threshold-generation (accessed August 12, 2009).

11. Kelly Evans and Sarah E. Needleman, "For Older Workers, a Reluctant Retirement," *Wall Street Journal*, December 8, 2009, http://online.wsj.com/article/SB126022997361080981.html?mod=igoogle_wsj_gadgv1& (accessed December 9, 2009).

12. Rampell, "As Layoffs Surge, Women May Pass Men in Job Force."

13. Maria Shriver, "The Shriver Report: A Women's Nation Changes Everything," edited by Heather Boushey and Ann O'Leary, The Center for American Progress, October 16, 2009, www.americanprogress.org/issues/2009/10/womans_nation.html (accessed November 26, 2009), 17.

14. "A National Dialogue: The Secretary of Education's Commission on the Future of Higher Education," www.ed.gov/about/bdscomm/list/hiedfuture/reports/equity.pdf (accessed November 30, 2009).

15. Bradford C. Johnson, James M. Manyika, and Lareina Yee, "The Next Revolution in Interactions," *McKinsey Quarterly* 4 (2005), 25.

16. Daniel Pink, *A Whole New Mind: Moving from the Information Age to the Conceptual Age* (New York: Riverhead Books, 2005), 39.

17. Thomas Friedman, *The World Is Flat: A Brief History of the Twenty-first Century* (New York: Farrar, Straus, and Giroux, 2005), 17.

18. Karl Fisch, Scott McLeod, and Jeff Brenman, "Did You Know 3.0," www.youtube.com/watch?v=cL9Wu2kWwSY (accessed May 14, 2009).

19. "FT Global 500, 2008," www.ft.com/reports/ft5002008 (accessed December 18, 2008).

20. "FT Global 500, 2005 - 2009," www.ft.com/reports/ft500-2009 (accessed November 27, 2009).

21. Niraj Sheth and Nathan Koppel, "With Times Tight, Even Lawyers Get Outsourced," November 26, 2008, http://livinglies.wordpress.com/2008/11/26/keep-those-motions-defenses-affirmative-defenses-notice-letters-counterclaims-and-complaints-coming-banks-are-feeling-the-pinch (accessed May 15, 2009).

22. Elizabeth Kelleher, "Work Is Changing as U.S. Companies Go Global," September 17, 2007, www.america.gov/st/peopleplace-english/2007/September/20070917165019berehellek1.978701e–02.html (accessed June 29, 2009).

23. Paul Teague, "P&G Is King of Collaboration," September 11, 2008, www.allbusiness.com/company-activities-management/operations/11683043-1.html (accessed November 30, 2009).

24. "Procter & Gamble Revolutionizes Collaboration with Cisco TelePresence," www.cisco.com/web/about/ac79/docs/wp/Procter_Gamble_Final.pdf (accessed November 30, 2009).

25. John Gantz, *The Diverse and Exploding Digital Universe* (Hopkinton, Mass.: EMC² Publications, 2008).

26. Ibid., 5.

27. www.facebook.com/press/info.php?statistics (accessed May 15, 2009).

28. Bret Swanson, "An Exabyte Here, An Exabyte There . . ." October 3, 2007, www.disco-tech.org/2007/10/an_exabyte_here_an_exabyte_the.php (accessed June 17, 2009).

29. Adam Bohannon, "Negotiating Identity in Internet Mediated Contexts" (paper submitted to Sun Microsystems, March 31, 2008), 4. Provided to authors via email.

30. Gantz, *The Diverse and Exploding Digital Universe.*

31. Central Intelligence Agency. *The World Factbook: United Kingdom.* Updated November 11, 2009. ww.cia.gov/library/publications/the-world-factbook/geos/uk.html (accessed November 27, 2009).

32. Randall Stross. "What Carriers Aren't Eager to Tell You About Texting," *New York Times,* December 26, 2008, www.nytimes.com/2008/12/28/business/28digi.html (accessed November 27, 2009).

33. Richard Wray. "UK Dotcom Tycoons Take On Apple with iPhone Competitor," *Guardian,* February 12, 2007, www.guardian.co.uk/technology/2007/feb/12/news.mobilephones (accessed August 13, 2009).

34. Angel Brady, "Free Spanish Tutor: Free iPhone/iPod Touch App from 24/7 Tutor," February 24, 2009, https://blogs.princeton.edu/hrc/2009/02/free-spanish-tutor-free-iphoneipod-touch-app-from-247-tutor.html (accessed June 18, 2009).

35. Thom Patterson, "Welcome to the 'Weisure' Lifestyle," CNN.com, May 11, 2009, www.cnn.com/2009/LIVING/worklife/05/11/weisure/index.html (accessed May 15, 2009).

36. Michael Sanserino, "Lawsuits Question After-Hours Demands of Email and Cellphones," *Wall Street Journal,* August 10, 2009, http://online.wsj.com/article/SB124986371466018299.html (accessed August 10, 2009).

37. Jacques Bughin, Michael Chui, and Andy Miller, "McKinsey Global Survey Results: How Companies Are Benefiting from Web 2.0," September 2009, www.mckinseyquarterly.com/links/35889 (accessed November 29, 2009).

38. Nortel Networks, "Position Paper: Hyperconnectivity Leads to Enterpise Transformation," 2008, www.nortel.com/solutions/unified_communications/collateral/nn123307.pdf (accessed February 25, 2010).

39. Socialtext, "6 Ways to Get Business Value from Social Software," www.socialtext.com/products/wp_businessvalue.php (accessed February 25, 2010).

40. Charlene Li and Josh Bernoff, *Groundswell: Winning in a World Transformed by Social Technologies* (Boston: Harvard Business Press, 2008), 9.

41. Scott Cook, "The Contribution Revolution: Letting Volunteers Build Your Business," *Harvard Business Review,* October 2008, http://hbr.harvardbusiness.org/2008/10/the-contribution-revolution/ar/1 (accessed November 1, 2009).

42. Ibid.

43. Gary Koelling, "Breaking It Down for Internal Communicators," January 30, 2008, http://garykoelling/?q=node/370.

44. Toru Iiyoshi and M. S. Vijay Kumar, *Opening Up Education: The Collective Advancement of Education Through Open Technology, Open Content, and Open Knowledge* (Cambridge, Mass.: MIT Press, 2008), xv.

45. Ibid.

46. Carolyn Hirschman, "Launching New Leaders," *Human Resource Executive*, August 2008, 43.

47. PricewaterhouseCoopers, "Managing Tomorrow's People," September 2008, www.pwc.com/gx/en/press-room/2008/human-capital-managing-people.jhtml (accessed November 30, 2009).

48. Don Tapscott, *Grown Up Digital: How the Net Generation Is Changing Your World* (New York: McGraw-Hill, 2009), 11.

49. Ibid., 6.

50. Ibid., 34–36.

CHAPTER 2: MULTIPLE GENERATIONS @ WORK

1. Rich Morin, "Most Middle-Aged Adults Are Rethinking Retirement Plans," Pew Research Center Publications, May 28, 2009, http://pewresearch.org/pubs/1234/the-threshold-generation (accessed August 12, 2009).

2. M. Z. Hemingway, "Wanted: Baby Boomers," *Federal Times*, September 15, 2007, www.federaltimes.com/index.php?S=2483622 (accessed December 18, 2008).

3. Ibid.

4. Ron Alsop, *The Trophy Kids Grow Up: How the Millennial Generation Is Shaking Up the Workplace* (San Francisco: Jossey-Bass, 2008).

5. Ibid., 4.

6. Tom Brokaw, *The Greatest Generation* (New York: Dell, 1998).

7. Don Tapscott, *Grown Up Digital: How the Net Generation Is Changing Your World* (New York: McGraw-Hill, 2009), 13.

8. Ibid., 14.

9. Rhea, "The Boomer Chronicles," www.thegeminiweb.com (accessed December 18, 2008).

10. Tom Peters, "The Brand Called You," *Fast Company*, August 1997, www.fastcompany.com/magazine/10/brandyou.html (December 3, 2009).

11. Tapscott, *Grown Up Digital*, 17.

12. Ibid.

13. Alison Macleod, "Generation Y: Unlocking the Talent of Young Managers" (London: Chartered Management Institute, 2008), 6.

14. PricewaterhouseCoopers, "Managing Tomorrow's People," September 2008, www.pwc.com/gx/en/managing-tomorrows-people/future-of-work/download.jhtml?WT.ac=mtp-future-hp-panel-2 (accessed November 27, 2009).

15. Ibid.

16. Ibid.

17. Carleen Hawn, "Time to Play, Money to Spend," March 23, 2007, http://money.cnn.com/magazines/business2/business2_archive/2007/04/01/8403359/index.htm (accessed December 21, 2008).

18. CTIA–The Wireless Association® and Harris Interactive, "Teenagers: A

Generation Unplugged," September 12, 2008, www.ctia.org/advocacy/research/index.cfm/AID/11483 (accessed December 17, 2009).

19. PricewaterhouseCoopers, "Managing Tomorrow's People."

20. Gary Curtis, Kelly Dempski, and Catherine Farley, "Does Your Company Have an IT Generation Gap?," *Outlook*, January 2009, www.accenture.com/Global//Research_and_Insights/Outlook/By_Issue/Y2009/YourCompanyIT GenerationGap.htm.

21. Ibid.

22. Adam Lashinsky, "Google Wins Again," CNN.com, January 18, 2008, http://money.cnn.com/2008/01/18/news/companies/google.fortune/index.htm (accessed January 29, 2008).

23. Donna Nebenzahl, "Managing the Generation Gap," Canada.com, www.canada.com/business/Managing+generation/1356792/story.html (accessed November 27, 2009).

24. Ibid.

25. Joyce Grillo, "Gen Y: How Millennials Are Changing the Workplace," *Diversity Executive*, May 10, 2009, www.diversity-executive.com/article.php?article=636 (accessed November 17, 2009).

26. Ibid.

27. PricewaterhouseCoopers, "Managing Tomorrow's People."

CHAPTER 3: PRINCIPLES OF 2020 ENGAGEMENT

1. William H. Macey and Benjamin Schneider, "The Meaning of Employee Engagement," *Industrial and Organizational Psychology* 1 (February 2008), 3–30.

2. Edgar Schein, *Organizational Culture and Leadership* (San Francisco: Jossey-Bass, 1992).

3. Gary Hamel, *The Future of Management* (Boston: Harvard Business School Press, 2007).

4. Ibid., 113.

5. Paul Hawken, Amory Lovins, and L. Hunter Lovins, *Natural Capitalism: Creating the Next Industrial Revolution* (New York: Back Bay Books, 2008).

6. Jessica Stillman, "Is Bad Corporate Governance to Blame for the Economic Mess?," BNET.com, December 16, 2008, http://blogs.bnet.com/bnet1/?p=773 (accessed September 10, 2009).

7. "Former Employees Live Life After Enron," *All Things Considered*, National Public Radio, January 30, 2006, www.npr.org/templates/story/story.php?storyId=5179137 (accessed November 30, 2009).

8. Libby Sartain, "The New Global Talent Marketplace," keynote address, 10th annual meeting of the SHRM Foundation Though Leaders Retreat, Rancho Mirage, Calif., September 22–23, 2008.

9. Kristin Weirick, "The Power of Employer Branding to Attract and Retain Talent," keynote address, 10th annual meeting of the SHRM Foundation Thought Leaders Retreat, Rancho Mirage, Calif., September 22–23, 2008.

10. Henri Tajfel and John C. Turner, "The Social Identity Theory of Group Behavior," in *Psychology of Interpersonal Relations*, vol. 2, ed. Steven Worchel and William G. Austin (Chicago: Nelson-Hall, 1985), 7–24.

11. "Qualcomm Careers—Life & Culture," www.qualcomm.com/careers/students/life.html (accessed December 20, 2008).

12. PricewaterhouseCoopers, "Managing Tomorrow's People," September 2008, www.pwc.com/gx/en/managing-tomorrows-people/future-of-work/download.jhtml?WT.ac=mtp-future-hp-panel-2 (accessed November 27, 2009)

13. "Corporate Social Responsibility," http://en.wikipedia.org/wiki/Corporate_Social_Responsibility (accessed December 21, 2008).

14. Sankar Sen and C. B. Bhattacharya, "Does Doing Good Always Lead to Doing Better? Consumer Reactions to Corporate Social Responsibility," *Journal of Marketing Research*, May 2001, 225–243.

15. "What Is 10,000 Women?," www.10000women.org/what.html (accessed December 20, 2008).

16. Ibid.

17. "Wireless Reach," www.qualcomm.com/citizenship/wireless_reach/index.html (accessed December 20, 2008).

18. "Intuit Operating Values," http://about.intuit.com/about_intuit/operating_values (accessed December 20, 2008).

19. "Corporate Social Responsibility," www.cisco.com/web/about/citizenship/index.html (accessed December 20, 2008).

20. "City Year," www.cityyear.org (accessed December 20, 2008).

21. "It's Time to Feel Better," CIGNA, http://itstimetofeelbetter.com/know_stuff/understanding_the_system.html (accessed December 20, 2008).

22. Freerice.com donates ten grains of rice through the United Nations World Food Programme for every correct answer to questions in the fields of art, chemistry, math, and so on.

CHAPTER 4: SOCIAL RECRUITING EMERGES

1. Kevin Smith, "Guest Post: 'How I Got My Job Through Twitter,'" Marketing Profs Daily Fix, March 12, 2009, www.mpdailyfix.com/2009/03/guest_post_how_i_got_my_job_th.html (accessed December 17, 2009).

2. Jobvite, "2009 Social Recruitment Survey Results," June 2009, www.jobvite.com/Recruiting/2009-Jobvite-Social-Recruitment-Survey.pdf (accessed November 27, 2009)

3. Michael Rendell et al., "Millennials at Work: Perspectives from a New Generation," PricewaterhouseCoopers, September 2008, www.ukmediacentre.pwc.com/imagelibrary/downloadMedia.asp?MediaDetailsID=1341 (accessed November 29, 2009).

4. PricewaterhouseCoopers, "Managing Tomorrow's People," September 2008, www.pwc.com/gx/en/press-room/2008/human-capital-managing-people.jhtml (accessed November 30, 2009).

5. "The Deloitte U.S. Firms Pre-College Outreach Program," Deloitte Talent Market Series, Volume 4, www.wstantonsmith.com/ICMFiles/Biofiles/PublicationFiles/Publication_4.pdf.

6. Ann Marie Chaker, "High Schools Add Classes Scripted by Corporations," *Wall Street Journal*, March 6, 2008, 1.

7. Ibid.

8. Ibid.

9. "The Green Dot," www.youtube.com/DeloitteFilmFest#p/search/0/id0uHBuhXtY (accessed December 8, 2009).

10. See www.youtube.com/KPMGGo.

11. Andrew Lipsman, "comScore Finds That 'Second Life' Has a Rapidly Growing and Global Base of Active Residents," May 4, 2007, www.comscore.com/press/release.asp?press=1425 (accessed February 24, 2009).

12. Kathleen Schalch, "Virtual Recruiting for Real-World Jobs," August 22, 2007, www.npr.org/templates/story/story.php?storyId=13851345 (accessed February 24, 2009).

13. Simone Brunozzi, "How I Got Hired by Amazon.com," May 22, 2008, www.brunozzi.com/en/2008/05/22/how-i-got-hired-by-amazoncom (accessed February 24, 2009).

14. Chantal Eustace, "VPD: Virtual Police Department," *Vancouver Sun*, May 29, 2007, www2.canada.com/vancouversun/news/story.html?id=0c37d98d c54f-44d3-9e72-0c19cf828565&k=56002 (accessed February 24, 2009).

15. Adam Ostrow, "Twitter Now Growing at a Staggering 1,382 Percent," Mashable, March 16, 2009, http://mashable.com/2009/03/16/Twitter-growth-rate-versus-facebook (accessed June 29, 2009).

16. Don Tapscott, *Growing Up Digital: The Rise of the Net Generation* (New York: McGraw-Hill, 1998), 228.

17. Ibid.

18. Amol Bengali, "The Latest WorkAsia Research Study by Watson Wyatt Worldwide," April 22, 2008, www.ayaanbayaan.com/?p=1435 (accessed February 24, 2009).

19. Tammy Erickson, "Parent-Approved Recruiting," *BusinessWeek*, October 8, 2008, www.businessweek.com/managing/content/oct2008/ca20081010_082535.htm (accessed February 28, 2009).

20. "SelectMinds Client Study Reveals the Financial Contributions of Corporate Social Networking Solutions," *Market Wire*, October 22, 2007.

21. Katherine Spencer Lee, "The Value of Corporate Alumni Social Networks," April 28, 2006, www.cioupdate.com/career/article.php/3602391/The-Value-of-Corporate-Alumni-Networks.htm (accessed September 10, 2009).

CHAPTER 5: ÜBER-CONNECT YOUR ORGANIZATION

1. Amanda Lenhart et al., "Adults and Social Network Websites," Pew Internet & American Life Project, December 2008, www.pewinternet.org/Reports/2009/Adults-and-Social-Network-Websites.aspx (accessed April 20, 2009).

2. Sarah Perez, "How to Reach Baby Boomers with Social Media," February 20, 2009, www.readwriteweb.com/archives/how_to_reach_baby_boomers_with_social_media.php (accessed April 20, 2009).

3. Jeremiah K. Owyang, "How to Reach Baby Boomers with Social Technologies," www.forrester.com/Research/Document/Excerpt/0,7211,46294,00.html (accessed August 12, 2009).

4. www.facebook.com/press/info.php?statistics (accessed June 3, 2009).

5. Nielsenwire, "Social Networking's New Global Footprint," March 9, 2009, http://blog.nielsen.com/nielsenwire/global/social-networking-new-global-footprint (accessed June 28, 2009).

6. Dave Rosenberg, "Social Networks, Blogs More Popular than E-mail," CNET.com, March 19, 2009, http://news.cnet.com/8301-13846_3-10200669 62.html (accessed April 20, 2009).

7. Nielsenwire, "Social Networking's New Global Footprint."
8. "Did You Know 4.0," http://www.youtube.com/watch?v=6ILQrUrEWe8 (accessed December 17, 2009), and from Brand Infiltration, www.brandinfiltration.com.
9. Max Chafkin, "The Customer Is the Company," *Inc.*, June 2008, www.inc.com/magazine/20080601/the-customer-is-the-company.html (accessed June 28, 2009).
10. Eric Edelstein, "How Big Is the Threadless Community?" January 2009, www.ericedelstein.com/2009/01/15/how-big-is-the-threadless-community (accessed November 28, 2009).
11. Chafkin, "The Customer Is the Company."
12. Bill Taylor, "John Fluevog: Ideas with Sole—In Tough Times, Tap the 'Hidden Genius' of Your Customers," http://blogs.harvardbusiness.org/taylor/flatmm/fluevog-video-transcript.pdf (accessed November 1, 2009).
13. Ibid.
14. Carrie Kozlowski, "Hi Choice Vanny," www.fluevog.com/files_2/open-source-chosen-choice.html (accessed April 20, 2009).
15. "Starbucks," http://en.wikipedia.org/w/index.php?title=Starbucks&oldid=298810229 (accessed June 28, 2009).
16. Michael Gray, "Starbucks Recipe for Social Media Success," May 14, 2009, www.dirjournal.com/articles/starbucks-social-media (accessed May 29, 2009).
17. "Ideas in Action Blog," http://blogs.starbucks.com/blogs/customer/default.aspx (accessed November 29, 2009).
18. "Starbucks," http://twitter.com/STARBUCKS (accessed January 18, 2010).
19. "Dunkin' Donuts," http://twitter.com/Dunkindonuts (accessed January 18, 2010).
20. "IBM," http://en.wikipedia.org/w/index.php?title=IBM&oldid=299067612 (accessed June 28, 2009).
21. "Bell Canada," http://en.wikipedia.org/w/index.php?title=Bell_Canada&oldid=298858531 (accessed June 27, 2009).
22. "Cerner," http://en.wikipedia.org/w/index.php?title=Cerner&oldid=282837799 (accessed April 9, 2009).
23. "JetBlue Airways," http://en.wikipedia.org/w/index.php?title=JetBlue_Airways&oldid=298379006 (accessed June 24, 2009).
24. "Nokia," http://en.wikipedia.org/w/index.php?title=Nokia&oldid=298892344 (accessed June 29, 2009).
25. Jack Ewing, "Nokia: Bring On the Employee Rants," *BusinessWeek*, June 22, 2009, www.businessweek.com/magazine/content/09_25/b4136050146630.htm (accessed December 17, 2009).
26. Rosta Farzan, Joan M. DiMicco, and Beth Brownholtz, *Spreading the Honey: A System for Maintaining an Online Community* (New York: ACM, 2009).
27. Ibid.
28. Charlene Li and Josh Bernoff, *Groundswell: Winning in a World Transformed by Social Technologies* (Boston: Harvard Business Press, 2008).
29. Noam Cohen, "Care to Write Army Doctrine? If You Have ID, Log Right On," *New York Times*, August 14, 2009, www.nytimes.com/2009/08/14/business/14army.html (accessed August 16, 2009).
30. Ibid.

31. Lieutenant General William Caldwell, "Learning from the Sacrifice of Others," Combined Arms Center Blog: Reflections by Frontier 6, July 13, 2009, http://usacac.leavenworth.army.mil/BLOG/blogs/why_i_serve/archive/2009/07/13/learning-from-the-sacrifice-of-others.aspx (accessed August 16, 2009).

32. Cohen, "Care to Write Army Doctrine?"

33. Jacques Bughin, Michael Chui, and Andy Miller, "McKinsey Global Survey Results: How Companies Are Benefiting from Web 2.0," September 2009, www.mckinseyquarterly.com/links/35889 (accessed November 29, 2009).

34. Ibid.

35. "Companies and Social Networks: Losing Face, a Tale of Two Airlines and Their Facebook Fiascos," *Economist*, November 6, 2008, www.economist.com/business/displaystory.cfm?story_id=12566818 (accessed April 20, 2009).

36. "Intel Social Media Guidelines," www.intel.com/sites/sitewide/en_US/social-media.htm (accessed November 28, 2009).

CHAPTER 6: THE SOCIAL LEARNING ECOSYSTEM

1. Norimitsu Onishi, "Thumbs Race as Japan's Best Sellers Go Cellular," *New York Times,* January 20, 2008, www.nytimes.com/2008/01/20/world/asia/20japan.html. In six months, the list changed from the top ten novels to the top five.

2. Peter Lyman and Hal R. Varian, "How Much Information?," October 27, 2003, www2.sims.berkeley.edu/research/projects/how-much-info-2003 (accessed June 24, 2009). The metrics for measuring the amount of information are highly debated, but there is widespread agreement that in most fields, knowledge generation is accelerating.

3. Ibid.

4. Robert Kelley, "Robert Kelley's Longitudinal Study with Knowledge Workers," www.kelleyideas.com (accessed December 3, 2009).

5. Malcolm Gladwell, *Outliers: The Story of Success* (New York: Hachette, 2008). Also see K. Anders Ericsson, Michael J. Prietula, and Edward T. Cokely, "The Making of an Expert," *Harvard Business Review*, July 2007, http://hbr.harvardbusiness.org/2007/07/the-making-of-an-expert/ar/1 (accessed December 3, 2009).

6. Center for Workforce Development, *The Teaching Firm: Where Productive Work and Learning Converge* (Newton, Mass.: Education Development Center, 1998).

7. This IBM case study is adapted with permission from a research report created by Bersin & Associates: Chris Howard, "Integrating Learning into the Enterprise: A Look at the IBM Enterprise Learning Portal," January 2008.

8. "Deloitte Announces $300 Million Investment in Its People," *Chief Learning Officer*, June 30, 2008, www.clomedia.com/industry_news/2008/June/3041/index.php (accessed March 3, 2009).

9. Anya Kamenetz, "Celebrity Calamity: A Game That Teaches Finance Through Stardom," *Fast Company*, February 18, 2009, www.fastcompany.com/blog/anya-kamenetz/green-day/help-im-celebritys-budgeter (accessed March 3, 2009).

10. Ibid.
11. Michael Schrage, *Serious Play: How the World's Best Companies Simulate to Innovate* (Boston: Harvard Business School Press, 2000).
12. EQMentor exchanges provided by Izzy Justice, CEO, EQMentor, Inc.
13. William C. Taylor and Polly G. Labarre, *Mavericks at Work: Why the Most Original Minds in Business Win* (New York: HarperCollins, 2006).
14. Clay Shirky, *Here Comes Everybody: The Power of Organizing Without Organizations* (New York: Penguin, 2008) 14.

CHAPTER 7: ACCELERATED LEADERSHIP
 1. Marshall Goldsmith, "The Long View," *Training + Development*, May 2008, 81; www.astd.org/NR/rdonlyres/E85805C9-8C2D-462D-880E-BA8F 1CAE634D/16659/76080580.pdf (accessed November 18, 2009).
 2. Jennifer Reingold, "Meet Your New Leader," *Fortune*, November 14, 2008, 146.
 3. Gary Hamel and Bill Breen, *The Future of Management* (Boston: Harvard Business School Press, 2007), 179.
 4. Hal Varian, "Hal Varian on How the Web Challenges Managers," *McKinsey Quarterly*, January 2009, www.mckinseyquarterly.com/Hal_Varian_on_ how_the_Web_challenges_managers_2286 (accessed May 27, 2009).
 5. Henry Mintzberg, "Rebuilding Companies as Communities," *Harvard Business Review*, July–August 2009, http://hbr.harvardbusiness.org/2009/07/ rebuilding-companies-as-communities/ar/1 (accessed December 17, 2009).
 6. Hamel and Breen, *The Future of Management*.
 7. Michael Pollan, *In Defense of Food: An Eater's Manifesto* (New York: Penguin, 2008).
 8. Stephen D. Reicher, S. Alexander Haslam, and Michael J. Platow, "The New Psychology of Leadership," *Scientific American Mind*, August–September 2007, www.scientificamerican.com/article.cfm?id=the-new-psychology-of-leadership (accessed December 17, 2009).
 9. Personal correspondence, May 18, 2009.
10. Steven N. Kaplan and Bernadette A. Minton, "How Has CEO Turnover Changed? Increasingly Performance Sensitive Boards and Increasingly Uneasy CEOs," July 2006, http://citeseerx.ist.psu.edu/viewdoc/download?doi=10.1.1 .64.5884&rep=rep1&type=pdf (accessed June 24, 2009).
11. Bronwyn Fryer and Thomas A. Stewart, "Cisco Sees the Future," *Harvard Business Review*, November 2008, http://hbr.harvardbusiness.org/2008/11/ cisco-sees-the-future/ar/1 (accessed December 3, 2009).
12. Ibid.
13. Brian Morrissey, "Q&A: Zappos CEO Tony Hsieh," *Adweek*, December 22, 2008, www.adweek.com/aw/content_display/news/strategy/ e3id78469d81136853904418d754416855e (accessed May 27, 2009).
14. Tony Hsieh, "How Twitter Can Make You a Better (and Happier) Person," January 25, 2009, http://blogs.zappos.com/blogs/ceo-and-coo-blog (accessed May 27, 2009).
15. Patricia Faulhaber, "Branding with Social Media: Zappos Builds Itself Using

Traditional and New Media," March 15, 2009, http://corporate-marketing-branding.suite101.com/article.cfm/branding_with_social_media (accessed May 27, 2009).

16. Wayne Niemi, "Zappos Milestone: Q&A with Tony Hsieh," May 6, 2009, www.wwd.com/footwear-news/zappos-milestone-qa-with-tony-hsieh-2121098 (accessed May 27, 2009).

17. Hsieh, "How Twitter Can Make You a Better (and Happier) Person."

18. Niemi, "Zappos Milestone: Q&A with Tony Hsieh."

19. "Zappos Core Values," http://about.zappos.com/our-unique-culture/zappos-core-values (accessed December 3, 2009).

20. Adam Bryant, "You Want Insights? Go to the Front Lines," *New York Times*, August 15, 2009, www.nytimes.com/2009/08/16/business/16corner .html?pagewanted=2&_r=1&sq=You%20Want%20Insights?%20 &st=cse&scp=1 (accessed November 15, 2009).

CHAPTER 8: TWENTY PREDICTIONS FOR THE 2020 WORKPLACE

1. Robert Cross and Robert Thomas, *Driving Results Through Social Networks: How Top Organizations Leverage Networks for Reform and Growth* (San Francisco: Jossey-Bass, 2009).

2. Lee Rainie and Janna Anderson, "The Future of the Internet III," December 14, 2008, www.pewinternet.org/Reports/2008/The-Future-of-the-Internet-III.aspx (accessed June 25, 2009).

3. Matt Hartley, "Making Way for the Mobile Decade," *Globe and Mail* (Toronto), May 25, 2009, www.theglobeandmail.com/news/technology/ download-decade/up-next-the-mobile-decade/article1145617 (accessed November 15, 2009).

4. Nidhi Verma, "Next-Generation Talent Management: Insights on How Workforce Trends Are Changing the Face of Talent Management," July 1, 2005, www.allbusiness.com/accounting/3487434-1.html (accessed June 25, 2009).

5. "2009 Talent Shortage Survey Results," *Manpower Inc.*, http://files.share holder.com/downloads/MAN/793144191x0x297372/dab9f206-75f4-40b7 -88fb-3ca81333140f/09TalentShortage_Results_USLetter_FINAL_FINAL .pdf (accessed December 9, 2009).

6. Ray Oldenburg, *The Great Good Place* (New York: Marlowe & Company, 1999).

7. Marco R. della Cava, "Working Out of a 'Third Place,'" *USA Today*, October 5, 2006, www.usatoday.com/life/2006-10-4-third-space_x.htm (accessed January 18, 2010).

8. Ibid.

9. See www.thenewpr.com/wiki/pmwiki.php?pagename=Resources.CEOBlogs List (accessed December 17, 2009).

10. Bill Marriott, "How Do I Blog?," *Marriott on the Move*, July 24, 2008, www.blogs.marriott.com/search/default.asp?item=2240720 (accessed December 5, 2009).

11. For Matt Blumberg's blog, visit http://onlyonce.blogs.com/onlyonce.For Mark Cuban's blog, visit http://blogmaverick.com.For Bob Lutz's blog, visit http:// fastlane.gmblogs.com.

12. Hsieh's Twitter feed may be found at http://twitter.com/Zappos.
13. World Without Oil may be found at www.worldwithoutoil.org.
14. Jeff Howe, "The Rise of Crowdsourcing," *Wired*, June 2006, www.wired
    .com/wired/archive/14.06/crowds.html (accessed June 25, 2009).
15. Jennifer Reingold, "A Job That Lets You Be Your Own Boss," CNN.com, Oc-
    tober 8, 2007, http://money.cnn.com/2007/10/08/magazines/fortune/goretex
    .fortune/index.htm (accessed June 3, 2009).
16. Personal interview with Pamela Tate, president of CAEL.
17. "It's 3 A.M.—Are You Checking Your E-mail Again?," July 30, 2008, http://
    corp.aol.com/press-releases/2008/07/it-s-3-am-are-you-checking-your-e-mail-
    again (accessed June 25, 2009).
18. Andrés Tapia, *The Inclusion Paradox: The Obama Era and the Transforma-
    tion of Global Diversity* (Lincolnshire, Ill.: Hewitt Associates, 2009).
19. Michelle Conlin, "Smashing the Clock," *BusinessWeek,* December 11, 2006,
    www.businessweek.com/magazine/content/06_50/b4013001.htm (accessed
    June 25, 2009).
20. Cone, Inc., in collaboration with AMP Agency, "The Millennial Generation:
    Pro-Social and Empowered to Change the World," www.coneinc.com/stuff/
    contentmgr/files/0/b45715685e62ca5c6ceb3e5a09f25bba/files/2006_cone_
    millennial_cause_study_white_paper.pdf (accessed June 25, 2009).
21. Annual Reports, www.nationalgrid.com/corporate/Investor+Relations/
    Annual+Reports (accessed January 15, 2010).
22. Christine Hobart, "Women Still Hold Less Than a Quarter of Senior Manage-
    ment Positions in Privately Held Businesses," Grant Thornton International,
    2009, www.grantthorntonibos.com/Press-room/2009/women_in_business
    .asp (accessed June 25, 2009).
23. "Fast Facts," National Center for Education Statistics, nces.ed.gov/fastfacts/
    (accessed January 18, 2010).
24. "Backstage 101," Sony, Sony.com/backstage101 (accessed January 18, 2010).
25. Jenna Wortham, "Apple's Game Changer, Downloading Now," *New York
    Times*, December 5, 2009, www.nytimes.com/2009/12/06/technology/06apps
    .html (accessed December 7, 2009).
26. "Telstra's 3Rs of Social Media Engagement," http://exchange.telstra.com.au/
    training/flip.html (accessed January 18, 2010).
27. Hillary Chura, "Hiring Is Rising in One Area: Low-Paid Interns," *New York
    Times*, November 28, 2009, www.nytimes.com/2009/11/28/
    your-money/28interns.html (accessed December 5, 2009).

CHAPTER 9: GET READY FOR THE FUTURE WORKPLACE

 1. Ed Frauenheim, "Class of '98: Hits and Misses on HR's Future," Workforce
    Management, December 22, 2008, www.workforce.com/section/09/feature/
    26/04/79/260483.html (accessed June 29, 2009).
 2. C. Bartlett and S. Ghoshal, *Managing Across Borders* (London: Hutchinson
    Business Books, 1989).
 3. Aimé Césaire, *Discourse on Colonialism*, translated by Joan Pinkham
    (New York and London: Monthly Review Press, 1972).
 4. United Nations Global Compact on Corporate Accountability,

www.humanrightsfirst.org/workers_rights/issues/gc/index.htm
(accessed June 29, 2009).

5. Gary Hamel and Bill Breen, *The Future of Management* (Boston: Harvard Business School Press, 2007).

6. Phred Dvorak, "Best Buy Taps Prediction Market," *Wall Street Journal*, September 16, 2008, http://online.wsj.com/article/SB122152452811139909.html (accessed June 29, 2009).

7. Karl W. Deutsch, *The Nerves of Government: Models of Political Communication and Control* (New York: Free Press, 1966).

8. Special thanks to Joseph Grenny for this thought-provoking question.

9. Nancy C. Lutkehaus, *Margaret Mead: The Making of an American Icon* (Princeton, N.J.: Princeton University Press, 2008).

10. We recommend the following books: Kerry Patterson, Joseph Grenny, David Maxfield, Ron McMillan, and Al Switzler, *Influencer: The Power to Change Anything* (New York: McGraw-Hill, 2008), and Kerry Patterson, Joseph Grenny, David Maxfield, Ron McMillan, and Al Switzler, *Crucial Confrontations: Tools for Talking About Broken Promises, Violated Expectations, and Bad Behavior* (New York: McGraw-Hill, 2005). VitalSmarts (www.vitalsmarts .com) has corresponding training programs as well.

11. Patterson, Grenny, Maxfield, McMillan, and Switzler, *Influencer*.

12. Edy Greenblatt, *Restore Yourself: The Antidote for Professional Exhaustion* (Los Angeles: Execu-Care Press, 2009).

13. Our five favorite business apps for the iPhone are:
   - FlightTrack Pro: Send your itinerary to plans@tripit.com, and it loads automatically to your phone. We have been updated on our phones by FlightTrack faster than by gate agents. Also load your friends' and family's itineraries for when you are picking them up at the airport.
   - Shazam: Hold your phone up to any music being played, and Shazam will identify the song and give you the iTunes link to buy it.
   - Tweetie: For posting to Twitter.
   - Encamp: To access Basecamp, a collaboration tool.
   - LinkedIn for iPhone: Allows you to access contacts and résumés from your phone.

14. Fluenz (www.fluenz.com) and Rosetta Stone (www.rosettastone.com), among others, offer kits for learning at home.

INDEX